"Once again, Penney Peirce has pierced the present collective spirit, and clearly describes the accelerating evolution of our global family. Penney is a pioneer who has long been scouting the territory of consciousness. *Transparency* will take you a very long way toward clarifying this evolutionary shift."
Carol Adrienne, PhD, *New York Times* bestselling author of *The Purpose of Your Life*

"Penney Peirce is a sweet mystic who reveals the visions and methods for creating a better reality from an inspired Now. *Transparency* is a peek into what is coming—a must-read for influencers and those ready to elevate, enlighten, and empower. Highly recommended!"
Nikolaj Rotne, cofounder of The Stillness Revolution and coauthor of *Everybody Present*

"*Transparency* is a book whose time has come! In it, Penney Peirce addresses our ability to transform fear and negative thinking into the essence of the divine. The resulting transparency produces genius, effortless results, joyful service, and unlimited possibilities."
Christy Whitman, *New York Times* bestselling author of *The Art of Having It All* and founder Quantum Success Coaching Academy

"Penney Peirce's new book is like a magic potion. Part vibrational medicine, part modern psychology, it speaks about personal alchemy—how we transform from dark, opaque, and dense into clear, sentient beings. Her book can help anyone who wants to walk this path toward enlightenment."
Nancy du Tertre, psychic detective, attorney, and author of *Psychic Intuition*

"Penney Peirce is on the cutting edge of consciousness, showing us a transcendent future with practical steps to take us there. If you're ready to cocreate a more honest, compassionate world, I recommend you stop everything and startreading *Transparency* right now!"
Edward Mannix, author of *Impossible Compassion* and founder of The LightWorker Accelerator™

TRANSPARENCY

Seeing Through to Our
Expanded Human Capacity

Penney Peirce

<small>FOREWORD BY JENNY BLAKE</small>

ATRIA BOOKS
New York London Toronto Sydney New Delhi

BEYOND WORDS
Hillsboro, Oregon

ATRIA
BOOKS

BEYOND WORDS

An Imprint of Simon & Schuster, Inc.
1230 Avenue of the Americas
New York, NY 10020

20827 N.W. Cornell Road, Suite 500
Hillsboro, Oregon 97124-9808
503-531-8700 / 503-531-8773 fax
www.beyondword.com

Managing editor: Lindsay S. Easterbrooks-Brown
Editor: Emily Han
Copyeditor: Jennifer Weaver-Neist
Proofreader: Madison Schultz
Design: Devon Smith
Composition: William H. Brunson Typography Services

First Beyond Words/Atria Books hardcover edition October 2017

ATRIA BOOKS and colophon are trademarks of Simon & Schuster, Inc.
BEYOND WORDS PUBLISHING and colophon are registered trademarks of Beyond Words Publishing. Beyond Words is an imprint of Simon & Schuster, Inc.

For more information about special discounts for bulk purchases, please contact Simon & Schuster Special Sales at 1-866-506-1949 or business@simonandschuster.com.
The Simon & Schuster Speakers Bureau can bring authors to your live event. For more information or to book an event, contact the Simon & Schuster Speakers Bureau at 1-866-248-3049 or visit our website at www.simonspeakers.com.

Manufactured in the United States of America

10 9 8 7 6 5 4 3 2 1

Library of Congress Cataloging-in-Publication Data:

Names: Peirce, Penney, author.
Title: Transparency : seeing through to our expanded human potential / Penney Peirce.
Description: New York : Atria Books ; Hillsboro, Oregon : Beyond Words, 2017. |
  Includes bibliographical references and index.
Identifiers: LCCN 2017015065 (print) | LCCN 2017030903 (ebook) |
  ISBN 9781501165481 (ebook) | ISBN 9781582706436 (pbk.) |
  ISBN 9781582706429 (hardback)
Subjects: LCSH: Intuition. | Perception.
Classification: LCC BF315.5 (ebook) | LCC BF315.5 .P4553 2017 (print) |
  DDC 158—dc23
LC record available at https://lccn.loc.gov/2017015065

The corporate mission of Beyond Words Publishing, Inc.: *Inspire to Integrity*

This book is dedicated to
my mother, Ruth Etoile Martin,
who grew to become Skip Peirce Eby,
a wonderful mix of world traveler,
multitalented artist, colorful storyteller,
historian, lover of life and learning,
friend to many, and mentor to me.

Contents

Foreword

You are in the presence of a master. Penney might not say that out loud herself—she's too transparent for that—but it's true. Penney Peirce's incredible body of work is an ongoing invitation to come home to yourself. Her incisive books are classics—references for how to be, how to navigate the complexity of life, work, relationships, major transitions, and the spaces in between. *Transparency* is the latest in this series of pioneering guidebooks.

In *Transparency*, you will learn how to replace your walls and secrets with the joy-producing abilities to see through the surface of things and be truly seen for all of who you are. You will find strength in vulnerability and radical trust in yourself and others. You will free yourself from worry and find enlightenment on the inside, in the small moments of the day, not just in some epic, faraway state of transcendent meditation. This book will show you how to create from your innate gifts, skyrocket your intuition, and ultimately find "release, relief, and childlike joy." I know this is possible because I have lived this *transformation-through-transparency* myself—from dark to light—thanks to Penney's guidance and presence.

If you are impatient with forewords like I am, you might be wondering who this stranger is, standing in the way between you and the juicy book you're about to read. I'm a fellow bookworm and an author who also studies how we can better navigate change. But perhaps my most important credential is the profound effect Penney Peirce has had on my life.

I have read every one of Penney's books, two or three times each, and I still learn something new every time. I am grateful to say that in the years and conversations since, she has become a mentor and great friend. Whether you are new to Penney's work or have been anxiously awaiting this latest book, as I was, you have come to the right place.

I lived in an opaque life and body for the first thirty-one years of my life. Although I seemed successful on the outside—working at a startup, then Google, then taking the leap into solopreneurship and moving to New York City when my first book came out in 2011—I was besieged by worry, anxiety, people-pleasing, and perfectionism. It permeated my days. Sure, I read dozens of self-help books with the best of 'em, but I truly didn't *understand* the material, let alone know how to integrate it. I could not yet feel, on a visceral level, the truth of the topics Penney covers with such clarity and depth: intuition, dream interpretation, frequency, inner blueprints, spherical and holographic perception, transparency, and so many others.

So I lived in a state of subtle suffering, even when it appeared life was going well. Nothing *should* be wrong, but it was. I went through too many cycles of burnout, depression, and soul-searching—more than I felt I could handle—without even knowing I had a soul.

It wasn't until my Apocalypse Year of 2013 (ever had one of those?) when everything started going haywire, that I threw my hands up on living this way. "I'm too sensitive for my own life," I remember thinking at the time. And then, "But it's as if Penney can read my mind." In *Frequency*, she describes the thoughts in this phase of transformation as, "I'm upset and afraid. Life is too intense and won't let up. My worst fears are taking shape. I can't control myself!" And she also says, "The question and answer exist together in each moment, and all is freely given—nothing is held back." That "perfect guidance exists as soon as you realize you need or want it." This reassured me and helped me trust what was happening.

Foreword

I bought *The Intuitive Way*, Penney's bestselling masterclass on inner wisdom, in 2014, but discovered I wasn't quite ready for it yet. I was just coming out of my fog, or as she describes it, the "dissolving stage" of transformation that each of us goes through as we transition from the (Too Much) Information Age into the Intuition Age. I do believe books jump off of the shelves (or into our Amazon carts) at the perfect time. Our souls tune in to the frequency of what we need to hear from the exact right person at the exact right time—the same way you have landed here and now with *Transparency*. A year after purchasing it, *The Intuitive Way* jumped off my bookshelf and said, "It's time."

I realized I was nervous about diving in. *What is all this "conscious body" talk about? Am I even capable of intuition? Gut instincts overwhelm me—and what if I learn things I don't want to know or admit?* Thankfully, my desire to expand, to live differently, and to come home to myself was stronger than my reservations. This started the deep immersion into Penney's work that changed my life.

I learned from Penney that intuition and coincidences are like radio stations—they are always on, we just have to tune in to them. We miss the majority of messages simply because our headphones aren't plugged in, or we aren't noticing the full range of intelligent, exciting, growth-inducing channels available to us. The more I followed Penney's instructions on how to honor my intuition and notice coincidences (then write them down), the faster and more furiously messages arrived. They were fascinating, delightful, and *fun*. I couldn't believe how much access I now had to the expanded wisdom and intelligence within me. And how, for the first time, I could truly hear my soul speaking and trust my innate talents.

I found a sweetness and relief in surrendering to my spiritual self. I started connecting with spirit guides and a personal council during meditation—something I would have rejected outright in my former opaque life. I immersed myself in the rest of Penney's books and soaked up every word. It was only after practicing the principles she outlines so clearly that the clouds parted and I realized I felt genuinely relaxed and calm. My days had a sense of grace and ease, and I felt faith in the Flow of my life. This was disorienting at first. *When is the other shoe going to drop?! I can't possibly feel this good for this many days in a row—something must be wrong.*

It is only now, years later, that I can say the opaque feeling and subtle suffering hasn't returned, even when I experience challenging life events. I have learned how to stay transparent, open, vulnerable, and in my home frequency—and return to it when I lose my way. I have dropped attachments to outcomes and surrendered completely to wherever life wants to take me. As Penney describes it, "The Flow becomes your best friend . . . you don't want to lock down any ideas—you want to leave space for everything to evolve and improve naturally."

When I wrote my first book, I was plagued by my inner critic. Writing felt arduous and intimidating. With my second book, *Pivot*, I followed Penney's advice and practiced her process. I included my book in my daily meditations. I talked to it. I asked it what next steps I could take so it could fly. I pictured it with wings, and asked what cuts to make so it wasn't weighed down by unnecessary information. I connected with the inner blueprint of the book—long before it was written—to access what might be most helpful for readers to hear, and how to go about finding a publisher. I tuned in to my intuition for every single aspect, from the content to the cover to the launch strategy.

Throughout the three-year process of working on the book, I adopted the mantra, "Let it be easy, let it be fun." I took the pressure off of hitting external markers of success, like sales figures and marketing metrics. If I fell out of my home frequency while working, I paused and recentered myself. Finally, after the book launched, I entered The Void—something that once terrified me—and told Penney I felt like I had entered a "goo state." She reassured me that it was all part of the Be/Spirit-Do/Mind-Have/Body creation cycle, and not to resist the natural dissolution of form and identity; I was just preparing for what's next.

I share my experience with a meaningful creative project—and with life—to confirm that Penney is someone who truly walks her talk. She lives these messages deeply, and works to understand the greater intelligence at work *as she is writing*. She does not presume to know all the answers up front. She sets her sights on enormous, meaty, spiritually significant topics, then makes herself transparent to receive and interpret the message so we can all understand it. She surrenders to the Flow and greater collective consciousness to beautifully translate what can be abstract and esoteric into practical, clear, soulful, and tactical terms.

As you read this book, I invite you to read from as transparent a state as possible. Open yourself up to Penney's words and wisdom. Allow concepts to jump off the page and transform the dark spots of your inner heat map—those fears and worries—into opportunities. Celebrate these opportunities. Practice radical acceptance *of yourself first and foremost* as you read these pages. Welcome the gap between where you are now and the fully transparent, surrendered state that Penney will guide you toward—a blueprint that already exists within you.

My mantra for writing *Pivot* was "If change is the only constant, let's get better at it." Penney Peirce is teaching us not just how we can become more agile at navigating change, but how to emerge as leaders in this new Intuition Age. So if you sometimes feel crazy for how you feel or think, know that you are not alone. Many are with you—Penney, myself, and every reader whose spirit graces these pages—for a start. We are all in this together, learning how to drop our protective, fearful, opaque shells and embrace our transparent gifts of lightness, superconsciousness, and full presence. It is this state—this *new perception* Penney talks about—that will reveal our astonishing human capacity for genius, miracles, and healing.

I hope you gain as much wisdom from *Transparency* as I did, and I thank you (and Penney) for this humbling opportunity to welcome you further inside.

Jenny Blake, author of *Pivot*
April 2017

To the Reader

All things are ready if our minds be so.
William Shakespeare

I've been fascinated with the subject of *transformation*—our quickening, or awakening process—my entire adult life. I've come to see that our sense of self and our reality are in a process of transmuting to something radically different. How will it work? What will we be like post-transformation?

I can easily say that this fascination ties strongly to my purpose: to immerse myself in the experience, understand the dynamics, embody the teachings, and share both the understanding and the experience of transformation with others who are ready. It's what inspires me to work deeply with people and what fuels my enthusiasm for writing, counseling, and teaching.

I'm always asking for a more detailed understanding of the process and the transformed state, always seeking to integrate the next nuances. When I receive a new insight, I'm so happy! But then the universe peels back another layer and I have a good laugh at the naïveté of my tiny left-brain consciousness that thought it had it all wrapped up! I realize there are many more nuances to transformation yet to be understood and integrated, and I remember how much I love the surprise of discovery.

I've been honing my intuition for many years, looking for the non-physical patterns of *energy-and-consciousness* (a term I use to remind us

that the two things are flip sides of the same coin and intricately connected) that shape our world; sometimes I think of myself as a private
eye, constantly searching out what's hidden. I learned to do this by giving personal life readings to thousands of people and discovering the
innumerable subtle dynamics of how the nonphysical realms—spirit,
mind, emotion, and energy—affect the body and personality. I also did
"research readings" for groups who wanted to look at future trends in
business, education, and other larger topics. My ongoing practice was to
continually ask myself: "Why did this happen? What's the underlying
cause of this? How does this behavior/event help the person/situation
evolve?" Year after year, one thing was consistent: energy, consciousness, and time seemed to be speeding up—relentlessly! Frequencies
were rising.

It's interesting how my intuitive revelations about transformation
seem timed to match the latest frequency increases affecting our planet,
bodies, emotions, and minds. I now see that certain knowledge can't be
known until we're on the same wavelength with it. This makes sense—
too much too soon and it all goes to waste. Perhaps, too, each stage
of transformation wants to be experienced and practiced fully before
we're ready for the next expansion of our worldview. So I live in what I
know, while also knowing there is no end, with faith that the next highly
vibrating insight will be doled out to me when the time is right.

If you aren't familiar with my work, let me sketch a quick picture
for you. I've been counseling, teaching, and writing about intuition (the
perception of transformation) and the dynamics of transformation since
1977. I still work individually with clients, tuning in to where they are
on their evolutionary path, helping them understand how they got stuck
and how to free their creative flow, and where their path might go next.
I was an interior and graphic designer earlier in my life, and I suppose I
see the dynamics of a person's, or an organization's, life as an interesting
design problem. Sort out the variables and find the most compassionate,
creative, appropriate, natural, simple solutions that support evolution.
And the variety of people's lives is so stimulating! I never tire of learning
how souls grow themselves.

I began writing books in 1997, with *The Intuitive Way: The Definitive Guide to Increasing Your Awareness*, which, over the years, has proved to be a sort of intuition-development bible. I followed that with books on being fully alert and mindful in the present moment, and working with dreams to develop 24-hour consciousness.

Then came two books that clarified key aspects of the transformation process. *Frequency: The Power of Personal Vibration* provided a roadmap through this psychological death-and-rebirth process, showing that the process isn't frightening and that it's totally doable in our lifetime. It helped readers learn to work with the subtle dynamics of energy to change their life.

Leap of Perception: The Transforming Power of Your Attention took the explanation further, describing how "old," linear, left-brain dominated perception could shift to "new," spherical-holographic, right-brain influenced perception, and how the Information Age reality would change to the Intuition Age as a result. It explained how the conscious use of attention would be the most important factor in the coming new reality, and described the new attention skills that would become second nature.

Now I've been receiving the next layer of the story. It focuses on the idea of *transparency* and how it can accelerate transformation and facilitate enlightenment. The idea began following me around and causing me to have experiences that demonstrated what transparency means. Details from my own life began to fill in the picture, and I knew this was the next natural progression in my series of books.

We Crave a Larger Context

In the last few years, I experienced the dissolution of familiar forms, friendships, habits, ways of defining life, and comfortable points of view. And my mother died suddenly, just as I began writing this book, stalling my forward progress for months but connecting me with the nonphysical realms in a new way. It seems the many insights that came from her passing needed time to surface and integrate in me so they could weave into the fabric of *Transparency*.

But in general, I have felt much less ambitious in the usual sense of the word. At the same time, I've felt more like my true self and what I need has come more effortlessly, rather than me having to chase it down. I don't worry much these days. This feels like transparency at work.

Along with these experiences has come a frustration with the various contractions I now feel so easily in other people's minds, emotions, and bodies. To me, many people seem dense, like they're living in an *opaque reality*—that thick, clouded state most of us assume is normal. They don't seem to want their worldview challenged, even by the most innocuous of new ideas. This self-protection makes me sad. Like a five-year-old, I always want to ask: "Can Sarah or Jimmie come out and play?" I want to be my soul with other people, but so many don't yet feel themselves as the soul. And yet, I know we wake up in waves, when it's right for us.

I have a sense that many of you are also reaching this point of frustration and impatience. As we open, heal wounds, release what's old, and joyfully embrace the surprise of the new that is constantly arising, it's easier to see through the various distracting behaviors caused by fear. We don't want to have to connect with others in that thick, semi-dead way. We want direct contact and sophisticated yet simple, truthful understanding. We want more rapport, love, kindness, and creativity—and more cocreation and sharing. We long for a shared experience, the sense of a collective self that knows about transformation in a more expansive, comprehensive way.

Psychologist Jacqueline Small has said, "At certain points along the journey, people begin to crave a larger context."[1] I think this is happening now. We are yearning to be our soul in our body and personality, consciously unfolding our life. We don't want anything to block the clarity of life's evolution. To really know this in our bones and cells, though, we must become transparent, or it's still a dim, filtered experience.

I'm naked to the bone,
With nakedness my shield.
Myself is what I wear:
I keep the spirit spare.
Theodore Roethke

To the Reader

Transparency Sneaks Up & Tricks Me

I notice, in retrospect, that the word *transparency* crept quietly into my previous books. As I explored the underlying meanings of transparency to outline this book, I actually forgot that the last chapter in *Frequency* was titled "Accelerating Toward Transparency." And in *Leap of Perception*, chapter 10 talks about how "Becoming Transparent Empowers the Flow." Even back in 1997, I wrote in *The Intuitive Way*:

> My intuition tells me that intuition is going to be the skill of the future. And that moving into the intuitive way of life and the Intuitive Age in history will bring profound transformations in our personal and societal worldviews, in the ways we relate to each other and manifest reality. To create the future and enter it gracefully, we must be able to know directly, now, without distortion. We must become transparent and fluid in our consciousness so we can dive in and swim with the universe's quantum particles and energy waves—like dolphins leaping alongside the prow of a fast-moving ship.[2]

It amuses me that clues were dropped into the mix of these earlier writings. It reassures me, too, that there is a great Sanity at work, cocreating with us.

For many years, I lived in Marin County, California, north of San Francisco's Golden Gate Bridge, a place known for its spirituality, artistic innovation, and interest in personal growth. I wrote all my books there, swaddled in the cozy like-mindedness of friends and colleagues. It was easy to be spiritual there. Though I had grown up moving every two years all over the country (my father was a troubleshooting management consultant for a large corporation), and had spent most of my early years in the Midwest states running through cornfields, riding horses, and swimming in quarries, I became a captive of Marin County and lost a sense of reality about the rest of the country. In my addiction to the

San Francisco Bay Area's wonderfully stimulating energy, oddly, I also became quite bored—though I didn't realize it fully.

When I wrote the last word of *Leap of Perception*—the final book I wrote in California—I was *instantly* hit with a tsunami-like wave of emotion, burst into tears, and sobbed intensely. My chest felt like it was bursting—with an odd mix of gratitude, surprise, and relief that seemed to come from beyond me. While this was happening, I heard a voice in my head say, "You're done." I immediately thought, "Well, maybe I'm going to die now." The voice somehow explained, without words, that I had completed an amount of work I had "contracted for" before I was born, to write a series of books about transformation. That I didn't have to write the books, but I really wanted to, so it was given to me as a "work."

Now I was free to write and choose whatever topic interested me, or not write. I could feel the end of the subtle pressure I'd been living with—what I might call a relentless motivation—and a huge spaciousness opened around me. Within a week, my landlord called to let me know she was selling the house I'd been renting for over twenty years! I had a couple months to move. It was as if the Flow, or Spirit, were ejecting me from Marin County like a seed from an exploding seedpod—now that I was "done."

Where to go? I tried on many ideas of places that were more affordable but which still had conscious, spiritually active, artistic people, and my intuition voted no on every one. What kept returning front and center was Florida—go live near my aging mother and her husband, and be available to help them. Life then picked me up and moved me, as though on a nonstop conveyor belt, to an area of the country where I imagined I would never fit in.

Next, instead of just renting, I found myself *buying* a house! Was my soul tricking me into committing to something I currently couldn't see the value in doing? Suddenly, I was living among warm-hearted but conservative, fundamentalist people.

When someone asked, "So what do you do?" I learned to avoid an awkward silence or a lecture about what the Bible thought about my views by saying, "I write self-help books." I was socializing with my mother's group of eighty- to ninety-year-old friends. Superficial conversation was easy, and they were all lively and fun, but I couldn't mention what I really thought about or what my deep truths were, because those sorts of comments were sure to fall flat.

"What am I doing here?" I thought. "Is *this* progress? Is *this* the next phase in my spiritual growth and transformation? Maybe this is the death knell of my career."

My inner voice chimed in occasionally with insights. "It's easy to be 'spiritual' when you're surrounded by like-minded thinkers and people on your wavelength. The so-called 'outside world' validates you. But can you be spiritual, and feel the way you like to feel, *anywhere?*"

When I began to feel compressed and restricted, even sacrificial, my logical left brain tried to make me feel better by saying, "But here you can expand your work—up the East Coast, into Europe, even back to the Midwest."

Immediately, my inner voice said, "It's not about expansion, it's about *exposure!* You don't have to project yourself out into more of the world, just let people see you. Don't protect yourself or hide; be transparent." This ran counter to my gut instinct that to show up and expose my truth and worldview might attract the wrong kind of attention and cause me to be in danger.

Nevertheless, I practiced dissolving any protective smoke, mirrors, or shields I might have inadvertently put up in my personal energy field. I practiced becoming my diamond-light self—the purer energy-and-consciousness me—and being a relaxed, clear space in the field of Florida.

One morning, I got up and found a note from the police taped to my front door, cautioning me about the danger of leaving my garage door open. Evidently, my garage door mysteriously went up in the middle of the night (I was positive I'd closed it!) and my conservative neighbor, who was somehow vigilant at that hour, called to report it. The police came into my house through my utility room, looked into my bedroom, saw that I was sound asleep, didn't wake me, left, and locked the doors behind them. When my neighbor told me what had happened, I was shocked. Yes, I'd allowed myself to be exposed and *had* been invaded—but by *protective forces.* Quite the testament to transparency!

We're entering the "Time of Great Ironies." What seems restrictive is really freeing. What seems dangerous is really protective. What seems safe is really detrimental. What seems problematic is really the answer. What seems easily spiritual is really numbing. What seems sacrificial is really an increase. It is the quest for and attainment of personal and collective transparency that reveals the deeper truths, and it brings with it some welcome humor and relief.

Deep Clearing & the End of Struggle

Understanding transformation is a matter of experiencing how the non-physical spiritual realms and physical life exist simultaneously in the same space and time—how they're simply different yet complementary, mutually sourcing, interpenetrating frequencies of the same universe. To know yourself as a soul, and matter as a frequency of spiritual energy, you must dissolve everything in the way—the *clutter* composed of fear, fixed beliefs, and unconsciously ingrained habits. These are filters that dim the soul's starlight and distort the translation of the soul's wisdom into form. Remove the clutter, and what's left is the transparent, diamond-like self. *To be transformed is to be transparent.*

I have addressed the clearing process in various ways in my previous books, but now it's in our face as never before. Perhaps we're getting down to the bottom of the bucket, where our core misperceptions about life reside—those last major residues of suffering. Feeling dense and opaque is becoming painful enough that it can't be ignored. We need a fresh way to see what the transformation process is doing, along with updated techniques to help us move through the eye of the needle with clarity and ease.

With this book I am dropping into the nuances of the last stages of the transformation process. I want to give you a whole new angle on how to understand, function successfully within, and come out the other side of what can seem like an extremely long, dark, cramped tunnel. *Transparency* will help you dissolve opacity and learn to live in transparency as a transparent person. These are crucial new skills.

When you're transparent, dividing lines melt, and all that's left is the true self—and it's everywhere, in everything and everyone, and that is a life-altering revelation that blooms and blooms. Feeling and remembering this is what I wish for all of us.

> Writing is a socially acceptable form
> of getting naked in public.
> Paulo Coelho

About This Book

Keep your heart clear and transparent,
and you will never be bound.
A single disturbed thought
creates ten thousand distractions.
Ryokan

This is a book about letting go of everything and receiving everything. It's about the irony of having no ego and an amazing personal presence, of not being intellectual and being a genius, of not needing to rescue the sufferers of the world and being a powerful force for healing. This book is about how becoming transparent empowers the good while seeming dangerous, how it lets you be empty and spacious while being full, and free while also belonging. This is a book about making enlightenment normal.

What's Been Happening to Us?

Many of you have noticed life's acceleration and its impact on your perception, identity, and reality. The frequency of matter and of our bodies, emotions, and thoughts has been steadily rising, causing us to feel uncomfortable and pressured, while also becoming ultrasensitive and more aware of the inner world of energy-and-consciousness.

You probably recognize some of the signs and symptoms of this quickening process—in fact, you've probably experienced a variety of them: the initial irritation of being in a body that's revving up for a leap, the unpredictable explosions of emotion or traumatic events that can feel oddly like re-enactments, the nagging sensation of treading water or feeling too far behind, the changing perception of time, the voluntary or involuntary loss of identity, the increasing discomfort with anything that feels old, slow, boring, snagged, sticky, dense, or controlling. You may be conscious of all sorts of subtle preverbal *energy information*—data transmitted via vibration—that you never noticed before.

At a deep level, as we've been adjusting ourselves to the high-frequency energy, preparing for a new self and reality without realizing it, we've also been unconsciously loosening the stuck places in our history, beliefs, and habits so we can clear them and be free to evolve. We're waking up to the immensity of what we *can be*; our capacity as human beings is expanding beyond what we've been able to imagine. If we pay attention, it's evident that we're experiencing a shift that starts in the nonphysical realms and materializes as a true transformation of life on earth. Is it any wonder that the word *miracle* is showing up everywhere these days?

This intensification of energy-and-consciousness on earth has been mapped for at least 16.4 billion years, if we are to believe the Mayan mathematicians and calendar makers. In our lifetimes alone, we've seen a geometric progression of knowledge, inventions, technology, and globalization. When we think about the speed with which the Industrial Age built momentum and the first printing press morphed into the first computer, or the first assembly line turned into the totally automated production facility—we realize how fast we slid into the Information Age.

The Information Age sped up and the advances in computing birthed the internet. The internet birthed social media, and mobile phones that are two-way video cameras and tiny computers. All this has empowered us to understand how intimately we are connected to each other, how available data is to anyone, and how fast communication can really fly. Yet we are reaching a point where the Information Age is too clogged, overwhelming, and on the verge of being boring. More information? It's not as exciting as it once was now that it's normal.

To deal with the pressure of assimilating the amount of information we can access, we have to find a new way of perceiving; the old, linear bit-by-bit or byte-by-byte method just won't cut it. We are diving headlong—right now—into the next phase of reality—the *Intuition Age*, where perception moves at the speed of light, in all directions, spherically and holographically. It is this particular shift of perception, caused by life's acceleration, that is behind the process of transformation affecting everyone and everything on the planet. And it is this same acceleration that is propelling us into the desire for transparency.

What Is Transparency?

In this book, we will explore the idea of transparency and what it means at a deep, personal level. What is transparency as it applies to your mind? To your emotions? To your body?

I'm not quite as concerned with the idea of transparency in politics, government, and the corporate world right now as I am with the ground-up, grassroots, inside-out development of transparency in people everywhere. It's transparent people who will demand, and create, transparent social systems. We'll definitely explore the potential for having transparent relationships, group endeavors, and organizations—and what it might be like as a critical mass of transparency occurs and we begin to live in a transparent world. We'll see how far we can imagine into the Intuition Age scenario, and we'll practice visualizing and feeling the new reality.

It's so important to have a treasure map that prompts you to watch for important landmarks along your path—and that's what I want this book to be for you. *Transparency* will help you clear the last remnants of your blockages in a smoother, faster way so you can create from your innate gifts and remember the fullness of who you are.

Once you learn to identify your own transparent state and stabilize it, you'll notice subtly different ways that life works. I mentioned irony in the previous section because many of the new insights you'll have about living transparently involve these sorts of "Oh, it's just the opposite of the way I thought!" surprises. This book will call out insights like these and help you understand how to become comfortable making them your new normal.

Seeing Through & Being Seen

It's easy to connect the concept of transparency with being honest and open. But to be that way, you need to embrace the vulnerability that comes with undefended visibility, which brings up huge issues of honesty and trust. This is a big undertaking! *Transparency* aims to help you become comfortable with being seen for who you are—flaws, mistakes, talents, and soul—the full catastrophe!

The ironic component of being seen is that it allows you to see through surface interferences in others and the world to the true core in anyone and anything. It's as though you suddenly have Superman's X-ray vision, and this enables you to reach just-right solutions, insights, and new knowledge in an instant, without all the arguing and struggle you're so used to. This book will help you develop your ability to "see through," so your intuition can skyrocket.

The Bridge Time

The new, transformed Intuition Age reality, in all its glorious transparency, is astonishing, but at the moment, we're dealing with a complex time of transition that often feels like an upheaval. Fears are surfacing everywhere, in individuals and groups, and as a result, many people are mired in chaos and confusion.

Our systems, like government, business, education, and family, are also in chaos and confusion as the new perception replaces the old, linear way of thinking. Old societal structures no longer function well and are breaking down. Some people are partially transparent, oscillating in and out of opacity, while others are still totally stuck in dense, defensive behavior.

The thought of becoming totally transparent can be terrifying when there is so much unconsciousness and reactionary behavior around us. *Transparency* will help you move through this seemingly dangerous bridge time at a pace that feels right for you.

Being Transparent in a Transparent World

Finally, this book sketches a picture of how things we've taken for granted in the old reality are likely to function in a transparent one. We see a version of things based on density and opacity right now, but if we can wake up and see through those illusions, what might happen to our experience of such things as ethics, time, healing, freedom, emotions, learning, birth, humor, business, entertainment, marriage/family, or innovation? What's possible when many people become transparent and work in transparent groups?

Subtle Distinctions

Transparency addresses many subtle confusions and fine-line distinctions. Does being transparent mean you become dangerously vulnerable? Or brutally honest? If you're transparent, is there anything there for people to recognize? Does uniqueness disappear? If you can see through the surface, will you become bored with life or depressed by what you see? Or might you ascend, never again to incarnate? If there are no secrets, what creates excitement in life? Or motivation? What are the ethics connected with transparency? What's the difference between a secret and a mystery?

The Structure of This Book

This book has a simple structure—just nine chapters and a "Final Thoughts" epilogue. The end of each chapter features a brief "Just to Recap" summary. As with my other guidebooks, *Transparency* provides anecdotes, examples, exercises, charts, diagrams, and inspirational quotes throughout to assist in left-right brain integration and to help you experience the points being made.

This book is not meant to be scholarly and academic but familiar, personal, and palpable while conveying sophisticated ideas that can stimulate thought and be applied practically. I want you to be able to understand and experientially integrate what I'm talking about. If I use potentially unfamiliar terms, I'll be sure to define them on the spot for you. And check the extensive glossary for many more definitions. Also, for clarity's sake, there are a few words that I use in lowercase when they apply to the physical reality, and in uppercase when they pertain to the spiritual reality, like light and Light.

As you work with *Transparency*, you'll go through stages of a developmental process. The flow of the content will first ground you in a summary of what's happening energetically on the planet and in our consciousness, how the Intuition Age is emerging, why we're ready for transparency, and what it is and isn't. Then we'll look at how we became so accustomed to living in an opaque reality with all its secrecy, lies, and hiding. Next, we'll contrast that with the new, transparent reality and how different it is. We need to know where we're headed. Once we have that understanding, we'll take a serious look at the challenges that face us in this bridge time, where people are waking up in waves. How can you focus on becoming transparent when other people are either opaque or partially transparent? How can the shift occur most easily?

Moving on, we'll focus on specific ways you can clear your clutter, improve your clarity, and minimize your oscillation in and out of transparency. Then we'll expand the concept of transparency to show how it can transform the quality of your interaction and cocreation with others. We'll dive into the ideas of "seeing through" and "being seen" and how these gifts can be used advantageously. What can you see through to? How is being seen a huge bonus?

Finally, the book examines how reality may evolve as humanity becomes more transparent and approaches enlightenment. What can you look forward to? What expanded capacities are rightfully yours?

At the end of each chapter, I've included a piece of my own inspired writing, a "Transparency Message" that comes from a state of higher frequency consciousness where my personality and normal writing voice are not in the forefront. If you read them slowly and deliberately or read them out loud to yourself, you may notice they convey a different rhythm and vibration than the regular text. Sometimes, holding one sentence or phrase in your mind for a few moments will reveal a hidden meaning.

As an extra benefit, in the end material, you'll find two indices— one to help you locate the various exercises, charts, and transparency messages and one to help you find the various lists of important points scattered through the chapters. And just so you know, I have changed the names of the people in the anecdotes I share, for privacy reasons.

Tips for Working with This Book

You can open this book anywhere, like an oracle, and read a sentence or a paragraph. Sometimes it's just what you need, like drawing a card in an oracle deck. You can ask yourself a question, and open the book spontaneously to find new perspective about an answer.

As with most of my books, *Transparency* is crammed with insights. Many people tell me they've read the previous books in my transformation series several times, or that one of them is always on their bedside table, or that they are user-friendly reference books. I say this so you'll take it slow; go through the chapters a paragraph at a time, an exercise at a time. *Feel into* the ideas and words. The material is often profound, yet it's also simple. If you stay in the moment, you'll find many things clicking.

It's Useful to Document Your Progress

By keeping a journal and writing about your experiences and insights, you can track your process of growth and make sure not to lose key revelations. This is a guidebook with exercises, and a journal is a perfect place to record the results you achieve when you do the exercises. What insights did you have? What difficulties or surprises did you encounter? What questions arose as a result of the exercise?

Between exercises, you might write about the things you notice during the week or the themes filling your dreams. You might ask your-self a question and answer yourself by writing directly from your core, with a totally open, innocent mind, letting a stream of words emerge as a spontaneous flow, without censorship.

In your journal, you can be creative; draw diagrams and sketches or have a section that serves as an idea storehouse, where you note things that have captured your attention—a song lyric, a synchronicity, a snippet of someone's conversation, an article, the silly behavior of a squirrel outside, or a book recommended by a friend. Record and decode your dreams, and transcribe the gist of the inner dialogues you have with yourself.

Write down the negative declarative statements your left brain makes so you can see these limiting thoughts on paper. Find elements of your life vision. List your loves and favorites, your distastes and pet peeves. You can go back later and review. What has your soul been trying to say? What are you really working on in your inner world?

You might even create a small study group to go through the book together over a period of weeks. Sharing your processes and insights can significantly accelerate everyone's integration of the material.

Next, in chapter 1, I summarize the important content of my two previous books—the flow of the transformation process and the basics of our leap of perception into the Intuition Age. Understanding this material lays the foundation for why transparency is the next natural step. If you'd like to explore this information further, I recommend you study *Frequency* and *Leap of Perception* in greater detail.

A word is not a crystal, transparent and unchanged; it is the skin
of a living thought and may vary greatly in color and content
according to the circumstances and time in which it is used.
Oliver Wendell Holmes

1

The Awakening

You are an explorer, and you represent our species,
and the greatest good you can do is to bring back a new idea,
because our world is endangered by the absence of good ideas.
Our world is in crisis because of the absence of consciousness.
Terence McKenna

Though it may seem like the world is falling apart, we are actually living in a very special time of global transformation—moving from the Information Age to the Intuition Age—and right now we're experiencing the early signs of this sweeping change.

In the past, transformation was experienced by individuals who isolated themselves from society—in monasteries, cloisters, and caves or as specially chosen souls in villages, like shamans and healers. They focused on their connection to the spiritual world with great diligence and discipline. Today, though, the experience is available to anyone willing to practice some key principles.

I briefly sketched some of the basic ideas pertaining to transformation in the previous two sections, but here in this chapter, I'll lay more groundwork so you can understand how the process itself is evolving and why transparency is the next step toward an illumined Intuition Age. Since this chapter is full of important material, it may help you to have a bit of an overview before diving in.

1. In Part 1, I describe how the transformation process functions, with the stages you are likely to experience along the way. At the end of this section you'll find a "Summing Up" chart that condenses the stages into bullet points.
2. Next, I talk about the big shift in consciousness, or leap of perception, out of linear perception into the spherical-holographic perception of the Intuition Age. This is divided into Part 2, which describes the functioning of *spherical perception*, and Part 3, which helps you understand *holographic perception*. Once you understand these two new aspects of perception, you'll see how they merge into a cohesive, highly expanded kind of knowing. At the end of both Part 2 and Part 3, you'll find similar "Summing Up" charts that condense the stages into bullet points.

I advise you to read this chapter slowly and use it as reference material. Often, a single sentence will be worth contemplating or even writing about.

PART 1: TRANSFORMATION DYNAMICS

The Inner Blueprint for Reality Is Changing

It may help to see transformation not as a sudden occurrence but as the natural continuation of a process that's been steadily progressing on earth for ages. It is not something that will affect everyone at once on a certain date; people will awaken at their own pace over a period of years. Nevertheless, life is ever-evolving and constantly transforming, and we are reaching an important crescendo. The pressure is on!

When you penetrate into the evolution and transformation of life on earth, you see that the pattern for its unfolding develops first in the nonphysical realms of energy-and-consciousness, creating an inner blueprint, which then precipitates into a physical process. This is the way all events and forms take shape. As the frequency of the inner energy-and-consciousness blueprint increases, reality materializes faster and functions according to more refined, elegant principles. The unseen and the seen always parallel each other. As evolution and transformation streamline, you and your life go through frequency-matching jumps or revisions. Letter-writing shifts to phone calls to Post-it notes and emails to texting with abbreviations to video chatting. As above, so below. Everything is accelerating.

Sometimes the higher pattern translates easily into form; you may experience this as sudden exciting innovations, perfect solutions to complex problems, or the magical convening of harmonious, like-minded groups. Yet all too often, the physical world is thick with negativity and overlays of long-term, locked-in beliefs and habits, and the higher energy can't penetrate the density to translate into new forms easily or accurately. Then the energy builds up until it can find a way to break through, often by creating cracks in the firmament—dramas, traumas, accidents, and shocks.

At a societal level, this might be events like the explosion of the space shuttle *Challenger* in 1986, September 11 in 2001, or the global financial crisis of 2007–2008. At a personal level, it might be the death of a loved one, the loss of a good job, or finding out you have a difficult disease. Though these breakthroughs are disruptive, they serve as wedges to open us to new realities and more expansive thinking. And yet, once some space is revealed, the higher pattern still has to find the right new physical expression around and through the confusion caused by the sudden breakthrough, which can take some time.

As reality's inner blueprint evolves toward transformation, it affects you personally in ripples or waves, like surf at the beach. When you're open, you roll with each wave, adjust to it, and clear any blockages in the way. This catalyzes positive change in your perception of how life works. For example, you might suddenly experience time differently, see how the nonphysical and physical worlds are merged, or realize you might not want to use so much willpower or plan too far ahead because goal-setting and accomplishment don't work the same way anymore.

The greater dynamic of what's happening, however, is little understood by people whose main focus is physical. They don't see the nonphysical part of the process yet and tend to assume the world is spiraling toward destruction. These people resist the wave and can be battered by it. Ironicially, the waves are actually helping us clear the clutter in the way of our transparency.

Without full comprehension of the stages of transformation, when the speed of life jumps up a notch or two, people rooted in the physical often panic and retreat into mental and emotional paralysis or reactionary behavior. This blocks the flow of the wave, makes things more difficult, creates chaos, and drains energy. Instead of welcoming the new energy, which can carry them through and beyond their stuckness, many people equate the early clearing stage of transformation with high pressure, negativity, stuckness, disillusionment, depression, overwhelm, or hopelessness.

Yet far from being negative, these contracted states are important precursors to clarity. They point the way to what needs to be dissolved; the waves are bringing these things to the surface. Clearing fear and negativity—and remembering your spiritual core identity—is what becoming transformed, or transparent, is all about. Then you can reframe your attitude about what's happening to eliminate unnecessary roadblocks and detours. You can take advantage of today's high-frequency energy and ride the wave instead of drowning in it.

Transformation Begins with a Shake-Up

For transformation to occur, attachment to the way your "old" reality has always functioned must be loosened, shaken, upset, and seen as dysfunctional, boring, and even painful. You must want something better. The first waves of people who wake up to this desire and sense the ultimate outcome, embrace the process as much as they can. They disengage enough from old beliefs and definitions that openings can occur; chinks can form in the walls so new energy and Light can pour through. You are certainly in these first waves.

The energy-and-consciousness that rises through the new porousness in your body, mind, and emotions—and even in society—brings glimpses of a better, easier, more enjoyable way of living. Once you catch sight of the potential new reality, you start tracking with the process and want more. The more you yearn and search, the bigger the openings become. The bigger the openings, the more of the transformed reality you can sense, understand, and handle. Yearning continues but now there's more certainty. You talk about what you notice, and other people become curious and wake up too.

We awaken in stages, as we're ready. It's true that you're never given more than you can handle, and as soon as you're ready for more, it comes.

> Both the descent of Truth into the lower nature and the ascent of the lower nature into the higher Truth are capable of solving the problem of problems, the illumination of human consciousness. They are equally effective and have an equal speed.
> Sri Chinmoy

The World Is Accelerating

The vehicle for shaking up the old reality and making life uncomfortable enough that people want to move beyond it is due to one phenomenon: *the acceleration of the frequency of energy in the planet.* We don't know what's causing it, but the acceleration affects matter and, thus, our bodies, which are made from matter. It also affects our experience of time—children grow up faster, results and repercussions to our words and deeds occur in less time, our computers and tech gadgets need updating more often, and innovations flood the marketplace.

The acceleration also affects the frequency of our emotions and the kind of thoughts we think. Emotions based in fear—like distrust, hatred, apathy, disdain, or envy—vibrate relatively slowly compared to emotions like love, joy, affection, enthusiasm, kindness, or appreciation. Thoughts that are fixed—opinions, beliefs, credos, and dogma, for example—vibrate at a lower frequency than thoughts that are fluid, such as inspiration, curiosity, imagination, or intuition.

As the vibration on earth accelerates, negative emotions and thoughts are more difficult to maintain. We eventually come to see them as a waste of time and life force—something that stalls our progress. We prefer higher frequency feeling and thinking that allow fluidity.

The Acceleration Causes Upheaval
in Body, Emotions & Mind

As your body increases its frequency, there is an initial increase in personal discomfort. We're used to functioning in a fairly methodical manner, often feeling separate from our body, which we sense as an object, not realizing that it is actually a collection of conscious parts and particles working harmoniously together.

With the acceleration, the body's energy increases—what was sluggish starts moving, and consciousness awakens inside the body. It becomes difficult to ignore your body now. As the body revs up, you might feel buzzy and electrical, overheated, or manic. Your heart might pound erratically, and you might be unable to relax or sleep. Parts of your body you've been overlooking might act up and call for attention by developing problems or pain.

A disturbed body easily produces disturbed emotions. For instance, if you're overheated and too electrical, you might become irritable or hot-headed and impulsive. If your heart is beating fast, you might experience panic attacks. But the main reason the acceleration triggers emotional release is that low-vibration emotions, old emotional wounds, and fears that have been denied and suppressed can no longer hide. They are being pried from old resting places and forced to move—up in vibration and up into your conscious mind, to be recognized and cleared.

As fear and pain surface, you may experience anxiety, hyperactivity, and aggression-avoidance behaviors. Your emotions might spike and dip, making you angry, high strung, or despondent. Is it any wonder that the incidence of bipolar disorder diagnoses in youth has increased stagger-ingly in recent years?

As your body and emotions shift to higher frequencies, your mind does too. Your thought processes might match the physical and emo-tional disturbances and become overactive, distracted, delusional, fixated on worry, stuck in negativity, or obsessive. Or your mental fixations may wobble with doubt, and suppressed, painful memories may suddenly become conscious.

Most of us are used to suppressing fear and denying any potential discomfort; this is a common mental coping mechanism. "What's bothering you?" "Nothing." "Are you OK?" "I'm fine." "What happened?" "It's complicated." We also routinely use strong beliefs, opinions, and habits as cover-ups so we don't have to feel terror and pain. These avoidance behaviors give us the illusion that we can live undisturbed in our head, oblivious and partially blind. But this is not possible anymore.

The transformation process is evolving your consciousness from fear to love. That means you have to dissolve the fears and emotional wounds you've been trying to avoid by understanding them with an open, neutral mind. And *that* means you have to face them, feel them, and decode them. When you do this, the negativity clears and you more quickly match the frequency of the accelerating wave that's been rolling through.

If you don't clear the negativity, it may reappear, amplified, as a real-life situation that parallels the reason the negativity became stuck in the first place. For instance, your mother was narcissistic and dominated you, and now that you've overcome your submissive nature and found a great job, you have a new boss who mows everyone down with his aggressive ego. Maybe you didn't clear *all* of this pattern. So you either clear the issue again or you try to resuppress and avoid it.

> They say that time changes things,
> but you actually have to change them yourself.
> Andy Warhol

Avoidance Complicates Your Life & Stops the Flow

If you decide you don't want to feel, understand, and dissolve your fear or upsets, you may try to push it all back down, distract yourself, and pretend none of it exists—all over again. This is frightening stuff, so it's common to react to it from the adrenal center, with fight-or-flight behaviors. If you're a fighter, you might use some form of control, domination, confrontation, intimidation, fortification, misdirection and trickery, cynicism, or stoicism. You might puff up to appear big and strong. You may take a counter-phobic, aggressive, even violent stance in life or develop hair-trigger defensiveness.

If you're more comfortable with flight (or even with freezing to appear invisible), you might avoid the issues by becoming spacy, unconscious, apathetic, or noncommittal. You might feign ignorance, distract yourself with addictive substances and behaviors, or fragment your awareness by trying to do the million things in front of you. That way, your attention span will be microscopic and you won't have time to notice much. You might give your power away to authority figures or act helpless, complaining about feeling unloved, deprived, or overwhelmed.

When the heightened energy scares you and you clench and resist it, it builds up force like water behind a dam and pushes harder to be released. If you continue to choose resistance rather than flow, life becomes intense and difficult, fills with negative experiences, then explodes, creating dramatic breakthroughs and breakups of old patterns. The acceleration cannot be stopped or plugged up for long!

> The largest part of what we call "personality" is determined by how we've opted to defend ourselves against anxiety and sadness.
> Alain de Botton

The more you resist this clearing phase of the transformation process, the more dramatic it becomes. Becoming defensive about the habits you developed to maintain security now brings up the opposite experience—the one you've resisted feeling. This is really a blessing, because with calm attention and presence, you can discover your deepest underlying blockages and clear them.

For example, if one person decides that being proactive, ambitious, wealthy, and powerful over others is the way to maintain security, the acceleration may cause her to lose her job, marriage, or investments, or to have a serious accident. She is thrust directly into the subconscious fears she's been avoiding, which may revolve around loss of control and failure. Embracing and being with the loss—without judgment—can lead her to reconnect with her true desires, see expanded possibilities, let people help her, and find a new definition of success.

On the other hand, if another person decides that being charming, likeable, helpful, pleasing, and humble are the keys to safety, he may experience someone taking something he said or did the wrong way. Maybe someone sues him, or he is ostracized from belonging to a group he values. Perhaps he uncharacteristically blows up at his powerful boss and is fired. Here, too, he finds himself facing his shadow side, which may be about avoiding anger and feelings of isolation. By being with the experience of aloneness, he can connect with soul and realize he likes himself as he is—he doesn't need to please people, he's not helpless, and there is a more courageous, authentic way to live.

> The man who never avoids what he actually is
> will soon change and elevate whatever he is.
> Vernon Howard

The Turning Point:
Disillusionment, Exhaustion & Ego Death

It's important to remember that the negative views that plague you are a figment of the left brain, which at its most contracted and dense, creates *ego*. My sense of ego is related to the left brain going too far and becoming calcified in its functioning. In the face of the acceleration, the left brain desperately tries to remain in control of reality via willpower and cleverness, to preserve its role as director of action and suppressor of frightening memories. Your left brain alone has no inspiration and is cut off from the rest of life; its perception is based on the past. Its actions are reactions, and its functions are analysis, definition, compartmentalization, isolation, and protection—so its interpretation of your experience is rarely expansive or evolutionary.

Your left brain must surrender control for you to transform. This is often called *ego death*. You don't have to be better than others, know everything ahead of time, have a plan for everything, or control other people's responses to you. As you drop these needs, the ego feels itself becoming useless, or "dying," and it can cause you to think dire, paranoid thoughts. Life can look dark and dangerous. Instead of understanding that a function of your brain is shifting, people often think they themselves are purpose-less or dying, or they project death and destruction onto the world at large. Witness the rise of suicide, terrorism, and Armageddon stories.

The last gasp of the more negative path to transformation is when you are finally so exhausted from avoiding, resisting, controlling, and resuppressing subconscious blocks, and so overwhelmed by complexity, that you just stop. There is nothing more you can do. Willpower and cleverness won't work. Wallowing in negative interpretations is too suffo-cating and heavy. The left brain's methods fall flat. At this point, you may feel disillusioned, unmotivated, or depressed. But actually, this is the turn-ing point! You've finally let go of *trying* to be successful, *trying* to make progress, even *trying* to understand. It is here that the left brain and ego are finally learning to become the servant to something greater and wiser.

In spite of yourself, you've begun to experience the open, slightly transparent mind. You're "getting out of your own way." All that's left is to be with what's happening, to be with yourself, to be with the confu-sion. And by simply "being with," and letting things be as they are, you return to an experience of your own "being," which was always present under the distractions. Now you, as your soul, can shine out, shedding Light on everything. Revelations emerge. Understanding and compas-sion dissolve fear. There is release, relief, and childlike joy.

The return to being is the doorway to transformation—when the left brain hands the reins to the right brain, the heart, the consciousness of the *unified field*, and the wise evolutionary Flow. As you step through, your shining identity emerges through the new experience of transpar-ency, along with a new world.

> There is an inner wakefulness
> that directs the dream,
> and that will eventually startle us back
> to the truth of who we are.
> **Rumi**

ACCELERATION SYMPTOMS & YOUR CHOICES

	Resist	Embrace
BODY	"Don't disturb my comfort level," overheating, fevers, rashes, allergies, aches & pains, heart pounding, exhaustion, frequent illnesses, feeling buzzy and overly electrical, actual nerve problems, insomnia, hyperactivity, unable to relax, high-vibrational illnesses like cancer or viruses, immobilization or restricted movement	"I welcome & use increased energy," vitality, endurance, release energy thru creativity, change diet, lose weight, detoxify, rejuvenate, move consciously and artfully, allow unusual sleep patterns, rapid healing, increase in abundance, trust instinct, make choices from truth & anxiety signals, decode energy information, read vibrations
EMOTION	"I don't want to feel it," fear, avoidance, pessimism, worry, lack of motivation, irritable, impatient, need for immediate gratification, erratic emotional release, dramas and traumas, intolerant of stimulation, overwhelm, bipolar behavior, hopelessness, defensiveness, hatred, violence	"Every feeling has a helpful message for me," more love, generosity, happiness, enthusiasm, optimism, trust, compassion, delight, motivation without will, love of the Flow and fluidity
MIND	"I don't want to know it," fixed beliefs, opinions, dogma, rules, short attention span, short-term memory loss, disorientation, ADHD, increased dualistic thinking, conflict, pessimism, argumentativeness, depression, disillusionment, apathy, stubbornness, focus on the past	"I know what I need to know right when I need to know it," meditation, mindfulness, being in the moment, trust intuition, innovation, creativity, inspiration, forgiveness, service, healing, optimism, surprise exploration and growth, focus on the present moment, power of attention

Fig. 1-1

The Positive Path through Transformation

You have a choice at every point along the way to evolve smoothly and rapidly, in harmony with the planet, or to struggle and suffer. When you embrace the heightened energy and the clearing process and don't fight them, they flow through you, lifting you to a higher vibration and increasing your love, understanding, and health. When positive energy increases, it's easier to face and penetrate old fears to find the simple truth inside. Every block and contraction you clear frees more transparent energy-and-consciousness that then helps you clear the next layer of clutter and the next.

This positive path through the acceleration/transformation process makes it easier to engage with what emerges in each moment, without judgment or recoil. It's all useful data. A surfacing fear simply points to an area that needs attention, sweetness, compassion, and patience. As you sit with the fear, it unclenches, tells you its story, and you gain calm perspective. Smiles return. You pass through the stages of transformation fluidly, and the experience feels like riding a magic carpet. The shifts come gently and the soul quietly saturates your personality, creating an entirely new perception of life. You feel like you've become your real self, peaceful and excited at the same time—like you finally get to do what you've always wanted to do.

Even when you've begun to see the Light, though, you can still be affected by other people's fears and may wrestle with *societal* beliefs in sacrifice and suffering. You gain insight, then backslide a bit. This is natural. Making the new reality normal requires a repeated choice to maintain your vibration at the level of soul, or what I've called your *home frequency*. We're breaking an ages-old habit, unlearning and relearning the principles of how we live, create, and grow. It requires patience and practice.

Moving Beyond the Industrial & Information Ages

In the world today, we see a growing polarization between people who welcome the acceleration with its psychological and spiritual growth, and those who close their minds so they can remain "comfortable" in their old ways. We see the beginning of the collapse of old structures based on fear and control. Large segments of society are progressing into chaos as old systems and ways of thinking fail to produce results. At the same time, other segments are progressing toward spiritual and mental clarity, innovative solutions to societal problems, and greater peace and abundance.

This acceleration has brought us from the slow Industrial Age, with its emphasis on physical, mechanical, linear (cause-and-effect) processes, into the Information Age, which emphasizes knowledge, access to increasing amounts of information, and the speed of data delivery and processing. We've evolved from a focus on body to mind. Our minds, however, are still dominated by left-brain, linear processing and compartmentalization.

We therefore try to integrate the vast amounts of information by multitasking as fast as is humanly possible or by skimming along the surface. "Just give me the bullet points!" As the Information Age speeds toward its leap into the next reality experience, the old mental reality of the Information Age is no longer competent, speedy, or expansive enough, and it will be eclipsed. Technology can only take us so far. Our own inherent gifts of consciousness will always be superior to our machines. We're moving now into direct knowing, into intuition, to total comprehension in the present moment—from mind to spirit.

> Everything we call real is made of things that
> cannot be regarded as real.
> Niels Bohr

Entering the Intuition Age:
It's a Vibrational World Now

The acceleration causes you to know yourself, everyone else, and everything else as energy-and-consciousness rather than as solid bodies or objects separated by empty space. You're vibrating at a higher frequency, and that means you can feel other forms vibrating too—each at its own particular frequency. You notice energy inside and between everything, then notice that energy is connected to consciousness. You notice that when you change your energy level, your consciousness changes; when you shift your consciousness, your energy shifts too. There's no space devoid of energy-and-consciousness. Energy, consciousness, and time are all interconnected. When the frequency rises, they all accelerate.

Just as you can feel how easy it is to communicate with someone "on your wavelength," you may notice that one tomato at the market has greater life force than another, or that classical music has a frequency that facilitates expanded states of mental or spiritual consciousness while rhythm and blues has a frequency that drops you deeply into your body and emotions. The vibrational world is full of a symphony of tones and states of being.

· · · · · · · · · · ·

Try This!

Feel Dissonant or Resonant Vibrations

1. List three people you know. Imagine each person's body radiating their personal vibration toward your body. As it meets yours and begins to pass through you, does it synchronize easily with yours? Or is it rough or "off" somehow? Imagine your personal vibration, focused at your home frequency, radiating toward and through them. Does it resonate easily? Does the person adapt to harmonize with you? Or is there a slight bit of dissonance? Is there a difference between the way you connect energetically with a good friend versus an acquaintance?

2. List three places you'd like to visit. Imagine you're actually there, in each experience, feeling the energy of the place. Read your body signals and the vibration of the land and people. How much resonance or dissonance do you have with each place?

3. List three tasks you need to do. Imagine yourself, and your body's experience, doing each one. See which task holds the greatest resonance for

14

your body, either because it matches your home frequency, or because it is on the universe's "urgent" list, or because it offers something you want right away. Rate them in order of your body's priority, not your mind's "shoulds."

. . . .

As you enter the Intuition Age, you become ultrasensitive and your energy-and-consciousness increases exponentially. As you successfully navigate the stages of opening and clearing, you adapt to the new speed of life, like a ship going through the locks to a new water level. Your emotions stabilize and you feel happier—more harmonious, enthusiastic, and positive.

The positive feelings beget a higher quality of thought; you stop complaining and criticizing, and trust your intuition. You open your mind to new ideas and are more curious. Positive imagination re-emerges, serving a renewed desire to create things that resonate with your destiny. Accessing knowledge and processing it in the Intuition Age is based on right-brain perception: empathy, telepathy, intuition, and compassion.

The old, contracted, dominating ego-self fades, revealing a greater potential self. Now you are a higher frequency personality, embodying more of your truth in everything you do. You have a very real *felt sense*—a convincing, living experience—of soul, in your body, all the time. Your options increase, your potential increases; you are not the same person— you are more of who you really are. Soul is no longer a concept; it's not something you *have*, separate and floating above you, connected by a string like a helium balloon. It's who you are; you are the Big You, not the fumbling juvenile you—and You are clear about what You want in life. As your identity evolves, you become a new kind of human with greatly expanded capacities and access to unlimited knowledge and love.

If it vibrates, it can be tuned. Everything is energy—violins, people, potato chips, thoughts, feelings, and events. They all vibrate.
Deena Zalkind Spear

SUMMING UP:
THE PHASES OF TRANSFORMATION

- The acceleration of the frequency of the earth affects your body, making it vibrate faster. This causes initial disturbances as you are moved beyond your physical comfort zone.

- The body's new higher vibration affects your emotions; old fears and emotional wounds that you've suppressed and denied can no longer remain hidden. Traumatic memories surface, become conscious, and you must face them.

- Since this is frightening material, there is a tendency to avoid facing it and to resuppress it. You may do this by using various adrenaline-based fight-or-flight methods. When low-vibration memories are resisted, the force of the acceleration builds up and eventually breaks through, causing even more drama and trauma.

- If you've been resisting and denying the energy of the acceleration and its need to clear your stuck, negative emotions, you may soon become drained and exhausted, disillusioned, or depressed. Nothing works and you're forced to stop using willpower. You must be still and let go of trying. Thinking negative thoughts just keeps you mired in the mud. You've reached a turning point.

- By relaxing and just being, by "being with" what is in each moment, you reconnect with your true self. You inadvertently shift from the left brain to your right brain. You enter the present moment. You expand. Now you have space for totally new thoughts and feelings to arise, and you have a new sense of yourself. You are sourcing yourself from your soul, and your intuition opens. You feel what it's really like to be in the Flow and trust it.

- You embrace the higher vibrations of body, emotion, and mind. You become healthier, happier, inspired, creative, and compassionate. You move with the frequencies yet understand that you have a core home frequency that never changes, that rises constantly from every particle in your body.

- You become intuitive, ultrasensitive, empathic, and telepathic, able to discern energy information directly from the unified field. You're conscious of energy, vibration, resonance, and frequency—and the principles of how energy-and-consciousness work.

- You can easily develop expanded human abilities that previously were considered supernatural.

Fig. 1-2

Chapter 1: The Awakening

Whether or not you can observe a thing depends upon the theory you use. It is the theory that decides what can be observed.
Albert Einstein

PART 2: MOVING BEYOND THE LINEAR

Understanding Spherical Perception

We make a stunning leap of perception as we enter the Intuition Age. With transformation, we actually move from one long-standing way of perceiving reality into a totally different kind of perception. To understand this, it helps to see that there are two underlying inner blueprints, or geometries of perception, that precipitate two different realities: *linear perception* and *spherical-holographic perception*. Spherical perception and holographic perception are slightly different but are so intertwined that in the end, they become one integrated thing. For purposes of clarity, though, we'll look at each aspect separately to better understand how it functions. It is spherical and holographic perception together that catalyze transformation; this is the new integrated perception of the Intuition Age. But first, let's take a look at linear perception.

Linear perception is an old way of knowing who we are and how life works. We've become so accustomed to it over the millennia that we can't imagine anything else and can barely even recognize it as a "thing." It is based on a model of reality that sees separation. Past, present, and future are lined up in a row, separated from each other by imaginary gaps, with energy functioning in a line, progressing sequentially toward goals. We have here and there, self and other, inside and outside, and the million either-or polarities that we move between via a line. We have timelines, storylines, lines of logic, mechanical processes, and the shortest distance between two points. *Linear perception is a function of the left brain.*

Your left brain governs analysis, description, proof, regulation, language, and rational, sequential, logical thinking. It reduces experience

17

to meanings that are separated into categories. Left-brain perception can easily make you feel isolated and the world can seem separate from you, and dangerous. Two of its primary rules are: (1) never be overwhelmed by negative emotion, and (2) avoid unproven change as much as possible.

Therefore, your left brain suppresses upsetting memories and knowledge, and makes negative declarative statements like, "I can't, or don't, do that. That's impossible!" It thus creates a kind of fake security. If you spend too much time in your left brain, it can become an addiction like anything else. You can identify with the behaviors and rhythms of that kind of consciousness and think you *are* the left brain. Then you may assume that reality functions the same limited way. It follows that objective science and technology with their logic and proof become more significant than subjective art and music, with their fluidity and unpredictability.

Linear, left-brain perception can cause energy to contract; it can slow and even stop the Flow. The result is that life cannot easily renew itself or flow into new cycles of creativity and growth. When you perceive through a filter of separation, the left brain can deny the soul's reality while validating the ego, keep you from being in the present moment, block guidance, perpetuate fear and scarcity, cause illness and mistakes, and create pain and suffering. As you begin to transform, though, linear perception seems inordinately slow, inefficient, sticky, boring, and restrictive.

Let's be clear—linear, left-brain perception is not "bad." It's just that it should no longer be the primary mode for knowing yourself and creating reality. Even after transformation, when we're living in the Intuition Age, we'll still use the left brain and we'll still understand linear perception. There will always be a use for this kind of mental functioning—it's what allows us to have individual self-consciousness and helps us get things done. Today, we still understand and use instinct, the perception of the reptile brain, though we see it as a smaller part of our intelligence. When dinosaurs roamed the earth, it provided the main organizing principle for reality.

Shifting to the Right Brain

So, we are unlearning the dominant human habit of perceiving from the left brain and thinking reality is like the left brain. We're learning to enter our right brain, explore the nature of its particular kind of perception—which some call "quantum perception"—and develop a liking for it.

The right brain is free flowing, nonverbal, nonmathematical, nonsequential, and its perception is not confined to specific spatial dimensions. It is integrative, perceiving the whole, and intuition is its natural form of perception. It doesn't use language at all, just direct experience and direct knowing via the senses, without description. There is no separation, no isolation of sensory input into specific sounds or images, no stopping anything. There is no willpower; everything works perfectly and doesn't need to be forced.

The right brain is the doorway to the *imaginal realm*, where all possibilities exist and abundance is normal. Here, you may receive large, comprehensive patterns of knowledge that are perceived with ultrasensitivity and a felt sense, where you understand all at once the data contained in different frequencies of energy. We might call it "heightened impressionability."

Dr. Jill Bolte Taylor, a neuroscientist who suffered a stroke and the complete disuse of her left brain for a period of time, describes the experience of living in her right brain as, "My consciousness soared into an all-knowingness, a 'being at one' with the universe, if you will. I could no longer clearly discern the physical boundaries of where I began and where I ended. I sensed the composition of my being as that of a fluid rather than that of a solid." She continues, saying that, "Even though my thoughts were no longer a constant stream of chatter about the external world and my relationship to it, I was conscious and constantly present within my mind."[1]

The easiest way to shift to your right brain is to become quiet and still. Be with the reality that's occurring in your present moment; don't try to change it or understand it, but engage with it, appreciate it, merging into the scene with its objects and open space. Feel into the reality and what's inside or under the reality—the inner blueprint, the vibrational pattern that's giving rise to the form. Feel how it's part of you.

The longer you pay attention, the more that's revealed. Soon you realize everything exists at once—harmoniously and consciously—with everything else. Everything is connected. The connections then take you into spiritual territory and you may have mystical insights about the Divine. *Right-brain perception has no experience of linear time because everything is totally in the present moment.*

The Present Moment Expands

Right-brain consciousness lets you break free from linear thinking. There is no sense of processes progressing or things improving over time. As you live more in the right brain and the Now, you notice a change in the amount of time it takes for results to occur. Creation and dissolution—moving from energy-and-consciousness to form, and from form to energy-and-consciousness—occur faster than ever before. It's natural to imagine anything and be able to materialize it, almost immediately. The idea and the result are both in the present moment. And your body, emotions, and mind adapt quickly to the latest wave of acceleration; it just seems normal to function at the new level.

Soon you realize that much more is contained in the present moment than you could have imagined. The Now mushrooms to include increasing amounts of the past and the future, all individual realities around the world, as well as the nonphysical dimensions—both inner space and outer space—and the beings who exist there. It becomes too difficult and useless to project your mind into the past and future or "over there"—as though other realities are separate from you—and you realize all the knowledge of what was, is, and can be is already in your big present moment with you. You don't have to reach for it or even wait for it very long. When you want or need it, it's there.

Living in the present moment is no longer a platitude; it's a discovery. When you keep your attention focused in the present moment, everything occurs in the present moment with you. The longer you hold your focus, the more knowledge and energy you can have; more layers and details are revealed through the mechanism of your own presence. The Now is capable of expanding to forever and infinity. Focusing your attention in the present moment reveals your soul's wisdom and your body's instinctive knowledge, and it enables you to access accurate guidance and insight from frequencies of consciousness you may never have tapped. *Mindfulness*—the art of paying attention to what you're noticing in the Now and why—becomes an important practice, one of the primary functions of the mind in the Intuition Age.

All matter originates and exists only by virtue of a force . . .
We must assume behind this force the existence of a conscious
and intelligent Mind. This Mind is the matrix of all matter.
Max Planck

You're Living in a Sphere, a Reality Ball

It takes some discipline to learn to be in the Now. We're so programmed to think about the past and future as separate locations that when the mind projects to either realm, we unconsciously assume we're leaving the present. Actually, the past and future are contained within the present moment! So you must learn to continually pull yourself back into your center and refocus on the Now. All of life occurs in the Now! The present moment is your place of power. It's where you realize your soul is actually in your body and spiritual energy is everywhere inside matter.

As you focus on living in the present moment, you learn to experience yourself as centered, as the nucleus of your reality, where your truest consciousness can be found. You realize you're always at the center of yourself, even when your mind wanders or your emotions run amok. Just be quiet and you-in-the-center reappears. When you quiet yourself and really sense the moment, you may notice that your energy-and-consciousness radiates from you—the centerpoint—in every direction, forming a perfect sphere, or ball of reality. Some people call this the *aura*. You are a ball of Light, a sphere of influence.

21

You realize your sphere is your present moment as well as your conscious mind, your personal energy field, your current reality, and your sense of self or identity—and it's fluid, not fixed. Your sphere vibrates at a particular frequency in any given moment. It's always a blend of your soul's true vibration and the feelings and thoughts you choose to focus on. Certain thoughts allow more of the soul to express freely while others block that expression. When you change your frequency, other changes match it—the size of your sphere, the way you experience yourself, what you know, and the possibilities in your reality. Throughout the day and night (in your dream world), your sphere changes frequency and size constantly, like a zoom lens on a camera, as you move in and out through the great universal Body of Knowledge, or the *unified field* of energy-and-consciousness.

Soften your focus, and your sphere expands to include more time, space, and knowledge. Sharpen your focus, and your sphere contracts to concentrate on fewer things more intensely. When your sphere expands, you resonate to higher dimensions and access more mental and spiritual knowledge. When your sphere contracts, you resonate to physical and emotional kinds of knowledge.

• • • • • • • • • • •

Try This!
Expand & Contract Your Sphere

1. Quiet yourself, and feel the scope of your present life, as though everything you're aware of is inside a spherical present moment. Notice that space and time are included in your sphere; you have a routine, projects in progress, relationships, movement and flows, repetitive thought patterns, desires and dreams.

2. Now imagine adding 50 percent more energy to your sphere, raising the frequency of your reality by 50 percent and expanding the scope of your life by 50 percent. Let that new amount of energy-and-consciousness bring greater confidence, exciting ideas, a better fit with people and opportunities, and an easier flow that brings just what's needed. Have you

remembered more about your interests and potential? What new developments do you see? What do you know now that you didn't before? How do you experience yourself, others, and life's possibilities now? Make notes in your journal about what this new reality looks and feels like.

3. Return to your regular present moment and life, then contract your sphere by 50 percent. Notice how your attention focuses differently, perhaps directing you to concentrate on something in particular. Do you tend to forget about certain things? Do you feel less visible? Less flexible? Write about your observations in your journal.

4. Come back to your normal present moment reality and see what ideas have come back with you. Notice from now on when you tend to expand or contract your sphere.

• • • • • • • • • • •

When you meditate, for example, your sphere expands to include the kind of knowledge that exists at higher frequencies. It is inspirational, peaceful, compassionate, and unitive, joining your individual earthly self with your higher spiritual self, and with the souls and hearts of all beings. You experience yourself as *I am Me* and *I am Us*. You may understand many great, universal truths. You may experience your history on earth, remembering many of your past lives and what you were learning.

If, on the other hand, you're concentrating on washing your car, your sphere contracts to focus on the nuances of the task at hand, and you're not aware of much that's universal. If you're in your normal comfort zone and someone criticizes you, the shock or fear reaction can cause your sphere to contract with self-doubt and defensiveness. Your world basically caves in with negativity, all you can focus on is overcoming insecurity, and you lose the connection to your real self. If you can recenter, focus on being the person you love to be, and radiate that home frequency again, your sphere expands and you feel much better.

Don't seek reality, just put an end to opinions.
Seng Ts'an

23

What You Learn from Your Sphere

When you learn to maintain the spherical model of reality, with you in the center, and never having to leave your center, a number of interesting things happen. You realize that anything you need is already inside your sphere. In fact, when it's time for something to change and evolve, the means of accomplishing it simply emerges from the sphere, as though the particles shape themselves into the next person, opportunity, or resource, and there it is! It doesn't come to you, you don't attract it—it comes out of you! And when it's time to be done with the trappings of a phase of accomplishment, the forms dissolve back into the pure energy of the sphere, available to be recombined into new realities.

Since everything happens inside your sphere, there is no actual "outside world" anymore. You can't get outside your sphere. If you think of a new thing, or visit a place you've never seen, your sphere has already expanded to include it. Other people are in your sphere, and you're in theirs. This helps you understand that there is always help—you are not alone but belong to a huge family of souls, who include each other and thus know about each other. This opens you to a desire to understand collective consciousness, interconnections, sharing, convening, and collaborating.

It's only when you're cut off from your own soul, isolated in one of those tiny, contracted, fear spheres, that a huge, dangerous, outside world seems to exist. When you're centered and realize there is no outside world, you also realize that souls work together to evolve collectively, and nothing is truly inimical. The world is in you, and at your home frequency, it is your best friend.

If everyone and everything is inside you, in your Now, there are many potential realities there too. Each reality vibrates at a specific frequency. Each reality is composed of many variables, and they all have their own subtly different frequencies as well. The variables you've combined to materialize your current life match your current vibration. When you become interested in other particular variables and their combinations, and place attention steadily on them, they can easily occur in your reality. *Attention allows materialization; lack of attention allows dissolution.*

For example, if you've finished with a job and sense you need a new career direction but don't know what to do, you're probably still focusing on the past and not working with the imaginal realm. As soon as you soften and open your mind, new ideas of what you might love to do can take shape in your sphere, and simultaneously, they seem possible. By maintaining attention on these ideas and the feelings that go with them, new opportunities arise in your life.

Your sphere is filled with the vibration you broadcast and acts like a set of instructions to the unified field, dictating what can materialize for you. Your sphere is like a flashlight beam illuminating and bringing to life sections at a time of the great unified field, which ultimately is your truest, most evolved self. You are the whole thing, but your sphere lets you experience varying frequencies of your entirety, one at a time. The possibilities that resonate with you vibrationally can occur in your world; those that don't cannot occur until you consciously match them with your frequency.

If you broadcast negative or limited thinking, for instance, your reality will contain negative, limited experiences and people, and you'll have a negative, limited experience of your own self. If you raise your vibration to match the planet's acceleration, you'll have situations that are fluid, rewarding, growth-oriented, dynamic, and supportive. And at times, when you-the-soul need you-the-personality to make a breakthrough, surprising opportunities and discoveries can appear out of the blue.

With the past and future absorbed into the present moment, your future is not "out there" anymore. *Your future is now a possible reality that vibrates at a higher (or perhaps lower) frequency of your current reality.* And there are billions of realities you can choose. If you place full attention on a possible reality, merge with it, and let your body, emotions, and mind adjust to the new frequency, it will likely materialize immediately, without having to go through a long, logical, developmental process. You'll simply experience a sequence of synchronicities and seemingly miraculous events, and *voilà*! Creating a new reality is just a matter of allowing your sphere to match a desired frequency.

SUMMING UP:
ELEMENTS OF SPHERICAL PERCEPTION

- Be silent and shift to right-brain perception. This opens you into the present moment and unified field.

- Enter the present moment fully, engage with what's occurring, and live from there.

- Notice that your energy-and-consciousness radiates equally in all directions, forming a sphere. Center yourself at the nucleus of your sphere. Realize you're always in the center.

- Understand that your sphere is your present moment, your reality, your conscious mind, and your current identity.

- Realize the moment—your sphere—contains more time (past and future), space (physical and nonphysical), knowledge, options, and other beings than you ever thought possible. Everything is inside you and available.

- See that there is no outside world; your sphere expands and contracts with your attention and frequency. If something becomes conscious, the sphere has already changed its scope to include it. You can't get outside your sphere. You are safe because, inside your sphere, everything is mutually supportive.

- In your sphere, dividing lines are gone. Physical and nonphysical worlds merge. Other people are in you and a part of you. Everything knows about everything else. What used to be separate convenes—left–right brain, head–heart, body–mind, soul–personality, self–others, inside–outside. You experience integration and greater unity.

- What used to be your future is now a potential reality. Place your attention on an imagined reality that pleases you, and match your frequency to it. Love it and it materializes, emerging out of your sphere.

Fig. 1-3

Chapter 1: The Awakening

He who does not trust enough will not be trusted.

Lao Tzu

Understanding Holographic Perception

Let's make a quick U-turn and go back for a moment to our shift from left- to right-brain perception. Certainly it takes focus and practice to develop the new skill of entering the right brain and experiencing life from that point of view. The goal is not to live constantly in that realm, though. In fact, it would be impossible. As long as you're here in the physical world, you need the left brain to focus your attention and thus create tangible realities to experience.

The world of the right brain is seamless, all inclusive, and not conscious of itself; perhaps it is the collective unconscious or collective superconscious. *The function of the left brain is to interrupt the continuum of the right brain so we can know things consciously.*

What we're trying to do is equalize the left and right brain's scope of consciousness and cooperation with each other. When you can use both equally, the next step is to balance and connect the two. You do that by using the right brain to access higher knowledge, remind you of truth and who you really are, rejuvenate you, and connect you to the greater consciousness of humanity, the earth, and the cosmos. Then you use the left brain to make your direct, intuitive experience of these expansive knowledge patterns conscious, translate inspirations into results, and communicate with others in the physical world.

Once you've created a result and described or defined a direct experience, you don't turn it to stone; you let go and move back to the right brain's imaginal realm again. You become quiet, enjoy the moment, and wait for a new vision to light you up. Back and forth, and around and around, like a figure eight—one kind of consciousness feeds the other, and on and on, smooth as silk. When this occurs, the scope of your sphere is unlimited. And yes, the left brain will provide helpful hints—e.g., "Don't let your toddler cross the road unattended," or "Friends don't let friends drive drunk."

• • • • • • • • • • • •

Try This!

Balance the Left & Right Sides of Your Brain

1. Sit quietly, with your back supported and your head level. Breathe in and out easily, slowly, deeply. Feel your brain inside your head. Imagine the two hemispheres of your brain, and notice whether one side seems larger than the other. Perhaps one side feels hard, one side soft. Or one feels darker, the other lighter. Just notice.

2. Imagine that between the two sides there is a partition. Reach in with your imaginary hand and pull out the partition. Now nothing is in the way, and the sides of your brain can communicate freely with each other.

3. Let the energy from the bigger, lighter, softer side flow into the smaller, darker, harder side and fill it, integrating and changing it in some way. Then do the reverse, letting the energy from the smaller, darker, harder side flow into its partner. Each time you do this exchange, let the two sides of your brain talk and give information to each other; you don't need to know what it is. Keep the back-and-forth exchange going until both sides feel equal and balanced.

4. Now notice your eyes, and adjust them in your imagination until they, too, feel equally sensitive and unstrained. Do the same thing with your ears until they feel equally open and alert.

5. Smile, feeling the left and right sides of your mouth and facial muscles. Adjust them so they are equally relaxed and your smile feels even.

• • • • • • • • • • • •

The Power of Centerpoints

This rocking between the brain hemispheres is akin to the movement between the physical and nonphysical realms, or the *round trip* between the quantum particle and the unified field, and back to the particle again. When the left and right sides of your brain integrate, you experience the merger of form and pure energy-and-consciousness. Now you can become aware of a centerpoint in the middle of your brain. It is the meeting place of heaven and earth—the unification point of your dualistic mind, often called the *eye that is single* or the *third eye*.

In esoteric teachings, this point corresponds with the pineal gland, and in meditation, it is considered the electromagnetic center of the body and the center of the experience of the individual self. When you focus attention for a while into this centerpoint, something interesting happens—a resonance begins that allows you to shift into other centerpoints via attention, and the centerpoint in the heart area is often the first stop.

From a Single Centerpoint to Multiple Centerpoints

The heart is where the soul integrates fully with the personality—that's why the heart is universally assumed to be the "seat of the soul." It is also called the place of the *hieros gamos*, or sacred union, of the energies of masculine/compassion and feminine/wisdom. The centerpoint in the heart generates the experience of the self connected intimately, with great understanding, to all forms of physical and nonphysical life.

The resonance of the heart center, partly because of its affinity for love and communion, helps you understand how every centerpoint resonates with every other centerpoint and how welcome you are to slide into any centerpoint in any dimension and share that experience. This is the basis of empathy—you can know the core experience of any other being or life-form by feeling into it with your attention.

And yet, the frequency of a centerpoint can act as a filter, causing you to understand other centerpoints of like vibration. When you experience yourself from the centerpoint in the heart, you're a being of compassion who can understand the hearts of all beings and even the essential nature of objects. When you experience yourself from the centerpoint in the head, you see yourself as a being of knowledge and can tune in to the collective mind of all beings. If you slide into the centerpoint at the base of your spine, you experience yourself as a purely physical being and can understand other bodies and the event-waves in the world.

If you flow into the centerpoint of a single cell, you experience yourself as part of a colony and understand the perfect interrelatedness of support and function. If you journey to the centerpoint of the earth, you experience yourself as a being composed of billions of life-forms and understand that level of complexity, as well as your connection to all other planets.

You can resonate into any centerpoint, at any frequency, and know that reality and the whole world from that particular viewpoint. This is holographic perception, where each part of the whole contains both an individual perspective and the entire experience of the whole.

To understand holographic perception, you must shift to the right brain to truly experience what can seem incredibly confusing when seen from the left brain and linear perception. The left brain perceives the experience of each centerpoint, one at a time, and gives the impression that you must jump in a linear fashion from one to another, and lose the experience of the first to gain the experience of the next. Some call this "attention blindness." To understand the combined experience of a number of centerpoints, all at once, the left brain requires a linear sequence of adding them together and attending to each new combined experience as it occurs. It's difficult to know great complexity as a whole.

To experience how any centerpoint contains the entirety of the whole, and to know that you can experience multiple centerpoints simultaneously, you must feel it and have a *direct experience* of it—and that comes from the intuitive right brain. If you focus too much, the holistic experience dissolves like a mirage. Only by remaining in the "soft mind" of the right brain can you feel how each point is both unique and a part of the whole and also know how the combined reality of a large number of centerpoints feels and functions—all at once! No sorting or separating required.

Centerpoints Expand to Become Fields & Whole Realities

There is an aspect of centerpoints that pertains to the concept of "as above, so below"—the idea that the macrocosmic and microcosmic versions of anything are related to each other, much as low C and high C are connected via resonance in music. Each centerpoint (microcosm) originally condenses from its ideal, nonphysical, spiritual source—a field of energy-and-consciousness (macrocosm). The centerpoint then acts as a seed, or inner blueprint, that can expand itself into a spherical reality that catalyzes a matching form. *Here's where holographic perception links intimately with spherical perception.*

For example, the spiritual qualities attributed to an oak tree (macrocosm in the nonphysical unified field) individualize as an acorn (microcosm in the particle-based physical world), which is a centerpoint whose expansion into a spherical reality catalyzes the physical oak tree. Every centerpoint is a potential spherical reality, and every reality has a centerpoint that contains and relays its core truth.

Your physical heart is a centerpoint that condensed from the field of your soul's compassion and understanding. It generates an electromagnetic field of radiance that's spherical in nature and accurately duplicates the unconditional love and wisdom of your soul. When you allow the heart's field to increase, it becomes a huge sphere you can live within that causes your whole life to be filled with love and understanding.

The power of the heart's centerpoint and field is enormous. Feeling how your heart functions, you can understand how you yourself function as a *hologram*: you are both the centerpoint (individual expression on earth) of your soul (a macrocosmic field) and you radiate the spherical field that catalyzes your physical reality. And, you resonate to all other souls' centers and fields, as well as the centers and fields of every object. Centerpoints and fields are in constant communication via resonance.

The choice between love and fear is made every moment in our
hearts and minds. That is where the peace process begins . . .
Like love, peace is extended. It cannot be brought from the world
to the heart. It must be brought from each heart to another,
and thus to all mankind.
Paul Ferrini

The Implications for Creativity

Let's say you want to change your life or invent something useful for society. With spherical-holographic perception, you remain in your center, with all possibilities inside your sphere with you. You might activate the vibration of the centerpoints in your heart, head, base of the spine, cells, and organs by placing attention fully on your own home frequency, and striking it like a tuning fork in your imagination.

Let that vibration expand until all the centerpoints become spheres, and let all the spheres merge into one huge sphere. Then allow that sphere to radiate farther, out to the level where the vibration of your "just right" new reality or invention exists. Be with that amount of self. Be quiet and receptive. Your attention will be drawn into a new centerpoint, and your old centerpoint will combine with it. As you adjust to the pattern inherent in this new seed-place, that centerpoint expands to reveal the new reality or new invention—and this reality is also "you." Keep being with the new reality, and the specific ideas, resources, and actions you need to create it physically will emerge.

Since all centerpoints resonate with each other, and since you can perceive multiple experiences at once, you can focus your attention at any frequency, shift your attention to that origin point, expand into its field or sphere, and know that reality—all without leaving, or losing, your own "home." This is how we'll travel through time and space, and this is how we'll know our many "past and future" lives—not in spaceships or time machines but via resonance with the billions of potential realities in the cosmos. It's travel—and knowledge of new worlds—via perception.

With spherical-holographic perception, you are phenomenally free. You no longer feel isolated and restricted. What you want to create happens effortlessly. Frustrations dissolve. Cause-and-effect thinking ceases to be the primary rule for materializing results; miraculous, mysterious, immediate results occur with no logical explanation. You feel intimately connected with your family of souls, who support you. You receive ideas easily, and trust the Flow and your perception in each moment. You understand more about the roundness of life. Processes become more cyclical and interrelated.

SUMMING UP:
ELEMENTS OF HOLOGRAPHIC PERCEPTION

- Focus yourself in the present moment, in the center of your sphere. Remember that you never leave the centerpoint.

- Balance the left and right sides of your brain, and the kinds of perception generated by each, by imagining there is no partition between the two sides and that the energy-and-consciousness of each flows into the other, back and forth, exchanging and integrating.

- Notice there is an intersection point between the two sides of your brain, a place where integration of knowing takes place. This is connected to the pineal gland, in the geometric center of your head. Some call it the third eye or the eye that is single.

- Occupy that centerpoint in the brain for a while, and a resonance begins that allows you to shift into the centerpoint in the heart. You may also notice you can shift into any centerpoint in any dimension via this resonance.

- Because the physical heart naturally radiates an electromagnetic field, it's easy to understand how centerpoints can "uncollapse" or radiate out to become spheres of energy-and-consciousness that precipitate physical realities. A healthy heart materializes directly from the soul and radiates the soul's qualities. The purer the translation, the more loving and wise your life is.

- While being at home in your own core, you can attune to any other centerpoint. This may be a new reality you're ready for. Merge with it, and the information it contains can balloon out to become a new experience that still feels like "you."

Fig. 1-4

Transparency

A human being has so many skins inside, covering the depths of
the heart. We know so many things, but we don't know ourselves!
Why, thirty or forty skins or hides, as thick and hard as an ox's or
bear's, cover the soul. Go into your own ground and
learn to know yourself there.

Meister Eckhart

Just to Recap...

We are going through a personal and societal transformation, experiencing an acceleration of energy-and-consciousness that affects the vibration of our planet and of our bodies. We may resist the heightened frequency at first since it takes us out of our comfort zone, irritates us, and scares us. Our emotions and minds are also experiencing the higher frequency, and this means the negative emotions we have denied or suppressed are surfacing to be cleared, and the fixed thoughts, beliefs, and habits we rely on for security are wobbling and malfunctioning. We may either embrace the process of loosening and clearing contracted feelings and thoughts, or we may try to resuppress and revalidate them through adrenaline-based, fight-or-flight methodologies.

If we avoid the flow of the acceleration, it builds up force like water behind a dam and eventually breaks through, causing even more drama and trauma. However, if we embrace the process and flow with it, we adapt to the new frequency of life and become clearer and more conscious of being our soul. The acceleration comes in waves.

If we continue to avoid and resist the acceleration, we become exhausted, depressed, and disillusioned. Eventually, nothing works. We are forced to stop, give up, and just be. This is the turning point where we let go of our left brain's dominance and shift to the right brain, where there is no language, no need to be successful. By being still, we allow the space for new developments to occur that are in tune with our destiny. This is the experience of ego death, where the phoenix (soul) rises from the ashes of the old reality.

Chapter 1: The Awakening

The acceleration causes time to speed up; it seems everything is happening in the present moment. We learn to focus attention in the moment and experience it as a sphere around us, with our mind, soul, and reality all inside our sphere. Realizing that the past and future are all in the present moment with us helps us understand that linear perception—where past, present, and future are separated along a line—is *old* and doesn't function well. We are shifting from the Information Age to the Intuition Age, where perception is based more in the unifying right brain.

We see that our sphere can expand and contract and that nothing is outside the sphere. We are in the nucleus or centerpoint of our sphere and we never leave that spot. But in our sphere with us are billions of different frequencies, and each is a centerpoint of another possible spherical reality. With our attention, we can focus on any centerpoint (or frequency), merge with it, and allow it to expand into a field. Now our reality changes; we experience the view of the world and of ourselves from that vantage point—all without leaving our own center. Every centerpoint knows every other centerpoint, and the whole of the unified field and the collective consciousness. This is spherical-holographic perception.

Spherical-holographic perception is intuitive and empathic; it uses the right brain and is the new perception of the Intuition Age. For us to be able to recognize the new perception and use it skillfully, we must complete the clearing of fear-based emotion and thought (contractions and clutter) that is such a crucial phase of the transformation process. It is this clearing process that leads us into transparency.

A person who has authentic presence...has an overwhelming
genuineness which might be somewhat frightening because it is
so true and honest and real....This is not just charisma.
The person...has...earned authentic presence by letting go, and
by giving up personal comfort and fixed mind.
Chögyam Trungpa

Transparency Message
WAKING UP

You are floating. In the velvety blue-black heaven-space, full of glossy diamond light, and you are dreaming of the life you will have. Images appear, you try on scenes, imagine yourself in them, see how they flow, how people occur, how lessons are learned. It's magical, how surprise events arise and fade into new scenes with new surprise events that are just right. The Flow carries the dream, sources it, and you punctuate it with your attention. You choose without logic. By feel, by what wants to happen. So easy. At a deep place inside, you are high on the joy of creating something perfect. Then in a twinkling, you are in another dark, more opaque space. A subtle shift. A moment of confusion. Yes! You are inside matter now.

As your life begins to unfold and unfurl, you feel sleepy. How did I get here? Who am I? Why am I in this darkened room? What do I know? Life events arise and fade and from the dark room, it all seems random. You have inherited contractions from family and humanity that freeze your energy-and-consciousness. You forget: the dream you made with the Flow. You can't remember: your creative joy. You can't see well through the opaque filter around your diamond mind, can't feel truth through the opaque filter around your radiant heart. You sink into dreamless sleep: something is going on around you but you don't know what. Choices are made but by whom? Who is living this life? You hear voices, receive impressions.

A surprise event occurs and matches exactly with the dream event you chose in the blue-black velvety world. Shiny light-rays break through. The perfect ease of correlation reminds you: this life is on purpose, this life is full of grace, this life is my life. I'm living the dream I created when I was wise. Now an effervescent

Chapter 1: The Awakening

energy bubbles up out of your cells, out of the air, the furniture, the food. It lifts you closer to the dream, to the joy. Here is the tiny glimpse of my truth! I want to know the whole dream I planted. I want to make choices that allow that dream life to be my life. I want my glossiness.

Be still. Don't reach. It's here, it's now, your whole dream life. Be still and let it come, and event by event occur in you, out of your substance. Patience and presence. Let the cloudy glass of tap water clear. Give away the contractions that aren't yours, let them soften and dissolve into the glossy light. Open your Eye. Wake up. Remember the dream glittering in the diamond light world. It is fluid. It evolves. It feeds you. It loves you, you love it. It is alive. You are alive at the same frequency. What the dream knows, you know. Wake up. You can know everything you know. The dream is inside you now. Receive it all. When you do, you are light and huge and high and wide: awake.

2

Transparency:
An Idea Whose Time Has Come

Three things cannot be long hidden:
the sun, the moon, and the truth.
The Buddha

By now you have a rough idea of how the transformation process works, and how the acceleration leads to a leap of perception from one way of knowing yourself and life to a dramatically different one. And you probably have a sense that much of the early part of the transformation process involves clearing your clutter—the fear-based emotions and thoughts that contract, slow, and distort the flow of energy-and-consciousness.

Every piece of clutter you dissolve back into clear light allows your highest *inner blueprint*—your soul's purpose or destiny—to translate fluidly and accurately into the form of your life. And the clearer you become, the easier it is to evolve along with the planet—with no snags, no stuckness, no suffering. This is the act of becoming transparent. *Transparency is a state of being that reveals the merger of the spiritual realm and the physical world, and eliminates any distortion between them.*

It is a state that allows you to remember who you really are and how ideally life can work. It is an experience of intimate connection to what's most real. But because the world has been functioning within a kind of opacity based on adherence to linear perception and fear-based behaviors, we've not understood the idea of transparency very well. Transparency in regard to accessing truthful information is beginning to sneak into our thoughts as an inalienable right, but it is only recently that a first big wave of people worldwide has become focused on waking up psychologically and spiritually to be able to experience total, holistic transparency.

In this chapter, we'll examine some of the ways transparency has been misunderstood or seen in a limited framework—from the concept of invisibility and camouflage to the current Information Age understanding of transparency as relating just to information and communication. Then we'll look at what transparency means as a function of the new Intuition Age.

The Evolution of Transparency

The past, in contrast to today with our growing consciousness movement, seems like the Dark Ages—when the gods were angry and punishing, sin was the original state of humankind, salvation was necessary, and safety might be achieved by following religious dogma or shamanistic rituals. In addition, superstition was rampant, intuition was seen as magical or blasphemous, and mystics were martyred.

The idea of transparency or spiritual enlightenment was incomprehensible to most people then. The rare, truly transparent people were sprinkled around the planet in tiny outposts, trying to maintain their Light against ignorant, fearful mobs who revered them one minute and persecuted them the next. They usually had to camouflage themselves or become reclusive to remain safe and radiate their Light. Let's look back a bit to see how our concept of transparency has evolved.

Tell people there's an invisible man in the sky who created the
universe, and the vast majority will believe you. Tell them the paint
is wet, and they have to touch it to be sure.
George Carlin

How Transparency Became
Confused with Invisibility

Back in the days of the various pantheons of gods and goddesses, people were not trying to be divine themselves; they may have been envious, but mainly they wanted to please the gods so they might conceive a healthy child, their crops would grow well, the weather would prove favorable, or they might have a successful trip to the land of the gods after death. Many primitive peoples did believe in the soul—that we have an invisible essence inside us that leaves at death to live on in an invisible world, along with other invisible entities, both angelic and demonic. They even had a sense that the invisible worlds had levels, from the lowest, often hell-like *astral plane* with its demons and troubled souls to the highest heaven realms, like Mount Olympus, the Garden of Eden, or Valhalla.

Throughout history, we've seen ourselves as physical beings living in a solid, physical world so separate from the invisible worlds that we routinely doubted anything was there. In this kind of reality, the closest we could come to the idea of transparency was a belief in the magical power of becoming invisible.

Human beings' earliest experiences were based on observation of nature combined with superstition about the gods—and this led to magical beliefs, ritual, sorcery, and a rich body of mythology and folklore. Chief among the benefits of magic was the ability to create invisibility. To be invisible was to cheekily become like the gods, and therefore have extra powers during one's life. Perhaps this is why the fascination with invisibility has had such a colorful, long life.

Becoming invisible was valuable for gaining advantage over other people. You could commit any sort of act in the midst of others without them knowing, or eavesdrop on important conversations to overcome an enemy, learn secrets, or formulate a plan for trickery, seduction, or criminal activity.

Usually it was a magical object or garment that conferred the power of invisibility, like a hat, ring, sword, wand, stone, flower, or even Harry Potter's cloak of invisibility. In many cases, the magical object granted the user invisibility from mortals, immortals, and supernatural entities. King Arthur had an invisibility cloak. The Greek hero Perseus had a helmet of darkness or invisibility, and a Sanskrit story tells of a Brahmin who becomes invisible by putting magic salve in his eyes.

An Apache Indian legend describes how a hero receives a cloak of invisibility from a lizard. Northeast Native American tribes venerate a supernatural horned serpent, perhaps something like a dragon, that bestows invisibility and shape-shifting "medicine" on those who defeat or help it. In addition, the use of invisible ink to write invisible messages goes back thousands of years.

As the fascination with invisibility moved into the realm of sorcery and witchcraft, practitioners relied on spells, incantations, invocations, and rituals. One spell, in Latin, opens with over thirty mystical names written in bat's blood. Another dictates that a special stone be wrapped in a bay laurel leaf and carried in the hand. Others simply recommend that the practitioner carry a black hen or frog under the right arm. Witches themselves can supposedly become invisible—as well as fly and shape-shift. And then, of course, the vampire is unable to be seen in a mirror.

> If God made a man in His own image,
> why aren't we all, like . . . invisible?
> Father Guido Sarducci, *Saturday Night Live* character

Invisibility in Religion & Metaphysics

These more superstitious ways of thinking about invisibility evolve somewhat with the advent of Spiritualism and a greater exploration into metaphysics. Spiritualists believe in communication with the dead, and that those who are in spirit (invisible in the invisible worlds) can partially materialize and dematerialize, especially during séances, which are held in darkened rooms. During these sessions, a medium can supposedly supply the entities with a vapor-like, malleable substance known as "ectoplasm," which the discarnate entities can use to form apparitions of their previous physical selves. Since ectoplasm is said to be sensitive to light and emotional and physical shocks, it's difficult to prove it exists. Spiritualist mediums have been widely investigated for deception and fraud and yet, sensing, and sometimes seeing, semi-invisible ghosts without the aid of séances is a worldwide phenomenon.

In metaphysics, invisibility might relate to the concept of shifting suddenly from the physical dimension to a higher one, or to a "parallel world," or alternate time period. Invisibility would be caused, basically, by the body's particles increasing in frequency until they dissolved into light. This relates to the idea of *dematerialization* of a body or object, or *teleportation*, where the body or object dematerializes and rematerializes in a different location. In esoteric teachings, ancient priests were trained to dematerialize their body by increasing the frequency of their consciousness, becoming less dense, accelerating molecular spin, and encompassing more light. Rematerializing was accomplished by slowing down their consciousness and vibratory rate.

H. Spencer Lewis, founder of the Rosicrucian Order, taught that invisibility could be achieved through the use of "clouds," or bodies of mist, called forth from the energy field surrounding us. Some postulate that this may refer to a cloud of free electrons that absorbs all light, and doesn't reflect or refract light. Consequently, the person surrounded by such a cloud would be invisible and an observer would see nothing. Perhaps this is similar to reports of how UFOs can suddenly vanish and reappear elsewhere, often surrounded by clouds that emerge from nowhere. This practice of disappearing in clouds is attributed to the various pantheons of ancient immortal gods and goddesses as well—might they have been intergalactic visitors?

Becoming invisible makes its way into some forms of religion. In the early stages of a yogi's progress toward enlightenment, he or she may develop any number of *siddhis*, or psychic powers, which include invisibility, changing shape, knowledge of past lives, reading the minds of others, knowledge of hidden things and the time of one's death, freedom from hunger and thirst, the ability to walk through space and time or to enter other bodies, and to become light or heavy at will. The *Yoga Sutras of Patanjali* advise that there is a practice called *samyana*—a combination of concentration, absorption, and trance—which when focused on the physical body, can suspend the power of another to see it. In effect, the body "disappears."[1] The use of these abilities for personal gain or vanity was considered to be an obstacle to spiritual development.

Christianity has the concept of *ascension*, the idea that certain enlightened individuals can shift directly into the higher frequency realms without dying first. Some have called it "entering Heaven alive." Jesus is resurrected from death and subsequently ascends. The Bible says, "And after He had said these things, He was lifted up while they were looking on, and a cloud received Him out of their sight."[2]

Similarly, Enoch, father of Methuselah, was "taken by God" and lifted to heaven. And Hiram Abiff, architect of Solomon's Temple and key figure in Freemasonry, was also resurrected in a Christ-like way. Esoteric teachings hold that there are many ascended masters who guide humankind, some ancient and some recent: Sanat Kumara, Sananda (Jesus), El Morya, Serapis Bey, Saint Germain, Pallas Athena, Kuthumi, Djwhal Khul, Hilarion, Quan Yin, Mary Magdalene, Buddha, and Krishna, to name a few. Ascended masters are reported to be able to materialize, dematerialize, and bilocate at will.

Buddhism has no direct focus on the idea of invisibility or the magic that might be used to create it. Instead, it focuses on emptiness, which may actually be the truest form or experience of invisibility—one that comes the closest to transparency. A story goes: Once, a master named Tao Shu settled next to a Taoist temple. The Taoist priests were irate at his presence and used every kind of magic to scare him away. However, he remained. After twenty years, the Taoist priests finally gave up. People asked Tao Shu, "What tricks did you use to beat the priests?" He replied, "I used emptiness. Taoist priests have magic and tricks. 'Having' is being finite, measurable, and exhaustible. I do not have any magic. 'Not having' means being infinite, inexhaustible, boundless, and immeasurable. Emptiness—not having—can overcome magic—having—by being broader and superior."

They can't have disappeared.
No ship that small has a cloaking device.
Captain Needa, *Star Wars* character, about the *Millennium Falcon*

Invisibility via Hypnosis, Mind Control & Cloaking

In most of these myths, folktales, and practices, invisibility is probably not a physical phenomenon at all. It's more likely that it is a function of temporary psychological blindness foisted upon others by controlling the mind through mass suggestion. One person becomes invisible because the others are effectively blinded by not trusting their own point of view. This brings to mind the Jedi mind-control tricks from the *Star Wars* films, especially the scene where Obi-Wan Kenobi tells the stormtroopers, "You don't need to see his identification." (They repeat it verbatim.) "These aren't the droids you're looking for." (They repeat it.) "He can go about his business . . ." (They repeat it.) And they allow Obi-Wan and Luke to "move along." Later Luke asks what happened and Obi-Wan tells him that the Force can have a strong influence on the weak-minded.[3]

Some modern hypnotists claim they can make individuals invisible to a hypnotized subject. Michael Talbot, in his book *The Holographic Universe*, tells a story about being taken to an event at his father's home where a hypnotist performed some amazing feats with a man from the audience, whose teenage daughter was also present. He was hypnotized in front of the group and given the suggestion that, upon awakening, his daughter would be invisible to him. When brought out of his trance state, he could not see his daughter, who was giggling right in front of him. In addition, when the hypnotist stood behind her and held a watch against the small of her back, the man was able to read the inscription on it as though he were looking right through her body. The man himself, afterward, hypothesized that he might have received the information about the watch telepathically.

> But as even the stupidest toddler knows,
> covering your eyes makes you invisible.
> Heidi Schulz

Another pseudo-invisibility technique is the phenomenon of camouflage, where the chameleon or squid becomes perfectly still and changes color to exactly match its surroundings. Thus, it is possible to hide in plain sight and seem invisible. Soldiers have given up bright uniforms and learned to use camouflage of various colors and patterns to blend in with their environment. The military has developed stealth technology for aircraft, a sort of radar invisibility that relies on shape to reduce reflected microwave radiation. (Black coloring and operating at night assist with this as well.) In the end, though, cloaking and hiding are not true invisibility, and they're not transparency either.

Some Drawbacks to Invisibility

There are definite moral implications to the concept of becoming invisible. Plato's opinion about any device that could facilitate invisibility was that it would eventually corrupt its owner, resulting in defeat and debauchery—the temptations of invisibility were just too great. J. R. R. Tolkien gives the same overall message about the power of the ring, which confers invisibility, in *The Lord of the Rings*.

H. G. Wells, in his famous novel *The Invisible Man*, has his main character, Griffin, a scientist who has devoted himself to research into optics, invent a way to change a body's refractive index to that of air so it doesn't absorb or reflect light. He carries out this procedure on himself, and does become invisible, but in the end, fails to reverse it, and only becomes visible again when he dies. Griffin says, "I went over the heads of the things a man reckons desirable. No doubt, invisibility made it possible to get them, but it made it impossible to enjoy them when they are got."[4]

· · · · · · · · · · ·

Try This!

Imagine You're Invisible

1. In your journal, make a list of the things you'd be curious to do if you were invisible.

2. Imagine yourself doing those things one by one, and write about the thoughts and emotions you have as a result. How do you feel about yourself?
3. Make a list of things you'd like to create or contribute to the world.
4. Imagine yourself trying to do those things one by one, while you're invisible. Write about the drawbacks, how successful you are, and the thoughts and emotions you have as a result. Were you able to cocreate with others? How well did you do when you realized you had to do everything by yourself? If you had to be invisible all your life, how would you feel?

. . . .

"Horizontal" & "Vertical" Transparency

It's no wonder there were moral implications and drawbacks to trying to become invisible—every form of finding that sort of transparency was limited to efforts in the physical world. And by omitting the spiritual truth, any knowledge gained remained extremely partial and thus fed into ignorance. Because motives for invisibility came from fear and feeling limited, the whole endeavor was bound up in old perception. *Invisibility is not transparency.*

As we begin to know transparency, we see it first operating with a focus only in the physical world. Transparency in physical reality refers to the quality of being able to transmit light so an object behind can be seen; or to an individual whose thoughts, feelings, and motives can be easily perceived; or to organizations that are open to public scrutiny. In this book, I'll refer to these forms of physically related transparency as *horizontal transparency*, meaning the motion and means are rooted in matter and person-to-person communication.

I want to address horizontal transparency in the Information Age, especially as it relates to government, business, and leadership. In the Information Age, we're still using old, linear perception, and seen from this vantage point, transparency implies that we're transmitting truth, or information, freely and without the distortion of fear, across to others in the physical world through the medium of left-brain, language-oriented communication.

The other kind of transparency I'm talking about in this book is a characteristic of our energy-and-consciousness. It's the totally clear perception that results when the soul integrates with the personality. As you clear yourself of fear and illusion, you experience *vertical transparency*, where the higher frequency, nonphysical energy-and-consciousness of the spiritual realm shines through the lens of your mind, emotions, and body to be made real in the world. This affects your perception, raising it in frequency to levels that are not limited by time and space. Fear does not exist at this frequency and the juvenile motivations that fueled the desire for invisibility seem laughable.

For now, we can eliminate the desire for our bodies to become physically transparent, like a jellyfish or a pane of glass. Eventually, as you and others light up more, and after your consciousness has become fully transparent, your body—and the whole physical world—may actually become nearly transparent, empowering you to dematerialize and ascend directly into a state of enlightenment. Is that science fiction? Who knows? Soon, though, in the Intuition Age, you'll use a combination of both horizontal and vertical transparency—a holistic transparency related to spherical-holographic perception. Let's examine a few of the ways we still see transparency partially and horizontally, as a function of the physical world alone.

> By giving people the power to share,
> we're making the world more transparent.
> Mark Zuckerberg

Horizontal Transparency in Government

In these end times of the Information Age, transparency is widely used to describe the ability of one person or party to access *information* from another, and we associate truth with good *information*. There is actually an official term now—"openness"—that refers to a policy that emphasizes free, unrestricted access to knowledge and information. Remember, though, that information is horizontal and left-brained, while wisdom is vertical, right-brained, heart-oriented, and of the soul.

It seems we're hearing the word *transparency* used more and more to describe the desire, or need, for honesty, ethics, and lack of corruption in business and government. This need for transparency in society is at an all-time high—because people are frustrated with secrecy, deception, and being manipulated. We want truth, not smokescreens! We don't want choices being made for us without our input. We want access to important commercial and governmental information that impacts us.

Despite media spins, propaganda, and stonewalling from officials, it's increasingly difficult for unethical or scandalous behavior to remain unnoticed. Because of communications technology, we have more access to, and thus demand for, relevant information. We've come to see it as our right, and we want it fast!

It's easy to see that transparency of this sort is strongly related to accountability. In a democracy, it is theoretically held that to be accountable, government must make its decisions public. Government officials are agents of their citizens, and therefore, their actions need to be known and approved of by the public. But government bureaucrats avoid transparency to protect their mistakes and greed. It's all too common for them to disclose information only to individuals who support their goals, which frequently revolve around amassing power and money. So, in a nutshell, lack of horizontal transparency tends to produce corruption.

> I hold the maxim no less applicable to public than
> to private affairs, that honesty is the best policy.
> George Washington

Were government officials transparent, they would inform the public of their plans, actions to implement the plans, mechanisms for checking that the plans had been accomplished, and if not, how the officials, who should be serving the public, could be punished or corrected. Without this form of honesty, the citizenry develops lack of faith in their leaders, and eventually, rebellions occur. Top-secret information is leaked to the public, whistle-blowers become common, mass online petitions are generated, and rabble-rousing, wildcard politicians become popular on the national stage. The willful lack of transparency, or collusion, by leaders is a form of the suppression of subconscious blockages I talked about in chapter 1. Keep resisting "ego death" and the accelerating, free flow of energy-and-consciousness—in this instance, truthful information—and drama, trauma, catastrophes, and explosions result.

Though many governments in the world have now adopted freedom-of-information laws (in our case, the Freedom of Information Act, or FOIA), information transparency is still limited, partly because the cost of offering the vast amounts of data to the public is astronomical. And in this era of terrorism, there are restrictions on access to information that might legitimately endanger national security—and much information can conveniently be made to fit that category, so it doesn't have to be revealed. According to the U.S. Department of Justice annual FOIA reports, more than 700,000 requests for information have been made each year since 2013.[5] The number of FOIA lawsuits has also increased dramatically, and recently, it was reported by the US House of Representatives Committee on Oversight and Government Reform that over 70 percent of the documents requested by the public were either ignored or heavily redacted by officials.[6] Journalists complain that it's difficult to obtain interviews, and that press officers, or "minders," must be on the phone during interviews.

In the Information Age, information is power, and those in government who resist the transformation process are likely to seek ego-fortification by controlling information flow. This eventually leads to authoritarianism, where the government legitimizes restrictive decisions based on the need to combat various "interest groups" and loosely defined "societal problems." And yet, there is a groundswell of attention pouring into the need for *radical transparency*—a phrase applied to governance, politics, software design, and business to describe approaches and actions that radically increase the openness of organizational process and data. Groups like Transparency International, the Sunlight

Foundation, the Open Data Institute, and ProPublica, to name a few, are working for freedom from corruption in government, politics, business, civil society, and daily life.

> In the twenty-first century, the countries that thrive will be
> the ones where citizens know their voices will be heard
> because the institutions are transparent.
> Joe Biden

Horizontal Transparency in Business & Leadership

Transparency in business could be as simple as the idea of providing an itemized receipt with a purchase. Or the obnoxious television ads for prescription drugs having to list all the gruesome side effects. Slowly, the business world is working to advance a new norm of transparency, one that reaches deep into the inner workings of the system. In business, a corporation is considered transparent when it allows access to information like financial records or its environmental impact. Does the corporation make its actions, like operations and decision-making, visible to observers? Is the information it reveals clear and accurate? Does it disclose its anticorruption program? Many companies are taking corporate integrity and transparency pledges, though many still hide shady insider dealings.

Today, large multinational corporations have the power of small nations. They are complex and opaque because they operate through networks of subsidiaries incorporated in different countries, under different legislation, while carrying out operations in yet other countries. These complex structures can easily hide tax evasion, illegal international practices, and bribes. And without transparency, many of these huge corporations are almost impossible to trace. Increasingly, local people want to know the impact of foreign corporations in their own territory.

The new Intuition Age consciousness is growing among the workforce; employees want to work in an environment that allows clarity and originality of thought, advancement, access to truth and key information, and trusting relationships among all the people. Open and honest communication supports the decision to trust rather than harbor suspicion; there is a high correlation between transparency and happiness (read employee engagement) in companies. Transparency not only helps employees function at maximum levels, it helps them plan and protect themselves—and be more of themselves.

It turns out that transparency, within and outside a company, can provide a huge competitive advantage. Internally, backstabbing and negative undercurrents are reduced when everyone knows what everyone else is working on and accomplishing, what their goals are, and even what they're each being paid—and that the compensation policy is fair and adhered to. Transparency also helps companies attract and retain top talent; replacing and retraining skilled employees who leave because of a poor working environment costs a lot.

Many potential customers now choose products and services based purely on concepts of transparency and social and environmental sustainability. A recent survey shows that 51 percent of people pay attention to factors like health, social impact, and transparency when buying food.[7] And there's nowhere where a lack of transparency shows more than in customer service; poor service easily equates with "something to hide." Getting the runaround and not being able to talk to a real human being on phone calls to companies resulted in 67 percent of customers hanging up mid-call, with 78 percent bailing on a purchase transaction.[8] A million people a week view tweets about customer service and roughly 80 percent of those tweets are critical.[9] In fact, surveys report that 86 percent of people say their buying decisions are influenced by negative online reviews.[10]

Technological advances like word processing, photocopying, personal computers, cell phone cameras, the internet, social media, and the Cloud have made it easier to generate, store, and disseminate information to more people, and the costs have been reduced as well. The Information Age is reaching its crescendo, and people are "friending," "liking," "pinning," and sharing their most intimate information with virtual strangers. It's not much of a stretch to realize they want the same sort of intimacy with their leaders.

People want to relate to their leaders and know they share similar human problems. They want to enter the leader's "personal space" and would rather see a video about the leader than read an article—that way they can read facial expressions and body language to evaluate how genuine the leader is. People also want to share in the direction their company is headed, and to know about problems that might undermine the company's success and their own future. Yet it is said that approximately half of all managers don't trust their leaders, largely because leaders hoard and control information as a source of power. Transparency in leadership today requires more personal engagement—more face-to-face connections, more frequent and candid communication, more sharing, more concern, more cocreating, more deep listening.

> Transparency may be the most disruptive and far-reaching innovation to come out of social media.
> Paul Gillin

Vertical Transparency in the Intuition Age

We've touched on the idea that back before the Industrial Age, transparency focused on the supposed "power of invisibility" being conferred by power objects or cloaking. In the Information Age, transparency has focused on the free flow of information and knowledge, especially in government and business. Both these interpretations are a result of seeing transparency as a horizontal function operating only in the world of form.

As we move into the Intuition Age and new perception, transparency takes on a new orientation. It becomes vertical as well. Now the nonphysical realm integrates with the physical, changing reality significantly. It is not about your body becoming see-through like the air, though. It's more that your mind and emotions become transparent, enabling you to see, feel, and know your soul and the workings of the spiritual realm—in your body, in your life, and in this world.

The invisible spiritual realms have always been merged with the physical world, but now we're at a high enough frequency to be able to feel and understand the ramifications of that. In days of old, our frequency was so low that heaven and earth seemed distinct and far apart; the abilities of the gods and goddesses seemed supernatural and out of reach of the ordinary person. Now, with our increasing vertical transparency, we're approaching the consciousness of those spiritual beings, and both the visible and invisible worlds are equally present in each moment as states of energy-and-consciousness. Here's a glimpse of how vertical transparency affects us:

1. **At the physical level**, vertical transparency provides an understanding of "perfect health," including qualities like fluidity, agility, adaptability, strength, and gentleness. You love your body for its loyal service and responsiveness to your feelings and thoughts. With focused attention, you find Light inside your body and matter. You may easily develop extraordinary human capacities, even to the extent of changing your appearance.

2. **At the emotional level**, vertical transparency brings an experience of calm, compassionate neutrality, with a natural tendency to welcome the new, to tilt toward joy and connection. Negative, fear-based emotions—like jealousy, insecurity, defensiveness, revenge, anger, rage, hatred, bitterness, arrogance, sorrow, depression, apathy, disappointment, shame, guilt, timidity, panic, obsession, greed, and disgust (I could go on!)—are reduced to a shadow of their former selves or are entirely gone. If someone who isn't fully transparent acts from negative emotion, you let it pass through and understand the core reason the person is focusing on fear and negativity. You remain in a position of compassion to assist the other person.

3. **At the mental level**, vertical transparency brings clarity of thought unclouded by the negative emotions that originally caused the left brain to make rigid declarative statements about what must and must not happen for you to stay safe. You no longer need beliefs, dogma, credos, and rules. You integrate right-brain perception with your logic, and function naturally and harmoniously according to innate universal principles, engaged with the sanity of the Flow, allowing spontaneous

turns and surprises. You prefer self-entertainment and are fascinated with fully engaged creativity. Your mind values stillness as well as movement, intuition as well as logic, art as well as science, overarching concepts as well as concrete detail. Your thoughts are more connective, collective, integrative, and expanded. You are honest. Just-right thoughts fall through into form in the blink of an eye.

4. **At the spiritual level**, vertical transparency brings ongoing revelation of greater truth, love, inspiration, and imagination to fuel the personality. You deeply trust yourself as the soul, and the collective consciousness of all beings. This kind of transparency brings authenticity that is immediately evident yet undefined. It reminds you of the awe-producing, perfect functioning of the inner, nonphysical realms—the profound harmony of the all-that-is.

> Inner silence works from the moment you begin to accrue it. What the old sorcerers were after was the final, dramatic end result of reaching that individual threshold of silence. The desired result is what the old sorcerers called "stopping the world," the moment when everything around us ceases to be what it's always been. This is the moment when sorcerers return to the true nature of man. The old sorcerers always called it "total freedom."
>
> Carlos Castaneda

An Idea Whose Time Has Come

Why is the world ready now for global horizontal *and* vertical transparency? It's the frequency! People around the world are connecting with each other via social media, and broadcast and cell phone networks. The internet speeds up access to every sort of data, every kind of personal story, every possible distortion of truth, and all the varieties of "reality TV" exaggeration. Everyone seems to be writing a book, creating podcasts, and making videos. We are flooded with truth and lies—and we want to burn off the fog. Horizontal transparency—honesty and authenticity concerning information and knowledge—helps us do that.

The importance of instantaneous connections with people on our wavelength, who share our interests, breeds a longing for intimacy. We want to find our soul partners, we want more depth and trust, we want our leaders to be our friends. We're looking for a global family experience, for commonality in diversity, and for the opportunity to make meaningful contributions to the world—not alone but in cocreative, harmonious teams. Vertical transparency accelerates these processes and expands our consciousness to be able to identify as global beings.

Transparency, both horizontal and vertical, increases the incidence of innovation and helps bring forth inventions and improvements to society, which can then be adopted widely at breakneck speed with little resistance. It is the increasing speed of life, the expansion of the present moment, and our leap into spherical-holographic perception that make us ready for a fully transparent self, life, and world. Those who are receptive are already forging the new pathways. Those who resist are being carried along and will open to personal transparency at their own rate. Eventually we'll see horizontal and vertical transparency merge to become an integrated state of crystal clear, global transparency functioning within spherical-holographic perception.

> There is only one thing stronger than all the armies of the world,
> and that is an idea whose time has come.
> Victor Hugo

Just to Recap...

Transparency is an idea that has not been fully understood until these transformational times. Historically, when the physical world seemed widely separated from the invisible land of the gods, people confused transparency with invisibility. They used various rituals, invocations, incantations, and magical objects to confer invisibility, though today we wonder whether it was all a form of mass hypnosis or mind control. As times evolved, forms of metaphysical skills, including the ability to dematerialize the body, were said to be obtained by shamans, yogis, high priests, and ascended masters. Certain religions, like Buddhism, held that becoming invisible was a mere trick, and that entering silence and emptiness was much more powerful.

Invisibility is not transparency. While we're still in the Information Age and using linear perception, transparency functions "horizontally"— person to person, organization to organization—concerned mainly with the free flow of information and knowledge.

Transparency in government, business, and leadership has been made easier and more requisite because of the speed of the internet, social media, and cellular networks. People are sharing themselves globally as never before. And yet, leaders and officials still hoard information and restrict its flow, because in the Information Age, information is power. In business, transparency is becoming a competitive edge. Business leaders are learning that employees want a more personal, shared relationship— more of a partnering than top-down direction.

Transparency in the Intuition Age takes on a more "vertical" aspect; the nonphysical realms merge with the physical world, the soul merges with the personality, and we receive great insight, revelation, inspiration, and positive qualities of feeling and thought. Negative, fear-based perception dissolves like a strange dream.

Transparency Message
THE YOU IN THE MIRROR

It's morning, you pull away from sleep, and you're up. There you are in the mirror, checking face, teeth, eyes, hair, body. You think it's you: oh, but it's just your coverings. Pause the talk. Be quiet and blank. Feel what's under. Who is here, inside this body? Who shapes this image? Be very still. Feel the presence of the

Transparency

observer—the big you with no name—in your body, all the way to your toes. Someone is here inside looking out through these eyes, feeling out through this skin. Noticing.

Look into the eyes in the mirror; the observer is there too. Your twin is noticing you. Find the shine in those eyes; call forth more shine. Watch the you in the mirror fill with Light and expand in presence, watch the eyes become bright like beacons, see them looking into you, calling forth more of you to match the you in the mirror. That you fills effortlessly with clear substance, releasing true essence into space. That one is magical and limitless, and capable of things you haven't yet dreamed. Keep watching with soft eyes. The you in the mirror is becoming transparent; the solidity dissolves. You can see through yourself, and soon the image is gone, totally clear. What's left is an impression in the air, a hyper-clear place in space where you still are: more intensely you than ever.

Feel into the transparency, sense the presence amplified to a high, almost radioactive vibration. You're there though you seem invisible: this is your true energy, who you really are. It is smooth and pure and hot and cool and joyful and calm and excited and wise and strong and committed and ready to respond to what comes. Let that energy transfer into you: yes, just match it. And now, the form in the mirror fills in again, and here you come, back into the world. Here you are, expanded, translucent, Light pouring from your eyes and wafting out of your skin, forming a cloud of gentle, happy Light all around you. You and the you in the mirror are truly identical. You are Light and you live in Light. The you in the mirror reminds you how much you can be. That one: is excited about being alive. That one: has another precious day to play, to remember. Own that you, be that you, you are that you. And now face, teeth, eyes, hair, body. And the new day, this white canvas.

3

The Opaque Reality:
Secrets, Lies & Old Perception

The Matrix is everywhere. It is all around us. Even now, in this very room. You can see it when you look out your window or when you turn on your television. You can feel it when you go to work, when you go to church, when you pay your taxes. It is the world that has been pulled over your eyes to blind you from the truth.

Morpheus, in *The Matrix*

Most of us live in opaque bodies in an opaque world. We do not see through to what's real and are rarely seen for who we truly are. We are resigned to an old, slow kind of perception in what's becoming a painfully dense—or opaque—reality. Think how much of our time, energy, and resources is spent on self-protection and defense, keeping secrets, lying, hiding, and living by outmoded mores. Think how much misunderstanding and waste result from the belief that we live in a destructive, inimical world instead of an evolving, compassionate one.

These things are symptomatic of a reality we've long considered to be inevitable. It's a reality where we live, partially hypnotized, believing we're at the mercy of uncontrollable, unfair, random forces that prevent us from becoming our totality. It's a reality where our original Light is dimmed and often blocked from penetrating into, flowing through, and radiating from us. This is the "old normal" way of life—the opaque reality.

In this chapter we'll delve into the origins of opacity, the beliefs that keep it in place, and the resulting culture of secrets, lies, and hiding that goes along with it.

59

Mia told me that she never gets what she wants. For her, things don't last or pan out the way she thinks they will. She worked in her family's business for years, but it wasn't her first choice, and she was numb from boredom. Finally, she decided to follow her dream and study graphic design. Midway through the program, she dropped out because she wasn't sure she was talented enough or could make a living from it.

Instead, she decided to teach yoga. It turned out Mia lived in a town that was too conservative for a successful yoga studio, so she gave that up. She decided to sell her house and move to a place that suited her growing spiritual and creative interests, with better light and a studio, but she had trouble with the broker, had to find a different one, and her home sat on the market for a year. Finally, her house sold, but the buyers backed out at the last minute. Mia was exhausted—and sad—from bucking a system that seemed to be against her. She wasn't sure she could even trust her own motives.

Josh encountered the opacity of the world when he tried to communicate his leading-edge, innovative ideas to his business partner concerning a bold new direction they might take to expand their company. He could feel how it would work and that it would be successful, but he was met with excuses and rationalizations about how difficult it would be, how their investors wouldn't back them, and how the ideas weren't "adjacent" enough to their current path.

Once Josh had become saturated with his new vision, he couldn't go back to the old trajectory. He faced a reality that, to him, was now limiting, dull, and off-purpose. He had a family to support, however, so should he sacrifice himself and his ideas and work at something he'd outgrown? Or break away and start his own company—all over again— with the financial insecurities and hours of overtime that would require?

And finally, young Georgia, at age eight, had always been open, compassionate, and intuitive, in spite of her family's skepticism about how she knew the things she did. They tried to correct her for being overly sensitive and dreamy. Nothing good could come of it, they advised. She'd need to develop a thicker skin and face reality. But Georgia couldn't shut herself down and didn't want to. Inside, she knew she had some wonderful abilities that would grow along with her.

Georgia faced living with the semi-blind, unconscious people in her family, as well as the teachers at school and many of the other kids her age. The programs on television were offensive and boring, so she retreated into her own world, reading, listening to music, and writing in her diary. She sensed there would be years of people judging her as abnormal before she met people on her wavelength and could really be herself.

These are examples of what I mean when I say we live in an opaque world. From not recognizing your own accurate insight to becoming almost crippled in the ability to move forward creatively, to the temptation to sacrifice yourself for survival, to the frustration of not being seen and validated for who you really are—we all face roadblocks like these as we grow up and learn to function in the "adult" world. There is a spiderweb of limiting beliefs, "shoulds," doubts, accepted procedures, and societal rules that snares the joyful, motivating spirit inside us. And, we are trained to believe the spiderweb is unavoidable and normal.

> A lack of transparency results in distrust
> and a deep sense of insecurity.
> **His Holiness the Dalai Lama**

So What Is Opacity?

Officially, opacity refers to something that doesn't transmit light and is impenetrable to sight. As I'm using the word, it refers to limited perception that blocks your view, making the world seem dense and rife with difficulty, sacrifice, and suffering. It prevents you from seeing through illusion.

Our bodies and most physical objects appear opaque and solid—they have a cohesion and density that tend to maintain shape and resist short-term change. With the exception of things like jellyfish and glass, we can't see into or through most solid objects—therefore, we think we can't know their inner workings, or if there are any at all. When life becomes opaque, it's often because we extend this idea about solidity to our own self: "Perhaps because I am physical, I can't be seen into or known for who I really am—and perhaps there *is* no inner world of Light."

The frequency of your focus—the vibration you're seeing from—can determine whether you see a table, rock, tree, or your own body as solid and opaque, or as made of vibrating particles with Light inside. When you perceive via the frequency of solidity, you see yourself and the world as solid and physical; the table behaves like a solid, reliable table. You and the table hold your own and resist each other. You have separate realities.

But when you look at it from a higher frequency, where you are an energy being vibrating in a world that is a sea of energy, the table appears to be a collection of particles floating together in space, blinking in and out of form—and it's quite porous. So are you. In this reality you can walk through the table. The table and you no longer have strong boundaries, and at this frequency, you are much more alike and nonresistant. You share an interpenetrating reality.

In an opaque reality, we forget our higher frequency identity—that we are beings of energy-and-consciousness, living in Light—and we fall into agreement with the masses who believe we are slow, solid, and separate. Perhaps this is the real meaning of "original sin." At any rate, it is the frequency of solidity that causes our experience of opacity, where we live mostly in shadow.

> If we're wrapping ourselves up to conceal any vulnerability,
> whatever happens to us has to go through all those extra layers.
> Sometimes love doesn't even reach where we truly live.
> Alexandra Katehakis

How Life Became Opaque

It's safe to say that what distinguishes us from other animals and forms of life is the development of the third level of our brain, the *neocortex*, with its left and right hemispheres. Because of this, we are capable of self-consciousness, self-motivation, personal growth, and understanding both the physical *and* nonphysical worlds. It is the left hemisphere—your left brain—that has created the frequency of solidity and contributed to the development of the opaque reality, all because of its superb ability to observe, focus, define, make things conscious, and reduce experience to meanings. Let's explore how.

1. **The left brain gives the perception of physicality and reality. To do this, it slows perception.** The left brain perceives by interrupting and stopping the continuum—the territory of the right brain—focusing on one part at a time. When it focuses, it leaves the high-frequency energy-and-consciousness of the unified field (the nonphysical realms) and spirals down in frequency to the vibration of a single idea. This slowing causes the idea to become more dense, and eventually, to crystallize and take shape physically. The idea of a sweet, juicy, round fruit becomes a smellable, biteable peach. So, focus and slowed perception cause the experience of the physical world. This is how we materialize things; what the left brain focuses on, we identify as real. After millennia, we've adopted the left brain's view as dominant—that we and life are mainly, or perhaps even totally, physical.

2. **The left brain produces the experience of separation.** When the left brain focuses, it perceives one part separate from the whole, and from other parts. It sees one thing at a time with selective attention. It's easy to see yourself as an individual body-personality and not see that you're also a soul connected to all souls. If you focus on having a problem, you don't see the bigger picture that contains the solution. Focus on yourself, then on another person, and it looks like there's a blank space between the two of you where the left brain glossed over the part of the unified field that's in between. *It looks like emptiness, but it's really absence of attention.* When you notice the gaps, it's easy to feel alienated from other people or your goals, which are always "over there." This slows your perception and makes operating in the physical world effortful and time-consuming.

3. **The left brain thinks in either-or terms.** Perceiving separation between things creates either-or consciousness. If you focus on others' needs, you don't recognize your own, and vice versa. Half of reality is always invisible. It's natural to fall into thinking about one *or* the other, comparing, judging, and narrowing your possibilities by feeling you must choose one. With this sort of split, the compartmentalizing left brain soon focuses on the concept of opposition, polarization, and conflict. It defines things in opposing pairs: form or emptiness, me or you, inside or outside, safe or dangerous, stillness or movement, etc. Having to choose sides and oppose something limits the scope of your life—you're always missing half of everything—and contributes to ignorance, energy drain, and sacrificial thinking. It also causes big logjams in the Flow.

4. **The left brain gives rise to linear perception.** For creativity to produce materialized results, the left brain says there must be a process, broken into steps and phases, a sequence of events or focal points progressing along a line. The vision is separate from the goal, which is separate from the plan, which is separate from the action, and it's all separate from the result. There is a linear path to accomplishment involving willpower and time. With such fragmentation, time slows from the instantaneous present moment, where things can happen all at once, to the sloggier division of time into past, present, and future, which are seen to be distinct territories separated by imaginary gaps along a line.

   With linear perception, the mind projects ahead to anticipate the future and behind to remember what worked or didn't work in the past. Every time your mind leaves the present moment, time slows and life seems stalled or snagged. When your mind projects in a linear way across time or space, accurate insight and choices can't be accessed because the soul's wisdom is only available in the here-and-now.

5. **The left brain causes insecurity and fearfulness.** When you become so used to the left-brain worldview—that there is just form and emptiness, that everything is physical, and that you are

just a body and personality—it can be hard to remember who you really are and how life can really work. You may forget to know the inner worlds where unity and compassion govern all. Is there a bigger You in the emptiness? It's easy to feel alone, abandoned, and terrified. You can be caught in a partiality that makes you sad, anxious, sacrificial, or angry. Negative emotions lower your frequency and opacity increases.

Linear perception causes you to feel separate from other people, places, objects, time periods, and your goals and dreams. Making connections and finding the attention-approval-love-success-happiness you seek becomes effortful. The belief in difficulty can make it seem that you're prohibited from attaining the experiences you crave. You may even jump to the conclusion that the Divine doesn't love you, or there *is* no higher power—and life becomes really dark.

6. **The left brain's need for definition causes contraction and blockages to the Flow.** As it collects information about the many partial views, the left brain categorizes and organizes, describes, makes decisions, and eventually creates rules, which are beliefs and fixed ideas. Most of these rules exist to help you avoid fear and "dangerous" mistakes. By acting like a severely over-protective, controlling parent, the left brain blocks the flow of new ideas, patterns, experiences, and growth. Rules and opinions cause contractions in the Flow and contribute to the need for secrets, lying, and wearing masks. Contractions cause snags, struggle, pain, confusion, frustration, self-doubt, thwarted love, and illness.

You can see from this brief sketch of symptoms that come from the overuse, overdependence on, and overidentification with the left brain, that they produce tremendous density—a low vibration of energy-and-consciousness—and partial blindness. Instead of seeing yourself as continuous, existing simultaneously and equally in the physical and nonphysical worlds, you see yourself as a wave somehow separate from the ocean. All these left-brain-generated symptoms create the darkened lens and the clutter I've mentioned previously. An opaque reality is the natural result.

SOME CAUSES OF THE OPAQUE REALITY vs. THE TRANSPARENT REALITY

Opaque Reality Low/Slow Frequency	• Physical/individual consciousness, only seeing the physical, isolation • Either-or thinking, polarity thinking, narrowing possibilities • Negative emotion, negative thinking, contractions of the Flow • Fixed ideas and rules, too much definition, partial view of life • Separation from soul, from others; fear of attack; need to defend • Linear perception; seeing gaps between things; breaking time into past, present, future; projecting the mind away from present moment • Lack of trust in self, others, the Flow
Transparent Reality High/Fast Frequency	• Connection to nonphysical realms and identity as soul • Naturally entitled to your destiny and self-expression • Positive emotion and thought; joyful creativity • Experience of oneness and belonging, safety • Trusting self, others, and the Flow; experiencing fluidity

Fig. 3-1

Chapter 3: The Opaque Reality

● ● ● ● ● ● ● ● ● ● ●

Try This!

How Much Influence Does Your Left Brain Have?

1. During the day, notice how often you think of yourself as physical. For example, needing to eat, wanting to lose weight, doing chores, or going to the gym. How often do you think of yourself as a soul? For example, meditating, reading inspiring books, feeling yourself observing the moment, or merging with the Flow. Assign a percentage to each. Write in your journal about this.

2. Pay attention to how you feel separate. Notice when you're focusing with selective attention on one thing—what are you not noticing at that same moment? How do you tell yourself that you're separate from someone or something you want? How often do you notice the gaps or empty spaces between things? Are they really empty? Write about this.

3. Notice how often you engage in either-or, polarity thinking during the day. Do you compare yourself to others or flip-flop about options for activity? Do you feel you must choose just one thing, and how does that narrow your life? What polarities have you been focusing on lately? Rich or poor, healthy or unhealthy, busy or resting, inspired or apathetic? Write about this.

4. See if you can discern when you're caught in linear perception. Are you thinking in terms of past, present, and future? The timeline to finish a project? The linear plot of a book or film? Can you feel how this slows you down? Write about this.

5. To what extent do you sense you've forgotten how things work in the higher realms? Do you feel like you're missing an experience of belonging? Is there any deep, core emotion—like grief or terror—that might be under your motives and behaviors? Write about how forgetting your connection to the nonphysical, spiritual world can cause insecurity or anxiety.

6. Where do you sense you have energy-and-consciousness contractions? Where is the Flow stuck in your life? In a certain part of your body? On a certain kind of emotional pattern? In fixed ideas, beliefs, and opinions? In habits and addictions? Why are you holding on or holding back? Write about these things.

● ● ● ● ● ● ● ● ● ● ●

Beliefs That Hold Opacity in Place

When you resign yourself to living in an opaque world, you generate limiting beliefs that seem like truth but actually affirm the opaque reality and old perception. For example, you might believe that certain emotional wounds, like PTSD or child abuse, are irreparable traumas lodged in the body and brain that cannot be healed or reversed. Or that when a loved one dies, you must hold on to the grief or guilt, or you lose the love. Or that aging is degeneration, that you lose brain cells, use up your finite resources, and become less than you've ever been. This sort of fatalism is an artifact of the opaque reality.

In the opaque reality, you may hold many ideas based on limitation, like: "I should choose one career path and stick with it. I can't be too needy, loud, greedy, silly, unfocused, or self-assured if I want to be popular and successful." It's a common belief that to tell about an idea before it's materialized will jinx it. Or that to avoid potential heartbreak, you shouldn't get too close to other people because love results in pain. And how about believing that the impossible cannot occur, or that this is the best you'll ever do, or that it's too late to change, or that the way you were raised prevents you from achieving your dreams? We often believe that our mistakes cannot be forgiven. Then there are the beliefs that begin with "I don't know," "I don't have," and "I can't."

> Only through becoming aware of yourself and your
> limitations can you be transparent with others.
> **Joanie Connell**

Some beliefs drop more deeply into negative territory, like the violence-inducing beliefs of hate groups: "An eye for an eye," keeping societal institutions separate and bloodlines pure, or condoning the killing of nonbelievers of one's own religion. Recently, according to Sir Paul Collier, a professor at Oxford University who focuses on public policy and twenty-first-century peace, there is a growing interest in understanding how subjective factors, like beliefs, correlate with conflict. He says that racist beliefs in the American South, for example, which were strongly entrenched for a century, broke quickly in the 1960s because of the youth movement's sense of being intimately connected to people everywhere. He says that researchers' challenge today is to figure out how to break belief systems that might perpetuate conflict.

I've just scratched the surface here, but you get the idea. How many of these cultural, largely unconscious, limiting beliefs affect your life right now? How many are you willing to question?

. . . .

Try This!

Turn Around Some Limiting Beliefs

1. Scan through your own beliefs about what you can't be, do, have, or know; what you believe is hopeless or impossible; what you dislike or hate; how life should function; even how you see life, death, an afterlife, sin, and what has to happen for you to reach "heaven." List these in your journal.

2. Take each belief and write the opposite of that statement. Or phrase each belief in a way where there can be a positive outcome or benefit. For example, turn "Life is blocking me from having what I want" into "Life is cooperating with me so I can see my own limiting beliefs." Or "I can't go to the gym because my back hurts" into "When I go to the gym, people help me work on healing my back problem."

. . . .

Secrets & Mysteries

When reality is opaque, when you can't see through to the truth, when you live with the shadows, it seems normal to not know things and to hold information and talent inside yourself that others never see. Some things show on the surface, but so much more lies hidden and secret like the bulk of a submerged iceberg. We have lived with this for thousands of years, and it's now routine to expect only partial perception and truth. For this reason, secrets are a big part of the opaque reality. A secret can be something you know that others don't, or that you don't want them to know. You may define the content of a secret as either good or bad.

To keep secrets is a normal function of the left brain, which separates experience into known or unknown, private or public, safe or dangerous. In fact, the origin of the word *secret* comes from the Latin *to separate or set apart*. When I hear the term "keeping secrets," I think of keeping chickens crammed in a coop or keeping valuables hidden away in a jewelry box. There's almost an aspect of hoarding involved.

For your soul, however, keeping secrets is an act of stalling and self-sacrifice because, for the soul, it's normal to know everything and anything. From that higher view, nothing can be set apart, all knowledge and experience fit together perfectly in the whole, and every bit helps evolve the entirety of the collective consciousness. These two views produce two motivations concerning secrets: the left brain wants to hide and protect secrets while the soul wants to discover and reveal them, so everyone can evolve faster and more easily.

> I realized that secrecy is actually to the detriment of my own peace
> of mind and self, and that I could still sustain my belief in privacy
> and be authentic and transparent at the same time.
> Alanis Morissette

Mysteries are different from secrets, although the words are often used interchangeably. A *mystery* is something difficult to understand or explain—a kind of knowledge that only experts or initiates are privy to. The origin of the word comes from the same root as the word *mystic*, implying that there is an element of contemplation and self-surrender required to obtain unity and high-frequency wisdom, and that it's possible to spiritually apprehend truths that are beyond the intellect. A mystery is something you suspect exists that could expand your reality.

Secrets exist at a fairly low level of vibration, and are usually connected with fear, isolation, sadness, or negative experience. They are static and prevent your effortless evolution. Mysteries, on the other hand, are connected with the collective unconscious; discovering one reveals the next layer of understanding of the universe. There's always more to know as we head into infinity. Mysteries lead you toward memory of the Light while secrets keep you in the dark.

You may be living at, say, 60 percent of your potential. The next 5 percent that you aren't aware of yet is not a secret, it's a mystery; it lives in the collective unconscious. And it will be drawn to the surface to become conscious and part of you, as soon as you realize the fullness of what you're already doing. Your soul is the ever-ready revealer. It wants to move you forward by dissolving blockages and leading you up the stairway to heaven. What's true of both secrets and mysteries, though, is that we are fascinated by them—we want to dig deep and uncover them—yet we also feel threatened by the prospect of them being revealed.

Why We Tolerate & Validate Secrets

Let me take this a step further and rough out an internal dialogue your left brain may have with itself about why it's important to keep secrets.

1. **I am limited to what exists in the physical world.** All I see is the form that's before me. All I know to do is what worked before. It's difficult to know more, create from the Void, or have abilities beyond the norm if I don't have proof that it's real.

2. **Since I can't see the nonphysical worlds, I doubt their reality, and the vagueness makes me feel fear and resistance.** I have the nagging feeling, though, that there is more to life and I am more than this, but I'm frustrated because the experience isn't physical, so I can't access it. I do sense that this bigger self has enough power to destroy the status quo, and I can't let that happen. My job is to maintain security. It's easier to ignore what's invisible or to make it wrong, silly, or taboo so I don't have to confront it and change. I'll

just pretend I'm not interested. Out of sight, out of mind. I can live in a small but secure world.

3. **The physical world is full of failure, disappointment, pain, struggle, and limitation.** The physical me is a product of history; I inherited my flaws from others. They were limited, so I am limited. My flaws produce mistakes. I do things I'm ashamed of, or I don't measure up. I am wounded and imperfect; I believe I'm innately bad. I remember what doesn't work and what's potentially dangerous before I remember what works magically. I doubt the miraculous or anything that's too easy. I focus attention on memory of criticism, wounds, mistakes, guilt, warnings, and loss. I am locked in to a negative worldview.

> If you tell the truth,
> you don't have to remember anything.
> Mark Twain

4. **To avoid rejection and judgment, I hide my flaws from others. I must project an image, wear masks.** I don't want others to see my vulnerabilities and judge or reject me, so I must cover my mistakes and flaws. I must hide these potentially damaging things and act in a dominating, pleasing, or disarming way. I have secrets I must protect. I must hold back and hold forth—I must project the image and kind of energy I want others to accept about me (even if I don't believe it myself), and try to create agreement between myself and the outside world. Then I must hide the fact that I'm trying to cover up my flaws because that would be another flaw. I must wear masks. At first, wearing masks is fun, like play, but it soon becomes a way of life. I identify with my masks.

5. **To maintain my secrets, I must lie. Since I don't see the real me, no one else does either.** I must lie about my deeper self and pretend that's OK. If I tell the same lie for a long time, or if I tell a big enough lie, people believe me. But really, I feel ashamed. The more lies I tell, the more potential and fictitious realities I must juggle, the

more I confuse and exhaust myself—and others. I don't trust others and they don't trust me.

· · · · · · · · · · ·

Try This!

Uncover a Few of Your Secrets

1. In your journal, make as complete a list as you can concerning the following:
   - What don't you want others to know about you? Why?
   - What don't you want to know about yourself? Why?
   - What do you project to others so they have the best impression of you? Why?
   - How do you think others misinterpret you? Why?
   - What don't you want to know about others? Why?
2. Now imagine that all these insecurities are remedied. Everything is known, all truths revealed. You're on the other side of the discomfort. Go back through each of the five categories and write about how it feels to have the information exposed. Are people more understanding than you thought? Does it lead you to want to improve yourself in some way? Is there more to the story concerning the background of your secrets that would help others understand you?

· · · · · · · · · · ·

6. **Seeing my own flaws makes me focus on others' flaws.** With my negative view, I easily see other people's flaws first, especially when they match my own experience. I actively look for their secrets. If I see other people's secrets and imperfections before they see mine, I can defend myself from them. I react defensively or aggressively when I think their secrets could be harmful to my survival. And I have a special radar that alerts me to others who are on the verge of discovering my secret vulnerabilities. Other people do the same with me.

7. **No one should see my good ideas or talents too much either.**
Because the outside world is dangerous and unfriendly, I basically
don't trust others. If I have good ideas, talents, good luck, or good
fortune, I shouldn't let people know because they will be jealous and
attack me or steal from me. I must keep the good things about me
secret, as well as the bad.

The result of convincing yourself that secrets are natural and necessary for survival is that you separate more and more from your soul
and core truth. "No one knows who I really am—not even me." All the
things you think you must hide from view, and the negative ideas you
hold about other people and the world, become the clutter that interferes
with your clarity. The effort it takes to hold back your own experience
and anticipate other people's secrets drains you; it takes energy to maintain secrets and lies.

All this leads to living life in a contracted state. When you hold,
clench, or rev your motor without moving forward, you most likely live
in a stalled, shaky state of perpetual anxiety. Your secrets are energy
turned in on itself—resulting in frozen, unavailable parts of your totality. The masks are forms of ego, what the left brain thinks you must do
to survive.

Eventually, this house of cards will fall; you may become ill, or the
foundations of your old security system might collapse. Some people's
secrets might actually kill them. All this hampers the magic of the Flow.
In the spiritual world, there are no boundaries, no secrets, no masks for
protection. At our core, we want to be free of this excess baggage!

Brad was a successful product designer at a high-powered Silicon
Valley tech company. He had been on a roll, contributing to the development of some of the most popular tech inventions of recent years.
At a certain point, for no apparent reason, his performance waned and
he couldn't find the inspiration to stay on the leading edge. He was
close to losing his job and his reputation. He decided to work with a
spiritually aware therapist to find the cause of his malaise, and they
discovered that Brad had a powerful secret he'd been afraid to face

or reveal to anyone. His grandfather, father, and older brother had all committed suicide, and he was now approaching the age at which his father had killed himself.

Brad had stuffed the fear that he would follow in his male relatives' footsteps—that this was a genetic propensity—deep in his subconscious mind. But now he couldn't ignore it. What would happen if anyone at work found out? Would they think him so damaged that he'd lose credibility or even his creative brilliance in design? Would he lose friends who felt sorry for him? Would he spiral down so far that he might actually consider killing himself?

Brad's counselor asked him to imagine a scenario where he exaggerated the fear of being so much like his male relatives that he came right up to the edge of the abyss and actually contemplated suicide. She asked him to sense how much power the magical number three had in convincing him that his fate was inevitable, and how much the anxiety was contributing to the reality. Then she had him imagine removing the mythology and anxiety altogether, that there was no "suicide gene" he could inherit.

She also had him imagine that he was a unique human being, with a destiny all his own, that his soul knew what it wanted to contribute to life, even what wonderful new inventions he might bring through, and that he had no need to leave this life. She asked him to feel how much natural joy and curiosity he had. Then she had him feel how his male relatives had their own issues, and how they might have even been connected in some karmic way that drew them to incarnate in a cluster.

As they worked through the levels, Brad saw that he had a choice, that he could create his life from this point forward in a unique way, and help heal the pain of his male relatives by moving beyond pain, shame, and self-recrimination. He could set an example and break the pattern.

Then the therapist asked Brad to imagine revealing his secret to his coworkers and friends. In his mind's eye, he was surprised to see that they were legitimately concerned for his well-being and wanted to help. No one judged him negatively. He saw that because he'd cleared his fear, no one else was afraid for him, or of him either. He could sense in his imagination that certain people might even feel empowered to tell him one of their secrets as well because they suddenly trusted him more. By removing the negative charge, Brad was fine with telling people or not telling people. This was a situation where, if left to fester, Brad's secret might have killed him. It's generally the case that when other people learn a dark secret and understand the pain and vulnerability underlying it, their compassion rises to the surface.

> There is not a crime, there is not a dodge, there is not a trick,
> there is not a swindle, there is not a vice which does
> not live by secrecy.
> Joseph Pulitzer

The Societal Code Around Secrets

Since life on earth—at least to date—supports the reality of having, keeping, and discovering secrets, we have developed a global societal code around this idea and its related behaviors. Governments have made the keeping of secrets and the surveillance necessary to discover secrets into an art form, or perhaps a way of life. Psychologists base much of their work on freeing people from detrimental secrets. Publicists for celebrities are masterful at crafting stories to cover over secret behaviors that might destroy reputations. Spin doctors in politics are experts at inventing lies and secrets about rivals and then exposing them.

The internet and social media now readily reveal information that was once secret and obscure; in fact, many believe the entire internet is being bugged and data-mined. Everything we think has been secret in society may soon be in the public domain. Let's take a look at some of the codes we hold as normal surrounding secrecy in our society.

1. **Secrets are necessary for safety and survival and must be protected.** At a personal level, you may believe your mistakes and sins will ruin you if others find out—that some inability or fear you have

will be so embarrassing that your reputation will suffer if others know. You therefore develop a variety of ways to camouflage the secrets through avoidance, misdirection, and lies. I just watched a marathon rerun of *Dexter*, the television show about the lovable serial killer and blood-spatter analyst, and realized much of my fascination was with how he cleverly deflects attention from his looming dark secrets, often at the crucial last minute.

A highly educated CFO I once knew was ashamed that he had been fired from his first big job. When he finally shared this with his staff, they didn't think less of him but totally understood and saw it in a positive light. What he thought was humiliating, they saw as equalizing. Often, the need to protect a secret takes more energy and does more harm than simply revealing it.

At an organizational level, though, especially with governments, some secrets do need to be confidential and top secret to prevent violence and war. On the other hand, many organizational secrets are protected by ambitious leaders who are safeguarding their path to power, and who may be willing to commit crimes to maintain their hidden agendas.

2. **Knowing secrets gives you power.** When you know something about someone else that they want to keep secret, you have leverage over them; you can blackmail them to achieve your own goals. And having secret knowledge that most people don't have makes you an expert, and sought after. All this feeds the ego, of course.

3. **Having secrets makes you attractive and interesting but also prevents people from trusting you.** It's often the people with smoldering secrets who we find sexy and attractive. We want to know what they know, or are attracted by their danger element; their aloofness makes us want to connect. And so, we may wonder: "If I reveal my secrets, will I be less mysterious and therefore less attractive to others?"

The opposite is also true. People who preserve secrets and lie to cover them up can arouse our suspicion. You might sense that this kind of person is "squirrely" or untrustworthy, that you don't know what's real for them. The danger element just as easily keeps people away. It might irritate you that you can't fully connect with them, that there's something in the way that prevents you from relaxing and enjoying them. You might reject them for this reason; it's just too much work to be with them.

4. **We must protect others from our secrets.** It's common to hide a secret because you think it will hurt a loved one to know it. The man or woman who hides having an affair from their spouse thinks revealing it would hurt their partner or destroy the relationship. And yet, the secret generally sabotages the relationship anyway. People try hiding addictions, illnesses, past mistakes, and family backgrounds, for example. When this occurs, the person being "protected" unfailingly senses that something is "off," responds with distrust, confronts the other with their suspicion, and is deflected with, "I don't know what you're talking about. Nothing is wrong." Or they may collude by keeping mum about the secret.

5. **We're supposed to keep secrets for others.** It's a well-known story—how people have trouble keeping someone else's secret that's been entrusted to them. They so often feel the burning need to confide in someone else and reveal the charged knowledge. This is the root of gossip—secrets about others shared freely with others, and the knowledge passes from one to another to another until "the whole world knows." We're supposed to honor other people's secrets, but if it's not our secret, we have no vested interest. Whether it's via gossip or outright deceit, revealing someone else's secret is a betrayal. Friendships, connections, and safety can be lost.

> Three may keep a secret if two of them are dead.
> Benjamin Franklin

We might wonder whether keeping secrets for others is even ethical. When someone asks me to keep their secret, I experience it as a burden that puts pressure on me. I didn't need to know this in the first place, and now what am I supposed to do with it? It's too disturbing to live with. Generally, I'm in the "Don't tell me" or "I will not keep your secret if you tell me" camp.

And then there's the situation where you discover something impacting another person that they *might* need to know: "Your husband is gambling at the racetrack." "Your mother is really your sister." "Your family doesn't want you to know you have cancer." Should you tell them?

In these cases, the choice to tell or not is an ethical one, and unique to each situation. It's most ethical to go to the original creator of the secret and ask them to reveal what's going on. If they don't, you could then go to the "victim" of the secret, or to the authorities if a criminal issue is involved. In some cases, saying nothing may be most compassionate; it's trusting that the situation knows how to work itself out on its own.

6. **We can sniff out secrets intuitively.** We want to know! When it comes to secrets, we can be like a dog digging up a bone—we keep going, dirt flying, until we get it. Remember, we are ultrasensitive these days, so when someone holds a secret, we feel the subtle anxiety around a topic, or the looming quality of a bubble that wants to pop.

We are more telepathic and empathic, so we often unconsciously read the secret in the other person's energy field and innocently come up with a similar idea on our own and start talking about it. If Jim holds a secret about being beaten as a child, for example, you may spontaneously think of telling him about an article you just read concerning the rise of child abuse. In certain instances, you may want to know a secret yet may be afraid to know it, because you might have to take responsibility for something. Or it might remind you of something you don't want to face. Be careful what you ask for.

7. **We secretly want to reveal our secrets.** Holding a secret takes energy and attention, and this can be tiring and isolating. Confessing or getting things "off your chest" is cathartic, and afterward, you feel better, more free, and able to be yourself. Yes, you run the risk of having other people jump to the wrong conclusions or act offended.

But there's probably a tactful way to speak of your secret that promotes understanding about your motives that can mitigate much of that. Knowing someone else's secrets can help you like the person more, and vice versa; we all like to find common ground. And no secret is that weird these days. The trend toward eliminating clutter that's causing your blind spots—by disclosing secrets and exposing lies—is growing.

> Secrets, silent, stony sit in the dark palaces of both our hearts: secrets weary of their tyranny: tyrants willing to be dethroned.
> James Joyce

8. **Secrets can be passed unconsciously through family lineages and act out through the generations in strange ways.** I have seen cases where, several generations back, a great-grandfather murdered someone. After that, in subsequent generations, the people in the family experienced various forms of violence and trauma. Some might commit suicide, or become abusers of their spouse or children. Others might turn to drugs and die of an overdose or violent crime. Others might have an unusually high percentage of their friends and family die throughout their life, making them feel cursed, guilty, and alone.

What's happening here is that the terrible secret—the murder—is telepathically sensed in a weird, vague way by the ensuing generations. The original event is hidden, but the idea of murder and the emotions surrounding the great-grandfather at the time he committed the crime—perhaps anger, terror, guilt, or grief—are still held in the energy field of the family. The cause of the family's misfortune is not genetic; it's the energy of the secret that remains, like a vibrating after-image. People are touching the secret and trying to deal with it, trying to make it conscious and taking it personally, without realizing it comes from an actual historical event.

I've also seen families where one child was fathered by someone the mother had an affair with. She kept it secret, and her husband thought it was his own child. However, over time, the husband judged or criticized that child unfairly and gave more favors to his biological children—while still believing he was the father of them all. Again, we are telepathic and instinctive; we sense things but don't often know how to describe the secrets.

9. **Secrets materialize as blocks to the experience of your full self or as the very thing you're hiding.** When you keep a secret, like you flunked fourth grade, you may work extra hard later and achieve advanced degrees in college, but you may always worry that you're still more ignorant than others, that you could fall behind and be at the effect of truly "smart" people. Or you could actually lose a job to a competitor. It's the charged energy around the secret that keeps your personal field patterned in a particular way and causes your reality to align accordingly. "What you resist persists," as they say.

10. **Eventually, secrets *will* be revealed and cleared.** Keeping secrets is abnormal to the soul, and obstructive to the Flow of creativity and evolution. The planet's acceleration and the increasing frequency of your own personality will break up the logjams sooner than later and sweep the information into consciousness. As you embrace what comes in each moment, seeking to understand the underlying reasons your energy-and-consciousness became stuck in the first place, you clear the contractions and fear that created your secrets and lies, and which have been keeping you from all the "good stuff." Keeping secrets will one day be seen as a silly old habit, and so unnecessary.

• • • • • • • • • • •

Try This!
What Do You Lie About?

In your journal, make as complete a list as you can concerning the following:

1. What behaviors do you rely on to feel safe? What masks (images you project) do you wear for others? Why do you wear each one? What would

happen if you dropped each mask and behaved honestly? What might you say or do?

2. What lies (excuses, justifications, avoidances) do you tell yourself? What lies do you tell others about yourself? What subjects do you typically avoid? When do you usually lie? What's the reason behind each lie? Imagine dropping each lie and telling the truth; what might happen in each situation?

3. On a scale of 1–10, how much do you feel that other people trust your authenticity? How might you improve that?

• • • • • • • • • • • •

We live in a culture of secrecy, where hiding and lying are accepted as natural, even though we don't like it. We want honesty, transparency, and authenticity in our loved ones, in our organizations and group experiences, and in our own self, so we can reach the heights of our capacity. At the same time, we're still hesitant to reveal our deep, dark truths for fear of being rejected or ruined.

Yet it's not just our secrets that cause an opaque reality, acting as clutter in our personal field of energy-and-consciousness. Many things can block the transmission of our natural Light—fixed beliefs, ego, unconscious fears, negative emotions and speech, the distracted mind, control and victim behaviors, too much linear-logical-left-brain perception, and even living only in our personal history and storyline. Though we're used to these things and see them as normal, by clinging to them, we stall our evolution.

> The great enemy of truth is very often not the lie—deliberate,
> contrived, and dishonest—but the myth—persistent, persuasive,
> and unrealistic. Too often we hold fast to the clichés of our
> forebears. We subject all facts to a prefabricated set of
> interpretations. We enjoy the comfort of opinion
> without the discomfort of thought.
> **John F. Kennedy**

Just to Recap...

We live in a world that seems opaque and shadowy, and we're resigned to sacrificing a huge amount of our potential and feeling helpless about it. We assume that being caught in the spiderweb of restriction and contraction is normal. It is the left brain, with its focus on analyzing, defining, describing, and separating ideas out from the background of the unified field, that causes the perception of stuckness and density we struggle with.

The left brain causes you to feel separate from the nonphysical realms and your own soul, as well as from other people and forms of life. It's easy to forget who you really are and how life functions at higher frequencies. You can also fall into either-or thinking and the polarities that lead to conflict and the narrowing of options. Once you've accepted the left-brain worldview as dominant, you can create a variety of belief systems that validate that reality, limiting your growth, joy, and love even more.

The opaque reality gives rise to the human habit of keeping secrets. Secrets are different from mysteries, which lead you toward the Light and greater knowledge. Secrets interfere with the Flow, keep energy-and-consciousness contracted, and inhibit greater knowledge. We are fascinated with secrets and mysteries, and want them revealed, while at the same time, we are often afraid of what will happen if they're brought to light.

The left brain has worked out a kind of logic that justifies the need for secrets: It's important to hide your flaws and vulnerabilities because the world is separate from you and dangerous. People only see what's on the surface anyway, so it's OK to hide, lie, and wear masks. You need to develop a special radar to see other people's secrets, in case the hidden parts of them are dangerous. And it's often necessary to hide your good ideas and talents as well, because people can become jealous and attack you. It also takes energy to keep secrets and to lie, and you can become exhausted or ill as a result.

We've developed a societal code around secrets because it's so normal to live a partially transparent life. That code makes you believe that having and protecting secrets is absolutely necessary for safety, that knowing secrets can confer power, and that having secrets makes you attractive. It also says that keeping secrets arouses suspicion and produces untrustworthiness, that you must protect others from your secrets, and keep the secrets of others when they confide in you.

At the same time, we crave knowing secrets, can sniff them out intuitively, and often want to confess our own secrets to others—to get things "off our chest." Secrets can be passed unconsciously through family lineages, from generation to generation, and can motivate aberrant behavior as family members grapple with uncovering the blockage. Finally, the code says that secrets often materialize as events in one's life. In the end, though, secrets and lies are so unnatural to the soul that the accelerating frequency on the planet will force them into consciousness to be cleared.

Transparency Message
HIDING YOUR LIGHT

The soul says, Shine out, shine on, shine always, in all ways. Your body emits my Light, your feelings relay my Light, your mind creates with my Light. The soul says, I want to flow in through out around up and down. I love the world of form as I love the pure land of Light; both are beautiful, both exquisite. I love taking shape authentically and dissolving again.

The soul says, Your fear is not real to me. Your blockages, your density, your thick greyness is not real to me; it is real to you. When you don't create with my fullness, you suffer; I don't. I don't know how to suffer. I only say Yes. When you don't remember me, that I am you, you suffer; I don't. I know I am you and I am in everything too.

Chapter 3: The Opaque Reality

When you spend your precious time not trusting, trying to survive, it stalls you, not me. I am eternal, I live in allowing, I have no future. Time is a dream. I have only love for you to know and use.

The soul says, The shadow world you live in is you hiding your Light, you are letting fear be greater than who you really are: you are me. The spiderweb you are caught in is you forgetting truth and not valuing it. Truth is like crystal clear water from a mountain spring: it gives eternal life. Come out of hiding, drop the heavy cloak of distrust, remove your dark glasses, feel me seeing.

The soul says, Trade places with me, look back upon yourself, feel yourself as me, saturating your body, fueling your feelings and thoughts, teaching you that the shadow world is a mirage. Feel yourself as me: uncluttered, fearless, kind, infinitely connected. I am seamless Love, uninterrupted Light. I am here for you because I am you. I cannot be gone.

4

The Transparent Reality:
Radical Trust, Flow & New Perception

O world invisible, we view thee,
O world intangible, we touch thee,
O world unknowable, we know thee,
Inapprehensible, we clutch thee!
Francis Thompson

When I began writing this book, I knew I would have to become more transparent myself to access the kind of insights I yearned for, then translate the information back through language so it would convey the experience of those higher states. I had been immersed for the previous four months in the practical and emotional work of closing my mother's estate after she died, and dealing with her many lovely belongings. All I'd been thinking about was sorting, categorizing, and distributing—figuring out which items were either personally or monetarily valuable, what to keep, where to donate the next load, and which of her friends might like what.

I knew I needed to begin the book, but how was I going to shift levels from the seemingly never-ending, mundane physical work, where my mind was so left-brained, shallow, and dull, to the super-clear, diamond-light space I required to do justice to this topic? From my viewpoint of being buried in the opaque mire of tasks, the difference in frequency felt like a gap that was nearly impossible to bridge.

And then, the day after the estate sale, when people came to take away the rest of my mother's possessions and the physical work was finally finished, I developed something like food poisoning, with an intestinal infection that lasted two weeks. During that time, I collapsed. I stopped eating my typical foods, and in fact, I hardly ate at all. When I recovered, I still didn't want to eat or drink the old habitual things, and ate only small amounts of a single food at a time. I lost twenty pounds without trying. I thought, "Is this my soul helping me 'lighten up' and be more transparent?" The illness had come spontaneously, like a punctuation mark, and I certainly felt more porous and open afterward. I began the book.

As I worked for a while, I realized I was now dealing with a kind of brain fog—an opacity in my mind that kept dragging me into spaciness. Once again, life provided some help—a colleague called out of the blue, raving about a healer he'd worked with recently who had cleared him of energetic blocks, and ever since, he'd been on an enthusiastic, creative roll. I followed up on that information and had a session with her. Over the next week, the fog slowly burned away.

There were more synchronicities to come—more incremental clearings, just when I needed them. That's the way it works. We teach ourselves to become transparent, bit by bit.

In this chapter, I want to help you discern the new reality we're aiming for and some of the ways you can make the shift. I'm sharing my little story with you because transparency is not as far away as you think. It seemed distant to me because I was physically and mentally fatigued, and pressuring myself to be instantly clear. I separated the state of inspired clarity from myself by making it a goal, futurizing it slightly, and making it "extra special"—so I made it difficult to experience.

Transparency Is Always There

The transparent reality had been there all along, in each present moment. It was in the simplicity of uncluttering my attention from food habits and in the fuzzy blankness I'd been resisting. It was even in the respectful way I had touched and thought about each of my mother's lifetime of things. The transparent reality is always available because it's our fundamental nature, our ground of being. We loop away from it with our mental constructions and explorations, then drop back in again.

I had been pushing so hard to move forward that I missed the obvious: It was time to "stop and drop"—back into my body, back into the simplicity of the moment's arising, and back into my interconnection with everything around me, both physical and nonphysical, so I might remember the state of my own peaceful, happy soul. Transparency miraculously appears out of that state if you just wait willingly, with full attention.

> There is another world, but it is in this one.
>
> W. B. Yeats

I also saw how I'd stopped the Flow with anxiety, willpower, and resistance and how important it was to trust the Flow. By trusting that the highly focused states I'd been in would easily shift to new, open, spacious states when I relaxed and "let things be," I allowed the Flow to release the contractions that had blocked me. *So, both being in the present moment and merging with the Flow are key components in the facilitation of transparency.*

It's important to remember that wanting to enter, understand, and live fully in the transparent reality requires trust in your own timing and path, in yourself as a soul who knows what to do, and in your personality's ability to notice the clues from your soul and act on them. Transparency arises naturally, like the sweet scent of a stargazer lily, from the essence of your being—especially when you're simple, still, and honest—and it surrounds you. It arises constantly, embraces you constantly, and calls you back when you stray too far into the dullness of the opaque reality.

> None of us knows what might happen even the next minute,
> yet still we go forward. Because we trust.
>
> Paulo Coelho

The transparent reality is the real reality; it underlies and inter-penetrates the physical world. Your physical reality can become more transparent as soon as you realize the transparency is already there, wait-ing to be activated by attention. You can actually feel the clearing occur when you place attention on that glossy, smooth, frictionless state. Sit and watch a glass of tap water become clear. Watch the mud sink to the bottom of a creek. Watch what's unnecessary dissolve from life. The action is so normal. Give yourself time.

Transparency comes from connecting your mind and feelings with your essential qualities of joy, appreciation, loving kindness, peaceful excitedness, and constancy. The only way to do that is quietly, patiently, with attention in the Now and on the presence in everything.

. . . .

Try This!

Let the Unnecessary Dissolve

1. Recall a time when you were caught in opacity—in an experience that felt strained, thick, dull, snagged, effortful, chaotic, or pressured. Remember how you may have felt sacrificial, contracted, superficial, or even tortured by doubt and fear. As you reimagine the situation and enter it again, you experience the frustrated or contracted feelings.

2. Notice that you're probably worrying—paying attention to what isn't work-ing, what you don't have, or how you can't do something. Make a note in your journal of these negative declarative statements, resistances, and feelings of limitation.

3. Adjust your attention so you think of the opaque experience as something with its own intelligence that you don't need to resist or invest too much energy in. It is what it is. You don't need to change it. Of itself, it may be quite neutral and worth doing, while some of the specific influences involved—like people or deadlines, or your thoughts and emotions—may cloud the experience. Which parts of the experience are unnecessary? List them in your journal.

4. Reimagine the situation, but this time, let the unnecessary parts dissolve back into the field, freeing up more energy. In your mind's eye, see how the situation—and your experience—transform.

5. Pull your attention out of the whole situation and let it, too, dissolve. Return to this moment. Breathe. Nothing prevents you from feeling the way you like to feel. It's OK to be blank for a while or to not do things the way you think you have to.

6. Now you're in the open state that facilitates transparency. Be willing to wait. Let the space inside your body and brain become clear as a diamond. Let the space all around you clear to the same level of glossiness. Any ideas or events can now simply fall through from your own higher dimensions. Give yourself permission to notice them whenever they show up and to engage with them. Now there is nothing unnecessary in the way.

· · · · · · · · · · · ·

Our Growing Hunger for Transparency

Yes, life is accelerating. Yes, you are beginning to identify yourself as a vibrational being of energy-and-consciousness. And yes, you are gradually matching your personal physical frequency with the frequency of the higher, nonphysical realms. Slowly, you are integrating the memory of the natural functioning of your spiritual roots, your spiritual "home," into your life on earth. The more you're aware of this occurring, the more impatient, intolerant, and bored you become with the opaque reality. From the depths of your being, you want systems and methods that work in concert with your increasingly fast spherical and holographic perception. You catch glimpses of the exciting ways new perception works, and you want to be free of limiting habits. Here are some of the ideas you may glimpse that trigger your growing hunger for the transparent reality.

1. **There are connections between energy and consciousness.** As the acceleration causes you to vibrate faster, you become aware of energy,

frequencies, the permeability and fluidity of the physical world, and how everything physical has an energetic counterpart. You understand yourself as a field, an inner blueprint, precipitating a physical self and reality shaped by purpose, thought, and feeling. *You want to learn to work and play with these principles of energy-and-consciousness because it can vastly improve the quality of your life.*

2. **There are higher dynamics of life in the nonphysical realms.** The acceleration causes the physical and nonphysical realms to interpenetrate; the veil of separation becomes extra thin. You remember how effortless life is in the spiritual realms and want the same thing in the here-and-now. *The nonphysical worlds are in your face, and you want to penetrate further into those inner realms and the knowledge they contain, rediscover how the universal laws work, experience it all directly, and work with it consciously.*

3. **Your new, higher frequency identity is so different from your old identity!** You are frustrated by the limitations imposed on you by the illusions of solidity and separation everyone takes for granted. There is natural bleed-through now from the nonphysical realms, and this changes the way you experience your identity. You sense the great freedom and belonging that can be yours. *You want to know who you are in the higher frequency dimensions. What is the experience of being your soul? What do you know and feel at that level? How does that translate into form and change you?*

4. **There's a new way to create and uncreate.** The acceleration draws you into the permanent present moment. It becomes normal to imagine anything and be able to materialize it immediately. There really is true abundance! You no longer need to steal, or believe in the haves and have-nots, or in the idea that loss is bad and gain is good, or that you're forever stuck in a reality you don't like. *You want to understand how the new materialization and dematerialization processes work. You want to dive into inspired, facile creativity.*

5. **You have direct, instantaneous, comprehensive knowing.** You realize that all knowledge is available in the present moment—your sphere—and is activated by attention. The end of the Information

Age brings a jamming up of data; information is everywhere, but there's a limit to the speed and effectiveness of linear processing. Your curiosity and impatience are stimulated. *You don't want knowing to be hard work; you want to know more now. You want holistic understanding, not just partial knowing. You want direct knowing, not slow knowing.*

6. **There is greatly increased right-brain intuitive sensitivity and empathic openness.** You're becoming ultrasensitive and empathic, so you receive subtle preverbal, prephysical, energy information—about everything and anything—effortlessly. You penetrate farther and have more nuanced understanding. Knowledge isn't just left-brained anymore. *You want to know what you know at these subtle, intuitive levels and also how to handle the overload of feeling so much more.*

7. **All you want is truth, depth, fullness, and destiny.** Superficiality becomes more evident, irritating, and boring; you want depth. You want the ideal, the real thing, the soul mates and soul group, the just-right ideas and actions, the elimination of waste. *You want truth and to be purposeful. You can feel your destiny very close; you want to know what it is, how to get into it, and do it.*

8. **Clearing clutter and being authentic is a top priority.** Blocks that caused your opacity—personal pain, suffering, and ignorance—are surfacing and clearing. You can no longer tolerate snags, blockages, barriers, and waste because they interfere with the higher frequency experience you crave. You want to see into the causes of fear to dissolve them. *You have no use for masks, secrets, ego, lies, hiding, wet-blanket overlays of old beliefs and habits, or actions that are inappropriate for each moment.*

9. **You experience a balance between personal self-consciousness and collective self-consciousness.** The rising frequency causes you to expand your identity to encompass *I am Me* and *I am Us.* You enjoy and use your alone time, and you're also focused on collective consciousness, interconnections, sharing, convening, and collaborating. You want to create things that are better than you could do by yourself alone. You don't need privacy or anonymity as protection, nor do you need immersion in groups to avoid subliminal anxiety.

You're excited about finding like-minded others and creating from shared knowledge, expertise, and respect.

10. **You realize transparency isn't frightening, it's sublime!** As you move beyond old, linear perception to new, spherical-holographic perception, your attitude and understanding about transparency change from fearful and resistant to normal and necessary. *Opacity doesn't work in the new perception; there are new rules of reality you're trying to understand, and positive, super-contemporary transformations of ordinary processes and institutions you're excited to help birth.*

11. **You realize you're ready. "Let's make the shift already!"** You are moving into this transformation inexorably, without even trying or consciously realizing it. You notice something big is underway, but how does it work, really? Are there stages? Is there a formula to help you understand? *You want and need to make this transformation from the opaque to the transparent reality more conscious and real at every level of yourself. You want to ease the shift and be there already!*

> You are not the oil, you are not the air—merely the point of combustion, the flash-point where the light is born. You are merely the lens in the beam. You can only receive, give, and possess the light as the lens does. If you seek yourself, you rob the lens of its transparency. You will know life and be acknowledged by it according to your degree of transparency—your capacity, that is, to vanish as an end and remain purely as a means.
>
> Dag Hammarskjöld

• • • • • • • • • •

Try This!

Rate Your Transparency Motivations

1. Read through the eleven categories in the previous section and feel how much your intuitive self understands and is motivated by each one. Rate each idea from 1–10, with 10 being the most motivating.

2. How aligned is your left-brain consciousness with each? Is there fear or skepticism? Are there "yes, buts"? Rate each idea from 1–10, with 10 being the most skeptical. Make notes about the left-brain's doubts.
3. Which ideas do you want to integrate more fully right away? Rate the ones that grab your attention first and that you'd like to develop and live by the most. Then list those that are a second priority.

• • • • • • • • • • •

Radical Trust: A Function of Transparency

Wikipedia defines *radical trust* as the confidence an organization has in its collaboration with online communities, specifically when using social media to cultivate relationships that provide useful feedback for the organization. I also see the term used in Christian writings with reference to placing one's total faith in God. But I mean something different and more comprehensive when I put these two words together, something that combines the ideas of trust in the physical world and trust in the inherent connection of the physical and nonphysical worlds.

Radical is a popular word today, giving the impression that we are speaking of an extreme version of something that excites big change. It actually means the quality of affecting the fundamental nature of something; something that is both far-reaching and thorough. It derives from *radix*, the Latin word for *root*, as in forming the root of something or perhaps getting to the root of something.

In my mind, combining radical with the idea of trust points to the concept of trusting not just one thing specifically but all things in all worlds. It means getting to the root of trust, the core truth of trust, and changing the way we understand how that experience can be applied universally and unconditionally. So *radical trust* might mean a state of unconditional trust for any single kind of trust—whether it be in yourself, in others, or in life—or it could describe a state of absolute trust—that perfect experience of peaceful surrender—in everything.

95

Radical trust is another key component of transparency. With trust, there is openness and permission; you allow energy-and-consciousness to flow into, through, and from you. There is no contraction or holding back, no negative thinking, no conditionality, no partiality. With radical trust, you welcome experiences from both the nonphysical and physical realms; the soul in its purity can source your experience, and the physical world, with all its crazy diversity and illusion, can source your experience as well. Welcoming everything without judgment helps remove blockages and clutter. If something negative arises, radical trust helps you remember there is useful information in every experience, so you don't contract with fear and jump away or clang the door shut.

With radical trust, you trust the Flow *and* yourself. You remember that you're always in the center of your reality and cannot lose yourself due to what's flowing through you. You are you, always radiating and living in your home frequency. All other frequencies have permission to exist—you can expand or contract your sphere to access any reality you wish—and nothing can affect you negatively unless you match a lower vibration (temporarily) and forget your own. And even if you do, it's just data, just a new experience—and it's easy to return to your core truth because you really can't leave it.

> The best way to find out if you can
> trust somebody is to trust them.
> **Ernest Hemingway**

When developing radical trust, we first need to look more deeply into the experience of trust in general. Many people think trust is a belief in the reliability, truth, ability, or strength of someone or something. I'd like you to feel into the experience of trust—it's not a "belief" lodged in the left brain but more a *knowing* that has become so ingrained that it feels totally normal. You might trust your dog to love you, or your home to shelter you. Trust comes with relaxation at a deep level, through a quality of softness, which comes from feeling totally safe. So how do we get there?

Trust in others naturally begins when you share love consistently with them. When you were a baby, if your parents fed you when you were hungry, picked you up when you cried, changed you when you were wet, and played with you when you were feeling playful, you naturally trusted them and let your love radiate. If they told you the truth and explained things to you as you grew up, you developed more trust and love; there is a congruence in this that relieves tension. Even learning about limits and discipline was seen as caretaking. If your parents validated your choices and let you make mistakes without punishment, you learned to trust yourself. This sort of trust is not a belief but a deep feeling of being connected and supported. Needs are being met, acceptance and love underlie it all, and there is joy in reciprocating.

If you didn't experience this kind of grounded trust growing up, you have to instill it in yourself later by making a *choice* to trust, or a choice to not pay so much attention to what might go wrong or how you might feel hurt. After you choose and have various experiences as a result, you sort them to find your truth: "I trust people who keep their word, who are authentic and spontaneously affectionate. I don't trust people who lie, hide, and manipulate." You validate the experiences where trust occurs naturally; you *teach yourself* how to trust and develop sensitivity to these states.

Trust is a function of being able to be yourself easily and enjoy being with others who are being their true self easily. Distrust is a function of doubt, isolation, and tension. Let's examine the areas you might want to focus on—and trust—to develop comprehensive, radical trust.

1. **You not only have a soul, you *are* your soul.** You and your soul are not separate. You don't "have" a soul like you have a car or a doctor's appointment; you can't acquire it or lose it. Your soul doesn't really evolve, it just gets covered by illusion after incarnating many times, and eventually burns away the blockages to remember itself fully. First, trust that this idea is true by simply entertaining the thought that it is. Then, when you're quiet and still, place focused attention on the idea. Stay with the idea and feel into it. Penetrate

into the experience of being your soul, right now, right here, 100 percent.

Your soul is in your body, in your emotions, in your mind, and in your whole personality (personal reality). Your soul—*you*—are running the show from inside. *You* know what you're doing. *You* are filling all your parts with high-frequency energy-and-consciousness. Imagine it, feel it, experience it fully. When you do, you won't have to trust that it's true. You'll know with every iota of yourself.

2. **There is a function of your mind—your Inner Perceiver—that causes you to notice what you notice.** What you notice is revealed to your personality by your soul via a teaching or guiding function of consciousness. It's been called the inner voice, the higher self, and sometimes, the Holy Spirit. I call it your Inner Perceiver, and it presents insights via your first thoughts and impressions. Make a choice to trust and validate this function of your mind—it's working for your optimal, most effortless evolution. If you pay close and loving attention to what and why you notice things, you can penetrate into the hidden messages and insights you're showing yourself.

When you routinely dialogue with your Inner Perceiver, you see wisdom at work. You may notice something negative that you-the-soul are trying to clear from you-the-personality. You may notice something that reminds you of the awe-inspiring, beautiful functioning of life. Or you may notice something that teaches you or leads to new creations. Trusting your own "right mind" becomes second nature when you relax into the Inner Perceiver's beneficent action.

3. **Your intuition and ultrasensitivity put you in touch with what's just right for you.** Make a choice to trust your right brain and body. You receive nonverbal signals and subtle energy information constantly, about people, groups, events, and various larger fields of data (e.g., countries, diseases and their cures, trends in technology, even rainforest dynamics). This information affects you all over and all at once, as a feeling pattern, though you may not relay it to your left brain to decipher it.

Place attention on when you receive an intuition or impression, how you notice it, and where it registers in your body. Ask yourself what it means. Make it conscious. Follow the guidance. Validate it. Soon you won't have to make yourself trust your intuition and sensitivity; these will be skills that are an integral part of your learning apparatus. Learn to trust intuition first, above left-brain generated proof, and watch yourself confidently base decisions on right-brain perception.

4. **When you trust others, they learn to trust you. When you trust yourself, others learn to trust themselves.** We've all trusted people who didn't keep agreements or abandoned, betrayed, or wounded us in dreadful ways. We're in the bridge time between the opaque reality and the transparent reality, and people are still immersed in fear beliefs and aggressive/defensive behaviors. How are we to trust others then? Isn't it naïve and dangerous?

We'll talk more about this in chapter 5, but basically, to develop radical trust, you must gradually make choices to increase your trust of others, from the easy kinds of people to the difficult ones, from friends and family, to acquaintances, to strangers, to enemies.

Fortunately, trusting others is something that can be "built." It begins, as do all other forms of trust, with a simple choice to entertain the truth of the idea that trust is a natural spiritual state—a state we are born from and actually still live within. Begin building trust by trusting *something*. If you can't trust a person's reliability, for example, you can still trust the fact that deep inside, other people are souls who love to love, just like you. A person may lie on a job application but be honest about their feelings. You can build more trust by finding the next thing you can trust. Look for it actively.

When you trust your intuition and ultrasensitivity, you develop skill in reading people, easily sensing when someone is holding back, lying, hiding a secret, or only partially invested in a relationship. When you encounter an untrustworthy person, the feeling state in your body is probably tight and contracted or jumpy and buzzy—compared to the deep comfort, safety, and freedom of expression you experience with someone who's in alignment with their own truth. You don't have to be fooled by someone else's shady character.

> Trust each other again and again. When the trust level gets high enough, people transcend apparent limits, discovering new and awesome abilities of which they were previously unaware.
> David Armistead

5. **When you need to work with people who don't feel trustworthy, you can still trust them to act according to their current ratio of fear to love.** Most often, people show or tell you how much you can rely on them, right up front. Even if they're charming or over-confident, your gut instinct will give you a warning sign if something seems fishy. If you gloss over those warnings, or overstep the boundaries and have expectations that the other can't or won't fulfill, you'll be rejected, disappointed, or wounded by that amount of your own overextension. They didn't hurt you; *you were counterintuitive—you overrode your intuition.*

   You can always trust in the soul of others—that deep down, everyone wants to evolve and lose the fear that's been holding them back, even those who have identified with fear-based behaviors, like criminals, terrorists, sociopaths, crooked politicians and business-people, or everyday narcissists. Let people know—telepathically *and* with overt validation when possible—that you trust that they are good. They will often try to live up to your vision of them.

6. **You can sense the trust quotient of groups and organizations as easily as you can with individuals.** Use your intuition and ultra-sensitivity to feel into a group's hidden dynamics. Pick up energy information from the spaces the groups occupy. How tense, linear, boxy, isolated, or strict do the group members feel? Or how loose, permissive, casual, uncaring, or distracted? If they don't match your frequency, don't become involved; you'll never really belong. Does the field of the group feel transparent and fluid yet crisp and

efficient? Or do you sense a shadow side—a dangerous iceberg looming under the surface of the group culture? Is there a good mix of contemporary/innovative and traditional/careful? Or is the group itself caught up in ego?

Make a choice to trust groups that are on your wavelength—groups that allow your full self-expression and also have clear parameters. Then let your Inner Perceiver show you ways to act with integrity within the group, so you help establish and reinforce trust in the group's activities.

> It is mutual trust, even more than mutual interest,
> that holds human associations together.
>
> H. L. Mencken

7. **You are an intrinsic part of the collective consciousness. You-the-soul have a plan for your lifetime—and you know how to cocreate it with other souls.** You-the-soul know how to engineer situations with all other souls to develop the pushes and pulls that direct you to experience your life lessons and express your talents. If you feel blocked, a breakthrough will be created. If you become overconfident, something will pop your balloon. You-the-personality always receive what you need—and other people help you in this because doing it is what they need. Just entertain the idea that this is true, that everything and everyone in your life have been there to help you grow toward full memory of who you are.

   Accept the idea that even strangers and rivals are working in concert with you. Place close and loving attention on how the experiences of your life—both positive and negative, the gains and the losses—have guided you toward new insights and actions. Anywhere you hold the idea of unfairness, look deeper.

8. **The Flow operates compassionately and with great sanity.** Your life materializes and dematerializes out of the Flow, which is really the collective consciousness of all souls and all beings evolving together and helping each other. The Flow functions in cycles

101

of Be/Spirit, to Do/Mind, to Have/Body, and back to Be/Spirit. In its abbreviated form, it can feel like action to pause to action, something to nothing to something, dream to result to dream, or desire to surrender to desire. Each phase and shift between phases is fun and interesting *if you engage fully.* Go with the Flow and everything works. Entertain the idea that you can totally trust the Flow, that it knows what it's doing and will bring you what you need when you need it—without you willing it to occur. Also trust that when the Flow gives you an idea or desire, it's because others need you to have it and do it so they can evolve too. Feel into the reality of how the Flow helps you create your day.

Getting Started with Trust

To develop radical trust, you must begin somewhere. Take a risk. It starts with choosing, or agreeing, to unconditionally trust at least one of the eight areas I outlined above. When trusting any idea seems scary or ridiculous, try it anyway but keep it light and fun—an experiment that leads to discovery. That's why I use the term "entertaining" ideas—think of these various ways of trusting as potential ideas or experiences you've invited over for a cozy dinner party. Learn about them by being with them and "acting as if" the trust is real and functional, all the while keeping your attention on how they actually are true.

Since it can be frightening to trust other people cold turkey, I suggest you start with one of the areas that concerns only you. How about trusting that you are your soul and you-the-soul are engineering your life from a clear, high-frequency perspective? Remind yourself of it consistently: "I'm my soul, and I'm present in my body and personality 100 percent. I know what I'm doing." Or "Somewhere inside me I already know what to do. I act when it feels just right." Say it and *feel it.* When your left brain chimes in with bossy demands or squashes innocent ideas for expanding yourself, remember the voice of the soul. It never says the word *should*, and it's never negative. The soul says, "I like, I love, I'm interested in, I am, I know, I experience, I do, I understand."

Try reframing the left-brain voice from the soul's perspective. Make a game of it. The left-brain voice might say, "I can't leave my boring job because I don't know how to find my right livelihood." The soul might say instead, "I know what I love, and I can combine a number of things I love to make a new kind of work. Even though I can't see the final answer right now, I know how to take the first small steps, and I know that if each step feels just right, the path will open up and expand. I'll get there because I'm unfolding my life in harmony."

Keep your attention on the idea of validating your identity as soul-in-the-body, soul-in-the-mind, soul-in-the-emotions, and soul-in-the-senses. *Feel what you say.* Soon it will be second nature, and you'll live in unconditional, radical trust concerning this truth.

> Negative emotion exists only when you are miscreating. And so, when you recognize that you are feeling negative emotion—no matter why, no matter how it got there, no matter what the situation is—stop doing whatever it is that you are doing and focus your thoughts on something that feels better.
>
> Esther Hicks/Abraham

You might move on to totally trusting that what you notice is what you need to notice, and it's coming from a wise part of yourself. You can choose to trust that there are hidden messages or teachings in what you notice, that what you desire shows up to lead you to new insights (not astray), and that everything helps you evolve to your highest frequency state of being. You can practice trusting that your intuitions are accurate, that your ultrasensitivity brings energy information that's useful. Trust that you don't have to know everything all at once! Trust the Flow to absolutely serve your growth.

When learning to trust your Inner Perceiver, you might ask it, "Why did I just notice a father cardinal feeding his half-grown baby at my bird-feeder?" Some insights may pop into your mind. Perhaps you're directing your attention to remember how your father nurtured you in his own way, so you can feel loved. Or you might want to remind yourself of how men express compassion. Or maybe there is something *you* need to feed and nurture so you can feel loving. Validate what you become conscious of by falling through the surface image or description into the inner experience. This way you open the pathway for vertical transparency that comes from trusting your relationship with your Inner Perceiver.

But what if you notice a desire to do something out of keeping with your upbringing, schooling, or current career direction? Are you leading yourself down the wrong path? Derailing yourself due to some dysfunctional tendency to sabotage your life? Can you trust your Inner Perceiver then? See if the urge will generate more compassion and soul-full-ness.

One of my clients is forging a successful practice as a business coach and trainer but also harbors a dream to become a model and belong to a great modeling agency. Can she trust an idea her left brain thinks is silly and self-serving? She needs to trust that the idea is not there by accident; it has had staying power. If she allows herself to do some modeling, perhaps with 30 percent of her time—or even if she just imagines doing it in 3-D and living color—she might build more confidence in front of audiences. She might find she likes herself better, or that she learns how to relay emotional states more accurately through her eyes and body postures, or that she just has fun feeling versions of herself in different outfits and becomes more self-expressive.

She might like the family feeling of an agency—of belonging with a group of people who share similar goals and lessons—and that might help her feel how she belongs with other kinds of people. Perhaps those new experiences and skills will eventually weave back into her coaching and training business. Maybe she'll star in her own videos or become a keynote speaker. Having radical trust in her own desires opens her to living a more transparent life, where more of her talents can shine through.

> When people honor each other, there is a trust established
> that leads to synergy, interdependence, and deep respect.
> Both parties make decisions and choices based on
> what is right, what is best, what is valued most highly.
> **Blaine Lee**

Building Trust with Intuition & Common Sense

It's true: trust is a choice. You either want to trust or you're too afraid to trust. You move forward or you stall and wallow. It's also true that trust is built. You begin with willingness. You experiment with allowing, receiving, and giving. You observe the dynamics of the way trust works—with your common sense. You feel and sense nuances and underlying conditions with your intuition. You experiment some more.

You notice the difference in the way it feels when you trust partially versus fully, or with doubt and skepticism versus innocence and cheerfulness. You notice how, when you give permission with no strings attached, the Flow resumes its harmonious movement to go to the perfect next place. Your comfort level with trust builds. When trust brings a success, you validate it by enjoying it consciously and even sharing the story with friends. The more you validate that trust works, the more you choose it.

If trust results in a partial success, there may be an important reason lurking just below the surface. Finding the underlying dynamic is part of building and choosing trust too. It requires trust in your intuition. For example: You chose to trust your intuition about which new job to take, and the one you chose turned out to have several egotistical, inept leaders, and the communication among your coworkers was clogged with hoarding and game-playing. Should you stop trusting your intuition? No! Other factors are at work. Perhaps some old personal programming tilted your choice toward the desire for safety, prestige, money, or power. So the option you chose was full of self-centered, materialistic people. As a result, seeing the effects of other people's egos directed your attention toward developing a more natural, compassionate kind of self-esteem and leadership in yourself. Perhaps you had unresolved emotional issues with a dominating parent, and the new bosses reactivated the pattern so you could clear it. By experiencing the surprise frustrations, you-the-soul made some clutter visible so it could be cleared through understanding. You tricked yourself into facing a few things!

When choosing trust, you may need to use your intuition to distinguish between real first impressions—your *truth and anxiety signals*—and wishful thinking, unconscious desires that come from avoiding fear, or lack of trust in your own destiny. With intuition, when you pay close attention to your body, you can learn to distinguish the false positives from the just-right next insights. Your anxiety signals feel dark and heavy, and cause your body to tighten, contract, or lean away from a certain choice. Your truth signals feel warm and light, causing a bubbling of energy, and you lean toward the choice.

Trust empowers your intuition to sharpen so that when you expect truth and can feel truth, you simply don't respond to partial or absent truth. With practice, you won't confuse your left brain's emotion-influenced "logic" or information generated by past action with the soul's simple, accurate responses, which arise from deep comfort.

Trust is related to surrendering but not in a helpless way. Trust is about granting permission but not to an unknown that you can't sense. There's a saying: "Praise Allah, and tie your camel to the post." To sur-render totally to the unknown is to give all the power to the nonphysical realms. And that naïveté can lead to some spectacular failures. You must also use your common sense and take care of the business at hand. To become transparent, you must merge the physical and nonphysical realms, experiencing clarity in both worlds.

You can believe in a higher power or a high-frequency universal consciousness, yet to know radical trust, you must experience that same high frequency in yourself. Attend to the dynamics of the energy-and-consciousness world and tend the results in the physical world; create interconnections. In other words, divine consciousness is in the unified field, and the unified field is in you, so divine consciousness is in you as well. Do you think you're a hole or gap in the field?

There is a related quote from the Bible: "Do not give what is holy to the dogs; nor cast your pearls before swine."[1] To build trust with others, it helps to use your intuition and sensitivity to read people: "Are they on my wavelength? If I give them more than they can understand or assim-ilate and they reject me, does it mean I shouldn't trust people? Or that I shouldn't trust my motives? What frequency of information matches the readiness of the listeners?"

Learning to intuitively gauge how much to give and how much you might receive from others is simply part of the experiment in observing how trust works. Your common sense will show you how to compassionately trust people as much as they can reciprocate, and perhaps how to help lead them into greater trust as well.

When you focus attention on developing radical trust and keep that idea at the front of your mind, working with the endeavor as a spiritual practice, you see why you have to trust failures or betrayals as well as successes. The failures are almost always due to a blind spot in your own consciousness or a lesson you-the-soul want to punch home dramatically. The other helpful thing is that when you develop one area of trust, it feeds into all the other areas of trust. Eventually, you experience radical trust.

. . . .

Try This!

Who, What & Why Don't You Trust?

1. Read back through the eight areas for trust-building listed on pages 97–102. For each, rate how much you experience it, from 1–10, with 10 being the most experienced. In your journal, for each area of trust, write about how and why you don't trust it.

2. Write about disappointing or wounding experiences you had that may have closed or blocked your desire to trust. Write about what you think could go wrong if you open unconditionally to trust each of the eight areas.

3. Write about how you do trust each of the eight areas. What experiences have you had that demonstrate the truth behind trusting? How have you learned that radical trust—trusting everything wholeheartedly, with faith in the Flow—creates greater transparency?

4. If there is a person you don't trust, write about why. How could you heal the distrust? You might be able to forgive them, but how can you find a new level of trust with them?

5. Focus on the idea of allowing. What do you allow? What do you monitor and censor? Apply this to knowledge, love, people, support, change,

freedom, etc. How can you increase your trust concerning allowing? Write about it.

6. Focus on the idea of receiving. What do you receive easily? Not so easily or not at all? How can you increase your trust concerning receiving? Write about it.

7. Focus on the idea of giving. What do you give easily? Not easily or not at all? Do you have conditions on giving? Do you ever give more than others can receive? How can you increase your trust concerning giving? Write about it.

• • • • • • • • • • •

New Attention Skills for the Transparent Reality

As you enter the Intuition Age and its transparent reality, you notice that life begins to function by different rules. Everything is fast, in the present moment, available, and direct. Behaviors based on fear backfire immediately. You notice that life doesn't function well when you use your mind in unskillful ways, like not trusting your intuition, or stopping the Flow, or projecting into the future or past, or thinking "outside your sphere." In fact, you notice that the skillful use of attention may be the most important ability you can develop—the thing that takes you furthest and grants the most profound success.

In my book *Leap of Perception* I describe in great detail some of the new attention skills we are developing to live successfully in an accelerated, transformed world. These are consciousness practices you can work with right now by breaking old habits, unlearning familiar types of thinking, and relearning new ways of paying attention. In addition to radical trust, here are some of the attention skills you can practice to help you ease gracefully into the transparent reality of the Intuition Age.

1. **Practice spherical-holographic perception.** In chapter 1, I described the shift from linear to spherical-holographic perception. You can affirm the new perception by remembering that you live inside a ball

of reality, that you're always in the center of the ball, and since the ball can change its scope, there is nothing outside the ball; it actually includes all things. There is no "over there" or "out there" separate from you. You cannot leave your sphere and don't need to. What seems to be outside your sphere is simply the collective unconscious—the amount of yourself you aren't paying attention to yet. The scope of your sphere simply expands or contracts like the zoom lens on a camera, matching the focus of your attention.

If you think of something new, your sphere has already expanded to encompass it. Inside your sphere, there are billions of possible frequencies floating in a field of energy-and-consciousness. They materialize as events, places, people, flows, objects, and ideas, and dematerialize back into the field again. Everything you're aware of is inside your sphere and you are interconnected with everything. That means at some level, you know about everything and it knows about you. This familial interconnection helps you understand safety and abundance.

With the holographic part of new perception, you experience how each centerpoint is the seed of a unique reality that also contains knowledge of the entirety—from an individual reality to the cosmos itself. You are the centerpoint, and your life is the field that radiates from the centerpoint. You can be in your own center and simultaneously place attention in another frequency, another centerpoint, and you can experience a different reality along with yours.

2. **Practice direct knowing.** As transformation occurs, your intuition deepens to direct knowing, and you rapidly perceive all at once, all through your body. Direct knowing is a heightened form of intuition that combines the comprehensive, nonverbal knowing of the right brain with the instinctive knowing of your body. Your organs, and even your cells, know something about the world. As your body becomes ultrasensitive, you receive insights as energy information that comes directly via vibration from the field around you.

Your ultrasensitivity leads you to become empathic, which then leads to compassion, the knowing of the soul. Direct knowing helps you become aware that the energy-and-consciousness inside your sphere is also part of your mind. Everything is conscious. Answers and insights emerge directly from your field in the present moment, when you need the information and when you ask. When you perceive with direct knowing, your left and right brain operate in a cooperative partnership.

3. **Practice undivided attention.** Attention can be focused on things from the point of view of linear or spherical-holographic perception. From the linear view, you measure attention by its span and see one thing at a time, which causes attention to be divided or fragmented. Now, at the end of the Information Age, processing huge amounts of data with linear, divided attention causes stress and mistakes due to multitasking, distraction, and speeding. With spherical-holographic perception, you can see many things at once and understand the interconnections without effort. Understanding becomes more refined, revealing energy-and-consciousness—and the soul—in everything.

Undivided attention removes the imaginary lines between things, helping you experience how the nonphysical realms are merged with the physical world and how nonphysical beings help do much of the work we used to do alone, as individuals. Undivided attention helps you develop the skills technology is currently trying to do *for* you.

You can practice undivided attention by holding your focus a minute longer on whatever you're noticing, then another minute, and penetrating a little further into the underlying reality. You can notice when you become distracted and why, and begin to practice being with each moment fully, appreciating and merging with it.

4. **Practice Flow attention.** When seen with linear perception, the Flow appears to be going somewhere, through space or into the future, the way a sine wave moves forward. With spherical-holographic perception, the Flow simply oscillates between the physical and nonphysical reality, dissolving and reforming again and again, from particle to wave to field and back through the wave to the particle again. When

you "go with the Flow," you allow right timing and natural motivation to coincide in an action that isn't dictated by willpower. You can't tell if you're doing the moving or if something bigger is moving you. You're not locked into a cause-and-effect process of creation.

The Flow never catapults you sharply into nothingness; it turns gradually through cycles of imagination, action, and results to open, restful, spaciousness and back to imagination. The Flow is the constantly evolving consciousness of all souls and all forms of life. It sources you and gives your creations to others who need them.

5. **Practice unified field attention.** As you experience the interpenetration of the physical and nonphysical worlds, you learn to notice and work with the fields that are inside every physical form—the inner blueprints. You experience how these fields precipitate forms and how you can, almost instantly, change the form of something by adjusting its inner blueprint. You also learn that you can adjust the frequency of your own field at will and be able to frequency-match other fields and read them for energy information. And when you keep your field vibrating at your home frequency—the vibration of your soul—others tend to match you by shifting into their own home frequency, which resonates harmoniously with yours.

Once you recognize the concept of fields, you can feel the unified field of the universal mind and cosmos as it interpenetrates your body, relationships, and even the inanimate objects in your daily life. Everything in the world is made of energy-and-consciousness, so everything is alive in some way. You have access to all the knowledge, all the patterns and realities, and all the possibilities contained in the unified field.

The universe is self-regenerating and eternal, constantly refreshing itself and in touch with every other part of itself instantaneously. Everything in it is giving, exchanging, and interacting with energy, coming in and out of existence at every level. The self has a field of influence on the world and vice versa, based on this energy.

Lynne McTaggart

6. **Practice collective-self attention.** Your identity ranges from you-the-personality in the physical world, to you as your relationships and groups, to the nonphysical experience of you-the-soul and your soul mates and soul groups, and eventually, to you as the entire unified field. With linear perception, you belong in relationships and groups, but with spherical-holographic perception, you *become* them. There are endless frequencies and foci of your self. You might understand the complexity of your expanded identity by realizing you've had many past-life incarnations, and you are the composite of all of them. Then include the experiences of all your ancestors passed to you through DNA and your overlapping energy fields. Keep including and soon you see that you have access to all lifetimes of all people simultaneously. You are a big situation!

   People of like vibration are beginning to show up magically in each other's fields and lives to work and create together, via resonance and the law of emergence. Organizations are changing from linear-hierarchical structures to more interconnected networks or matrix-like structures, where contribution, compensation, and responsibility are more evenly distributed. When you practice collective-self consciousness, you experience a new level of intimacy. You experience the true meaning of fellowship and communion, and a new kind of ethics based on compassion. With these new values, you are careful not to be "violent" in even the subtlest ways, and you realize that any form of self-sacrifice hurts others, which also hurts you.

7. **Practice shaping the imaginal realm.** The imaginal realm is similar to the *many-worlds theory* in quantum physics. It's like the higher level of the universal mind—and of the soul—where all possibilities exist and anything can be created. The ideas are there for the choosing, free to anyone who places attention on them. Imagination is a powerful, creative force. It is how you create your life. You bring your imaginations into form by paying close and loving attention to them, and by feeling into them, giving your body a tangible, felt sense that the potential reality is actually phys-

ically real. And soon, *it is*. Attention causes the higher frequency inner blueprint to slow down and eventually crystallize in the three-dimensional world. You can re-imagine and revise a reality you've created by changing the variables you combine in your imagination.

If your imagination has become stagnant from taking in other people's imaginations (via television or books, for example), or if you've been programmed to think imagination is silly, you can rebuild your imagination muscle by playing with ideas, creating little movies in your mind, tweaking the variables, and entertaining yourself with made-up scenarios. You can go to the imaginal realm as if it's a real place where you can have magical, effortless, creative experiences. You can imagine better realities for others as well as yourself. And it's important to remember that everyone is imagining their reality simultaneously, and the different preferences combine to create the world we all share. Imagination is sourced by joy.

8. **Practice opening new human capacities.** You soon change your idea of what's normal for people to be able to do. In the Intuition Age and the transparent reality, what used to be supernatural becomes natural. It used to be that only superheroes had superpowers, but things like telepathy, clairvoyance, and mediumship are already becoming common. Psychic abilities and expanded powers are a result of bringing patterns from the nonphysical world into the physical without reducing their frequency.

Technology hints at abilities we all have inherently, and we will always be several steps ahead of technology—learning, or remembering, how to do things that are beyond its scope. Many expanded capacities may develop softly and gradually as your frequency increases and the need for them arises. One new ability may connect to a variety of others, then deepen. There are principles of energy-and-consciousness that affect phenomena on earth that we don't understand yet, but they will be revealed in the transparent reality. Anything is possible in the nonphysical realms, and part of what keeps new human abilities from becoming physical is lack of imagination and the belief that they're only possible for superheroes or ascended masters.

9. **Practice "pretend dying."** In the transparent reality, your idea and experience of dying transform. When you experience the merger of the nonphysical and physical worlds—how the process of involution and evolution, of materialization and dematerialization, are continuous—you feel how life is ever-present. There is physical life and nonphysical life; nothing ends, life just changes frequency and cycles around and around. You understand that there is really no such thing as death—unless you see captivity in ego as a kind of death.

Many people have had near-death experiences or have explored after-death states in deep meditation. They report there is a progression of experience after death in the nonphysical realms, and the early stages involve removing blockages and clutter. The next stages pertain to sorting through and understanding what has been learned in the lifetime through a filter of compassion. After that, you remember how living in the nonphysical dimensions functions, and you continue to learn and create in the imaginal realm.

Learning to do these things consciously, while still physical, can make the actual experience of "transitioning" effortless and joyful. I call this practicing "pretend dying"—doing the work you might normally do during and immediately after death, now, in your mind, emotions, and body. This way, you can have a new life without death. It's also useful to build skill with direct knowing, telepathy, compassion, and imagination in preparation for nonphysical life, because these are skills you'll use when out of the body. As we become increasingly transparent, we may not need to die and be reborn to experience both the nonphysical and physical aspects of ourselves; we may simply ascend and descend.

The transparent reality promises to be truly astounding in its efficiency, joyfulness, and its empowerment of individuals, groups, and organizations. Knowledge and innovation will grow exponentially, and compassion will be the new evolutionary force.

> This world, which we think so solidly real, is a shadow out of
> which and beyond which we may at any time pass. It is an
> abstraction from a more fundamental and dimensionally larger
> world—a more fundamental world abstracted from a still more
> fundamental and dimensionally larger world, and so on to infinity . . .
> You can prove the existence of a dimensionally larger world
> by focusing your attention on an invisible state and imagining
> that you see and feel it.
> Neville Goddard

Just to Recap...

As you shift into the Intuition Age and its transparent reality, you will notice a few key things that help you experience transparency. First, you notice that when you leave the present moment and project ahead or put pressure on yourself to be more or better, you block the experience of transparency, which arises when you're calm, still, and centered in the here-and-now. You also notice that if you stop or stall the Flow through fear or negative thinking, you block the experience of transparency, which is a function of allowing the Flow to bring what you need and dissolve what you don't need. Clearing what's unnecessary—the clutter in life—is an important part of this. In addition, you notice that trust is a key component of transparency. Trust is about unconditional allowing, receiving, and giving.

You are becoming curious and hungry for the transparent reality due to the effects of the acceleration of energy on the planet and in yourself. There are many new glimmers you're noticing about how the Intuition Age will function that motivate you to make deep changes. For example, you want to know about the dynamics of the higher nonphysical realms, your identity as a soul and as a collective group consciousness, how materialization really works, and what's possible to know when everything is available.

To experience transparency, you need to develop radical trust, which means absolutely trusting yourself as a soul—that you-the-soul guide the unfolding of your life and fuel the function of your Inner Perceiver, which helps you notice what you notice for good reasons. You also need to develop absolute trust in other people and groups. To do that—especially in this bridge time between the old and new realities—you must work with intuition and common sense, since many people are still caught in fear behaviors, lies, and woundedness.

You can trust that at the core, everyone is a soul and we all want to love and be loved. Even if others are walled off from their soul experience, you can telepathically communicate this to them. You can also read people so you know how much others are able to receive and give. Being betrayed, for example, is not the other person's fault; it's because you didn't read them accurately enough or acted counter-intuitively to override your intuition. Finally, you need to agree to absolutely trust life itself, and how it occurs as a cocreation of your own soul and all other souls, in a mutually supportive, coevolutionary way.

Developing radical trust often begins with a choice to experiment with one area of trust. Hold the idea lightly and keep attention focused on the practice of trusting. Observe neutrally how it works. Validate when it does, and when there are partial results, look below the surface to find the reason for the interference. Continue to work with your intuition. Radical trust can be built; the left brain just needs to be convinced of it. Trust is related to surrendering but not in a helpless way. It's important to realize that the divine higher power or high-frequency consciousness is in the nonphysical realms but also in the physical world, *and in us.* You can expand to the heavens and also "tie your camel to the post," using your common sense.

Finally, there are a number of new attention skills that we are developing to enter and live successfully in the Intuition Age, or transparent reality. You are learning to practice spherical-holographic perception, direct knowing, undivided attention, flow attention, unified field attention, collective-self attention, shaping the imaginal realm, opening new human capacities, and "pretend dying."

Transparency Message
OPEN OPEN OPEN

We, the nonphysical beings, your teachers, helpers, friends, colleagues, family members, and benefactors, are here, right now, with you, as soon as you place attention on us. Placing attention on the idea of us or on our vibration calls us instantly into existence in the higher frequencies of your field. We emerge from the background, from whatever frequency we've been exploring. In our reality, we can be in many frequencies simultaneously. If you feel cut off from people, please start with us. We can re-instill your experience of belonging, supporting, and being supported.

Call us and trust that we hear you. We have unconditional trust in you and caring for you, and we give it constantly at higher frequency levels where you also exist, where assistance is our entertainment. We all play and exchange freely. We would gladly drop closer to your physical and mental vibration. Just think of us, invite us into your frequency, and open to feel us.

We can penetrate into the physical world and even share space with you in your body. We do not interfere but telepathically and kinesthetically seed ideas into your field, ideas you ask us to help you remember, which then bubble up and you think they are your own, and they are. We have no space to cross to reach you, and we are masters at shifting our frequency instantly to any inviting vibration, even to the nth degree of a variation. We are not caught in fear: we see clearly. You share your life pattern with us fully, and we cooperate in assisting your growth so you maintain perfect attunement with the acceleration of the planet.

We understand resonance at a level you cannot yet comprehend and we know how to help you start a resonance inside your field that will accurately precipitate into a form you need. At the highest frequency levels, you already trust your interweaving and interpenetration with us. You trust it to such a degree that you don't sense us as different from you. We all love.

If you wish to develop radical trust in your physical life, where you so often live in the illusion of fragmented consciousness, first expand into imagining our shared existence at these high frequencies. Then slowly spiral down in lovely loops, bringing the oneness with you through the mind, the emotions, and into the radiant body that underlies your physical body. Rest a moment, allow the knowing to register in the cells. When you are attuned to your next-higher frequency, you see colors more vividly, smell the clarity in the air, feel the love in the plants and animals, and hear the unvoiced messages whispering.

Open to us and you open to your soul, to the souls of other physical people, and to the essence of every form. Be open and also observant. Wait to know, and you know immediately. Trust us all, and you receive and give with ultimate proficiency. "We" are all inside the physical world. Come find us.

5

The Bridge Time:
Life in a Partially Transparent World

Life is pleasant. Death is peaceful.
It's the transition that's troublesome.

Isaac Asimov

All this talk about developing radical trust, spherical-holographic perception, and becoming transparent in the Intuition Age is certainly idealistic, and perhaps it's a far-off fantasy if you take into account the state of the world as it has always been and still is today. Dramatic, shocking news is covered by journalists before positive, contributory developments, and we hear about frightening environmental changes and international upheavals immediately. The negativity in the world certainly seems pervasive and devastating. It's difficult to sense how life is progressing toward a transformation for the better when it seems like Armageddon is just around the corner.

If you look with eyes that see only the physical world, and if you give more weight to negative events than to the goodness of people, the explosions of hatred, violence, and suffering look overwhelming and can paralyze you or make you want to retaliate in kind. If you let that happen, the dominators, dictators, and terrorists win. And you remain in the opaque reality with them.

The truth is that we are experiencing a chaotic, confusing bridge time between two different perceptual realities. In this chapter, we'll take a thorough look at this sticky, turbulent time of transition, and discuss ways to minimize the shock of moving from one kind of reality to a very different one—especially where you might stand out from the crowd in ways that seem dangerous.

Understanding the Bridge Time

Let's remember: In the old opaque reality, there is an "outside world" full of people who believe in fear and lack a steady connection with heart, soul, and spirit. Both ego and self-sacrifice are glorified. Suspicion, evil, and catastrophe can seem omnipresent. It's easy to expect the worst from people and not dare to live up to your full potential for fear of reprisals from jealous outsiders. If you see yourself as separate and isolated, or don't occupy your body and life fully, being invaded or attacked on various levels is likely—and then self-defense, secrets, hiding, and deception seem necessary. Life defaults to "power over" and survival of the fittest.

In contrast, in the new transparent reality, there is no outside world, no past and future. There is just one vast, present moment with all possible realities floating in it, existing at different frequencies. Match your mind, body, and emotions to any frequency, and that version of yourself and that reality can occur. Other people are inside your sphere and there is mutual support and frequency-matching—so the people you interact with match your thoughts and emotional state at any given moment. If you focus on a compassionate ground of being, you get mutually supportive people. If you place attention, even unconsciously, on a fear-based reality, you get fear-based people. And yet, it's as easy to be safe as it is to be in danger.

In the transparent reality of the new Intuition Age, all knowledge and possibilities are inside your sphere as well, so you have instant access to anything you need. The new reality fosters healing, cocreation, innovation, and evolution. This sort of life might seem utopian to people who've never peeked outside the old, dystopian reality. But the more you open your intuition and compassion, perceive from your right brain and unity consciousness, and stay focused in the present moment, trusting the Flow, the more real the transparent reality becomes.

We are gods in the chrysalis.
Dale Carnegie

The new transparent reality sounds pretty great, right? But we're not there yet. We're in that uncomfortable chrysalis to butterfly stage, partway into and through the doorway to a transformed life. It would be great if we could just weave a cocoon around ourselves and spend some quiet time in the dark, allowing our molecules to rearrange themselves, then pop out all beautiful and perfect! Unfortunately—or fortunately—ours is a *conscious* transformation process fueled by individual choice and attention. You and I have the privilege of living through this unusual time period when the magic happens—not for one or two, but for many.

We are in the bridge time when some people are already becoming transparent, some are just discovering the idea of transparency and transformation, others are chafing under the dynamics of the opaque reality but don't see an alternative, and still others are dedicated to and defensive about the opaque reality because it's familiar and real. For those of us who are actively on the path to transparency, it's challenging to stabilize our new perception in the face of people who doubt, ridicule, and oppose personal and societal transformation.

In the early stages of this bridge time, you're probably dipping your big toe into the *possibility* of having your world be safe, open, and fluid in a positive, creative way. You're giving yourself experiences that you can compare: "Here's how it works in the old reality, here's how it works in the new one. Hmmm. Yes, I'm slowly convincing myself that the benefits of the new reality are true. But let me check it again just to be sure."

Can we *all* really transform and change the entire world? You want to believe it but your residual programming probably says it's a silly, naïve pipe dream. You might think, "If I become transparent before others do, I'll end up being a victim of the remaining negative, opaque people. I can't be too successful or let people know how easy things have become for me. I can't reveal all my secrets; I'll have to keep my transparency a secret."

But this is not the way it works. Dissolving fear and solidity creates an elegant, highly functional, safe, joy-based reality—even when others are still in various degrees of opacity. Not everyone has to agree with you for you to have your own experience of transparency.

Opening Pandora's Box

I mentioned in chapter 1 that a big part of the transformation process concerns clearing the subconscious mind, or dissolving the clutter that interferes with the free flow of your soul's wisdom into and through your personality. Clutter is the only thing, really, that prevents you from experiencing your natural, inherent transparency. The frequency of the planet and of our bodies has eclipsed the low vibration of fear suppressed in the nether regions—the subconscious blocks we've never wanted to face.

Now those subterranean vaults of fear are wide open, and as with Pandora's Box, all the little demons and torturous thoughts fly out and up into your conscious mind, which is your daily reality. Collective fears flood into the collective conscious mind of society, which is the news and current events. When a personal fear surfaces, it's likely to cause a related fear-based situation to occur in your life. For instance, a memory may surface of you dying young in another life, and now a friend's child is in the hospital with leukemia and you feel unusually disturbed by it. When societal fears surface, a country may find itself electing a fear-based, controlling or dictatorial leader, or moving toward revolution. Though the process of clearing clutter can seem like punishment, you (and we) actually have the chance to drill down to the underlying causal beliefs, to clear the fear through understanding, compassion, and right action.

Everyone else is experiencing the flood of released personal disturbances and the re-enactment of past dramas too. Life has become intense! The bridge time is about this global clearing of your own individual fears combined with humanity's collective fears. It seems chaotic and dark, as though it may continue ad infinitum, but it's a necessary and critical step toward transparency and enlightenment. It will not last forever—evolution will see to that.

So many people are still ignorant about the opportunity at hand, however; they don't yet understand that a profound transformation—for the better—is underway. They certainly don't see how the flood of negativity, and what seems to be out-of-control growth in areas like the Internet of Things (IoT) and artificial intelligence (AI), could be a positive step in the right direction. (Do I want a helpful robot that reports my every move to Big Brother? Do I want trackers implanted in my children so I always know where they are?) It seems to many people, who keep their eyes on what's going wrong or could go wrong, that the world is headed for destruction. They thus maintain a constant level of anxiety and dread, which materializes more anxiety and dread.

As Pandora's Box opens, what was already fear-based—for example, behaviors developed to fight and avoid fear, and behaviors that heighten fear—become more exaggerated and prevalent. We move around in an atmosphere tainted by anxiety, and it is always foremost on our mind, even when we sleep—if we sleep. The result is that life becomes fragmented, unpredictable, and chaotic. It may seem like clear people must fight against this disruption and upheaval, but that would be the wrong move.

> If you trade your authenticity for safety, you may experience the following: anxiety, depression, eating disorders, addiction, rage, blame, resentment, and inexplicable grief.
> Brené Brown

Seeing Past Polarity

When you're focused in the opaque reality, fear causes you to be hyper-alert to polarization and conflict, which can lead to extreme positions and "extremists." There are the violent, hate-filled people and the peaceful, love-filled people, the realists and the visionaries, the workers and the slackers, the faithful and the infidels, the liberals and the conservatives, the poor and insanely rich. The physical world seems "real," while the nonphysical world is a fanciful dream of a heaven that might not actually exist, or that could exist if one has enough faith.

Today, in the opaque reality, people take sides and grow ever further apart, which prevents them from understanding each other's point of view. Remember the O. J. Simpson trial, where there was such a racial divide that neither side could comprehend how the other side's logic or perception was functioning? What was obvious to one was totally baffling to the other. It is this belief in opposition and polarization that keeps spiritual and physical experiences separate from each other, and prevents transparency.

When your attention focuses on some terrible mass shooting in the news, or the ugly mudslinging of political opponents, or the plight of millions of refugees, your left brain automatically wants to divide the world into good guys and bad guys. As soon as that happens, you're stuck in opacity. If you think you have to choose between the earthly reality that seems so bad and the heavenly reality that seems so good, you're stuck in opacity. *All either-or polarities are a symptom of old perception and the opaque reality*.

As you enter transparency, you leave that oppositional world. The spiritual and physical realms interpenetrate, sourcing each other every millisecond. Separation dissolves. Fear dissolves. There is no more polarity. All positions exist together, complementing each other, without opposition. Your right brain and heart set the tone. You don't buy into the idea that the world is a place of suffering. You don't take sides or resist the negativity because at a deep level you experience that *polarity is not the real reality—unity is*. The more you remember to choose to live in the new perception and develop transparency, the less energy the old reality has. It's not attractive anymore. Then you don't need to fight the old reality; instead, you eclipse it. You move to a level of understanding beyond the old model, allowing the old model to be inside your sphere, but you don't match its vibration.

The unconscious is not a demoniacal monster,
but a natural entity which, as far as moral sense, aesthetic taste,
and intellectual judgment go, is completely neutral. It only becomes
dangerous when our conscious attitude to it is hopelessly wrong.
To the degree that we repress it, its danger increases.
Carl Jung

Overwhelmed by Negativity & Narcissism

With Pandora's Box wide open, we see previously suppressed secrets and lies everywhere—the many scandals, taboos, hatreds, nondenial denials, excuses, and abuses that have already come to light. We're swimming in a sea of muck, and everyone seems to have a short fuse. With the advent of reality TV, people moved beyond the older form of the "roast," where a celebrity would be humorously put down by friends. We can now view the shocking ugliness of the subconscious mind in a way that is seductive, direct, and safe; no humor is necessary to water it down.

We can be privately fascinated with what has always been considered bad and be free to ridicule and "punk" others, and express meanness, sarcasm, frustration, and hostility. Let's crawl through the home of a hoarder and make fun of him! Let's focus on the nastiest stage mother who wounds children; or the outrageous, narcissistic wives of the *nouveau riche*, who only think about bling; or the cattiest, meanest teenage girls who are incapable of supporting each other; or the favored boyfriend who is rejected at the last minute for another man by the beautiful bachelorette. Defensive and offensive behaviors are now glorified, as if they are something to be emulated. And given the permission, many people do emulate these behaviors.

Collective fear stimulates herd instinct, and tends to
produce ferocity toward those who are not
regarded as members of the herd.
Bertrand Russell

Now the subconscious mind is emptying into online media. Parents who experienced a tragic loss of a child are reamed out on Twitter and Facebook for being bad caretakers. Cyber-bullying is rampant among teens. We're awash in negative reviews and vitriolic opinions. There is a term for this: *mob shaming*. On the internet, some people cry out for *others* to be more transparent, while maintaining their own right to privately project criticism from afar.

When researching trust online, I found pages of *memes*—virally transmitted social ideas, often represented as sayings in graphic boxes. So many were negative and based on disillusionment and ignorance, like: "Trust is like an eraser; it gets smaller and smaller after every mistake." Or "Be careful who you trust; the devil was once an angel." Or "Don't trust too much, don't love too much, don't hope too much, because that too much can hurt you so much."

What we see in the media carries over into real life. Road rage is rampant—probably because people resent having to interrupt their texting-while-driving to remember to turn or exit the highway. Or they're outraged that someone dared to make them feel inferior by passing them. School shootings are carried out most often by alienated, bullied boys getting their revenge. We're afraid to inadvertently offend someone out in public for fear they'll pull out a gun and shoot us. What's really going on?

Does having the freedom to spew bile at others really help reduce the pressure of our internal stress—our deep need to clear our own fear? Does it lead to us facing our own wounds? Or does the distraction of projecting the pain onto others stall us from becoming clear? Are people identifying with the mean and violent characters depicted in the media, finding a sense of belonging and identity in a group of the disaffected, so that these behaviors are reinforced instead of being lived through and eliminated? Those who over-identify with the rebel/revolutionary archetype and feel good about themselves because they're "bad" can easily become stuck in this odd variation of ego. This resistance thinking can cut off the life force, and the result can be increased negative repercussions—and perhaps, even an early death.

Chapter 5: The Bridge Time

A wise man who I loved very much once said:
"Let's stop finding a new witch of the week and burning them at the
stake. We are all horrible and wonderful and figuring it out."
Stephanie Wittels Wachs

The Plus Side of Freeing Negativity

All this negativity is no more prevalent than it's always been—it's just not being suppressed and denied, so it's much more visible and tactile now. The chaos of the bridge time is really about the soul's deep desire to disgorge and dissolve what's false from the subconscious mind, while the left brain/ego desperately tries to maintain and protect its known territory. There is a positive function in all this—the bridge time helps you see what used to be invisible. Perhaps you notice that your own fears are happening to *other people* in the media—both in real life and in movies—and you achieve some perspective about what's been holding you back. Maybe you develop more compassion when you see others being disrespected, humiliated, and shamed publically online. Maybe you now notice liars and egotists more than ever before and resolve to heal places in yourself that feel vulnerable and insecure.

Jon Ronson, a Welsh journalist, in his book *So You've Been Publically Shamed*, takes an interesting, positive view on public shaming: "When we deployed shame, we were utilizing an immensely powerful tool. It was coercive, borderless, and increasing in speed and influence. Hierarchies were being leveled out. The silenced were getting a voice. It was like the democratization of justice."[1] Perhaps some of our short-fused, entitled-to-be-negative behavior is actually fueling transformation, helping to expose outdated thinking, and breaking up what needs to be dissolved.

It's true that societal structures that rely on ego, hoarding, will-power, and control are beginning to crumble. Hierarchies are becoming outdated. What's worked in the past—like blind reliance on the oil industry or organized religion, for example—is less viable now. And even though we're seeing the death throes of organizational ego and outworn societal habits, there is still a need for courageous whistle-blowers and those speaking "truth to power." It's all about making the subconscious conscious so some Light can shine through and we can become fully transparent.

There are ironies here: Your soul is trying to clear your subconscious mind of old wounds—to free you—yet the clearing process with its flood of negativity can be a quagmire. People with a poor sense of self may identify with the surfacing negative thoughts and behaviors and validate their woundedness all over again. Or the extreme of low self-esteem can cause people to flip to the opposite extreme—narcissism and brazen ego expression. We're seeing people take millions of "selfies," start sentences with the word *me*, crave fame for doing almost anything, and expect to make a six-figure income upon graduating from college.

The clearing process is about the soul shining through, but if you don't have a clear sense of self to begin with, you might try to manufacture one with willpower. This is understandable. To develop a spiritually based sense of self—the experience of soul—where it's been blocked, narcissism and self-importance may be a first step. From there, people may be able to relax about themselves, open their minds and hearts, and come closer to the truth. Eventually, they may realize that extreme, audacious ego is no different than extreme victim ego—it's all just a trap.

The emptying of Pandora's Box will not go on forever. We can't stand the saturation in ugliness and meanness for long, because it's essentially anti-soul and anti-evolution. At heart, we want to grow and improve. Mob shaming, cyber-bullying, and explosions of frustration that become attacks are mainly a venting of pent-up, blocked energy-and-consciousness that comes from not experiencing the soul. Luckily, our frequency continues to increase, and that means any kind of stuckness—even a fixation on being-good-by-being-bad—will soon be swept along, broken up, and transformed in the swift current of evolution.

> If everyone is thinking alike,
> then somebody isn't thinking.
> **General George S. Patton Jr.**

The Temptation to Backslide

Global transparency begins with one person: you! You must want to be free of your paralyzing clutter, free to be authentically creative, and free to grow into more of your possibilities. You must know how to work with the clearing process—how it oscillates and how you naturally rock back and forth between opacity and transparency. The more you choose transparency and face and transmute your fears, the longer you remain transparent. Of course, you can be knocked out of your clarity by old beliefs and habits, and by people who are fighting the acceleration. Best to be prepared so you don't backslide into old thinking! During the bridge time, here are some things that can be expected.

1. **When you talk about transformation, new perception, and transparency, people respond differently.** Some respond with a blank stare, thinking it's too complicated, confusing, dangerous, "out there," or futuristic. Or it's just not in their reality yet. Other people may react defensively because the new thought pattern threatens their current belief system. Some respond with curiosity or know just what you're talking about. Learning to use your intuition to sense which category people are in is important. So is learning to communicate to people at different levels of readiness. If you react to being rejected by people who don't match your frequency, you backslide.
2. **Since you're in a process of clearing your own clutter, you can be tripped up by sudden negative occurrences and dramas in your life.** Don't be surprised if you occasionally backslide into negative thinking or a negative self-image during the clearing process. It's important to remember that these events and inner dialogues are seeded to you-the-personality by you-the-soul, so you can understand the erroneous underlying perceptions that got you stuck in the first place. Don't let your own process trip you up! It's always about evolution.
3. **Since everyone else is clearing their clutter too, you can be inundated by the increasing negativity in the world.** When you notice other people dealing with their own traumas and challenges, you

may overlap with them; in other words, a similar issue may surface for you as well but in a different area of life. It's important not to separate your reality into "me and them," but instead use everything you notice as fodder for your own clarification process.

4. **Your increasing ultrasensitivity can cause you to be extra-disturbed by the chaos in the world.** You may feel you need to withdraw and be alone or distract yourself with an addiction. You may feel pressured to make sense of the overwhelming amount of linear data and nonlinear energy information you're receiving. You may also feel the need to rescue others from their suffering. When you merge with others, you can be fooled into feeling that their pain is yours, and if you constantly pay attention to others and not to yourself, you'll feel drained and exhausted. Remember, you have your own center and home frequency that puts everything in perspective for you. You can access information from the field around you, then check to see if it makes sense. If you forget that you know how to be clear and that others have their own process of clearing their own clutter, you backslide.

5. **It may take several rounds to clear each chunk of clutter as you learn not to indulge in negative thinking.** You may become discouraged or impatient, thinking, "I did that already! Why is it happening again?" If you think this way, you backslide. Remind yourself that you didn't do anything wrong—it's just that some patterns run deep, and the belief in them is longstanding. You may clear them in layers. Be patient and extra kind with yourself. Stay with what arises in each moment, and honor the fact that it's surfacing. Each time something surfaces, it's new. When you finally clear it, it won't come back with the same charge. You'll feel neutral or even bored with the issue, and you'll have more vitality.

6. **If you look at the transparency process from a left-brain viewpoint, transforming the world's consciousness may seem like an impossible, disheartening task.** Because the left brain perceives in a linear fashion, it sees transformation and transparency as a *process* moving in stages from past to future, through time and space. But

transparency is a state of being that's natural to the soul; it underlies the crazy assumptions we've bought into concerning life on earth. It is already everywhere and is the predominant reality. Transparency has the real power. The transformation of the planet to a transparent reality will occur in the vast present moment, through nonlinear means and the attainment of a critical mass of people that tip the scales all at once. You can't "figure it out" or project its date of occurrence. Don't project ahead and fall into disappointment or despair over the impossibility of it all, or you backslide.

7. **You may underestimate the value of achieving your own transparency.** Again, when seen from the left-brain point of view, one person becoming transparent in a sea of opaque people seems like nothing—an event with no impact. Ironically, it's just the opposite. Since all other beings exist inside your sphere, when you become clear, they become clear to some degree. You telepathically communicate this view of them instantly through time and space, which helps motivate them. When more individuals become clear and include each other, the idea of mass transparency becomes more normal.

> The air is full of our cries.
> But habit is a great deadener.
> Samuel Beckett

What Do You Feed with Your Attention?

Unlearning an old habit and relearning a new one is a matter of shifting your attention—totally—from one focus to another. When feeling captive of the negativity swirling about you, it helps to bring some consciousness to the process of turning your mindset around. The first thing to remember is that *what you place your attention on comes alive* and becomes real to you.

There is a key concept in *A Course in Miracles*—basically, it says that if, in any given moment, you experience love (by choosing the unity view), you don't know fear, and if you experience fear (by choosing the linear, separated view), you don't know love. So in this bridge time, if you watch the news every night or read the paper religiously, you may feel inundated by what's dysfunctional and overwhelming in the world. You may feel you can barely keep up with progress and will soon be left behind in a morass of ignorance. That focus is the filter that creates an opaque reality.

> "Ginny!" said Mr. Weasley, flabbergasted. "Haven't I taught you anything? What have I always told you? Never trust anything that can think for itself if you can't see where it keeps its brain."
> J. K. Rowling

On the other hand, if you're stepping into transparency and new perception, you may read uplifting books, attend workshops to develop new consciousness skills, meditate, practice mindfulness, and find your life dream. You may not be interested in the news anymore, or even television programs that are too shallow or dark. You're not avoiding the world's negativity out of resistance (that just feeds the opaque reality), you're simply not investing attention in it. You're still noticing the world events you need to notice. In fact, you might use some of them as fuel for your spiritual growth. Perhaps it's correct for you to become involved in petitions or a demonstration, or to work with a nonprofit organization. Focusing on the Light within all beings and events, and on the evolutionary nature of life, is a filter that creates a transparent reality.

You always have a choice. And it's through repeated choice that your reality takes one path or another. Even if you're on a path of self-improvement and spiritual growth, it's still a daunting task to not participate in negativity. You might check to see if you derive any strange satisfaction from feeling helpless or like a victim of circumstances. If you default to panic, anxiety, or worry in times of stress, you stall yourself from making the shift into clarity. You might examine the reasons you unconsciously choose to contract and feel deflated or jacked up to an abnormally high pitch. Honestly, it's unnecessary.

When a negative event occurs, you don't need to revisit the past and old beliefs and "react." It's just as easy to be neutral and just be with the situation without voting on it. Be the observer and don't take things personally, as though you're wrong or flawed in some way. Give yourself a moment to feel from the soul's point of view. Think about the deeper meaning of what happened.

> Look on every exit as being
> an entrance somewhere else.
>
> **Tom Stoppard**

So, which reality do you feed with your attention? How much do you tolerate being a victim of the opaque reality? How much do you know instinctively and intuitively that the transparent reality is the real reality? Which reality do you want to live in? *It's high time to choose and make your choice permanent.*

When you choose to move through the doorway into the transparent reality of the Intuition Age, it becomes your life work, or your spiritual practice, and your destiny flows freely from that. If you don't want to live in the unconsciousness of the bridge time for an unnecessarily long time, consciously choosing helps; it tips the scales in the right direction. The new reality can occur in an instant each time you choose and *feel the truth of the new perception.* Yes, you stray back to old perception for a while, but if you've really chosen, you easily remember to recenter yourself and return to your preferred state. Each time you forget and remember again, it's easier to remain in the new reality.

· · · · · · · · · · ·

Try This!

Make a Solid Choice for Transparency

1. Close your eyes, be quiet, center yourself. Feel how it is to live in the old, linear reality with its polarization, fear, anger, self-sacrifice, and slow progress.

Notice how your body responds. Does it contract or expand? Then imagine living in the new, transparent, Intuition Age reality, where there is unity, support, freedom to create, ease of self-expression, and safety. How does your body respond? Does it expand or contract? Which state do you prefer?

2. Ask yourself the following questions and write about your answers.
   - Do you believe it's possible to change your own reality?
   - Do you believe it's possible to influence other people's reality by setting a good example?
   - Are there any "yes, buts" or hesitations involved in your ideas?
   - Are you ready to choose the new transparent reality?
   - Are you ready to commit to the daily practice of choosing and creating the new reality with your attention? This involves rechoosing repeatedly until the new habit stabilizes.
   - Which reality do you choose with 100 percent of your being? Examine your choice and write about why.

3. How will you remind yourself to shift from the old reality to the new? Write about some ways to remember and practice the shift.

· · · · · · · · · · ·

Identifying Your Stressors

It helps to understand the stressors that cause you to backslide into negative, fatalistic thinking at the first sign of a challenge or difficulty. Does seeing animals or the elderly neglected or abused do it? How about a big drop in the stock market, someone giving you an insulting gesture as they pass you on the highway, a friend gossiping about you, a boss ignoring you when you bring up a good idea, the cost of healthcare and food, not getting into your first choice for college, or the cheaply manufactured product that falls apart a week after purchase? If you isolate your own particular triggers, you can be on the lookout for times when you backslide, so you can recover more quickly. Then, work with each trigger at a deeper level to find the underlying fear belief, and see why you give it power over you.

Chapter 5: The Bridge Time

The greatest weapon against stress is our ability to
choose one thought over another.
William James

LT is a successful, visionary businessman and consultant to large corporations. He is innovative, understands systems and trends, and also has a strong intuitive/spiritual side, practices yoga, and likes to sculpt and paint. We often discuss new ideas, and I always enjoy his balanced left and right brain. Recently, we were talking about how he was noticing the bridge time affecting business.

He recounted a number of his frustrations. He said he knew himself and his competencies pretty well and had many visions of accomplishment (he called them expectations) based on that understanding. Yet he consistently found that the people he wanted to sell his visions to were not able to see the value or how they might combine the ideas with their own products or services to create something better and more profitable. Or the people who capitalized on his ideas weren't able to understand and further the underlying motives that caused him to develop the ideas in the first place.

People were in ruts based on habit and old perception, and the leadership in many companies seemed more suspicious and guarded than ever before. LT said one company he had looked forward to working with insisted he sign a noncompete agreement, which, in effect, would have crippled him from using his own technology and systems with other companies, and therefore would have prevented much beneficial progress for other business segments. And yet, he saw so much potential in working with this company that he was tempted to argue with them and make a case against the noncompete.

He said in his imagination, he could see how much energy making the argument would take and how exhausting it would be, and that it probably wouldn't work, given the stubborn mindset of the leaders. It was this sort of ignorance and blindness that caused his energy to sink into dejection. He said it was hard to find people who truly "got" him and that not being able to work with people on his wavelength made him feel he would not be able to reach his optimal potential in this lifetime. And those thoughts really brought him down.

I said I knew there were many entrepreneurs and innovative business leaders who were thinking ahead and beginning to understand the transformational shift we are living through, even if they didn't call it that yet. There were plenty of people to work with at a level that would bring more of his genius to the fore and allow him to have a sense of family with his clients and colleagues. I said that working with businesses in the bridge time is similar to working with individuals—there will be many people who aren't on our frequency or wavelength, many who don't understand what's happening yet.

Unless it's your life purpose to be a teacher, trying to lead people to new perception can be draining and a waste of time. So bless them, let them be the way they are, and move on. They'll get it in their own time. Reaffirm your home frequency and truth, live in it, saturate with it, and radiate it. The people who are ready and want what you have will mysteriously emerge from your field.

LT was looking for clients among businesses that were too set in their old ways. Those had been the kind of companies he'd worked with over the past twenty years, as the Information Age was building steam. He had been brilliant at helping them in their mental processing and making linear perception more efficient, but he had outstripped his own past knowledge. LT needed to acknowledge that he was different now. He was moving through the bridge time, where his old pattern and expectations were changing significantly. His old inner blueprint was still trying to materialize a reality similar to what he was used to creating, while his new inner blueprint wanted to create a new reality.

LT's stressors—feeling sadness, or even grief, over the lack of communion with others, and frustration over people's ignorance, unwillingness to learn, and his inability to accurately place his own inspirational innovations in the world to further his humanitarian motives—had been returning him to a default setting in his brain. He had been stalling his expansion because of those unconscious "yes, buts." Under the stressors there were some erroneous ideas: That he might be forced to feel, and accept, that he was totally isolated and an outcast. That nothing he had to offer was of real value. That he might never feel the fullness of who he is while in the physical world. That to feel himself, he needed validation from others, from the "outside world."

Dealing with those core fears, reframing each one of them, and experiencing the opposite truth allowed LT to come from a different, more solid place where he could then see his motivations as his destiny. He could see that of course his ideas would help many people. And *of course* the times were ripe for more leaders to understand the transparent reality of the Intuition Age.

He practiced feeling the truth in these statements and integrating the experience into his body: "I am connected to everyone in the physical and nonphysical worlds. It's easy to communicate with people on my frequency. People on my wavelength value who I am and what I know and do. The ones who are ready to cocreate with me simply show up through synchronicity. I enjoy the fullness of who I am, and I know there is more to me that I haven't accessed yet. It will come through when the time is right. I value other people for who they are and not for their agreement with me."

. . . .

Try This!

Prevent Backsliding into Opacity

Use the following chart to do some deep diving into the things that trip you up and cause you to backslide into old perception just as you're making headway toward transparency. In your journal, write about your own dynamic. What are your triggers? What are your habitual reactions? What are the erroneous underlying beliefs that have been holding these habits in place? (Keep notes so you can use the insights in the next exercise.)

. . . .

DISCOVER YOUR STRESSORS

What Are Your First Knee-Jerk Reactions?

FIGHT	FLIGHT	FREEZE
• I feel offended • I feel violated • I feel rebellious • I feel angry, violent	• I feel scared • I feel anxious • I feel restless, impatient • I feel unconscious, blank	• I feel hurt, sad • I feel paralyzed, helpless • I feel ashamed, guilty • I feel paranoid

What Triggers Your Reactions?

FIGHT	FLIGHT	FREEZE
• Insensitivity in others • Ignorance in others • Domination by victims & egotists • Being disrespected • Being manipulated • Betrayal • Being criticized • Feeling pressured	• Illness, injury • Poor performance, failure, mistakes • Invisibility (feeling invisible to others) • Loss, sudden change (death, divorce, finances, child leaving home) • Lack of attention or approval from others	• Overwhelm, enmeshment • Mental & physical abuse • Limitation, captivity, imprisonment • Abandonment, isolation & loneliness • Suffering & pain of others

(Continued on next page)

The components of anxiety, stress, fear, and anger do not exist independently of you in the world. They simply do not exist in the physical world, even though we talk about them as if they do.

Wayne Dyer

DISCOVER YOUR STRESSORS

What Do You Typically Do?

FIGHT	FLIGHT	FREEZE
• Blame others • Attack others verbally or physically • Act more clever and control others • Act impulsively or irrationally	• Avoid the situation, run away, leave your body • Lie • Blame yourself • Become pessimistic • Indulge in an addiction • Distract yourself	• Do nothing, hide • Keep secrets • Turn the tension inside yourself • Become apathetic, depressed • Get sick, sleep

What Are Your Underlying, Erroneous Core Beliefs?

• I am alone in the universe
• The world is a place of pain and suffering
• I'll never be able to be my real self
• There is no safety or security in the world

• No one loves me or supports me
• There's no escape from evil & ignorance
• I'm inherently bad and unlucky
• People are inherently bad

Fig. 5-1

Reframing & Eclipsing

There's a positive side to any negative action or event. Living through the bridge time without backsliding involves shifting negativity and fear to the plus side, and finding the openheartedness that can result from seeing snags and challenges from the soul's-eye view. In the physical world, there are certainly plenty of cruel, hateful actions, and I'm not saying they should be tolerated—just used in a way that allows you to find growth, or that "teaching moment" that keeps your heart open. When you reframe a negative situation, you leave the facts alone but challenge the assumptions by changing the viewpoint. This way, the entire meaning can shift, and your reality can more easily change from opaque to transparent.

When the left brain steps in to define a situation as negative, the Flow stops, and creativity stops as well. You are suddenly cut off from compassion and understanding. One way to prevent the opaque reality and opaque people from pulling you back into the muck is to turn the left brain's negative declarative statements around to the opposite—see what the soul might say about the same thing with its broader wisdom and deeper love. When you feel the positive reality, even in your imagination, the Flow returns and your creativity can now go somewhere.

For example, the left brain might declare, "I have an insurmountable problem and there is no good solution." The soul might say, "I created a learning opportunity and a chance to cocreate a better situation with others. There are innumerable options for moving forward." Perhaps the left brain declares, "I was born with a weakness for picking bad relationships." The soul has a different take on things: "I've created experiences to fully develop my sense of trust and how to read other people's level of openness."

Perhaps someone born with a physical handicap is really learning and teaching others about resilience and inner beauty. Or the person who is paralyzed is learning and teaching about what freedom really means at every level of the self. You might reframe something you previously thought impossible by saying, "This idea is absolutely possible, and I will learn to do it step by step as I go along. And other people will help me."

. . . .

Try This!
Clear Subconscious Blocks By Reframing

1. Think back over the past month and recall the times you've felt frustrated, stuck, disappointed, sad, angry, hurt, disillusioned, blank, or offended. Go back into the situation and feel the sensations. Remember how you reacted

and what exactly you reacted to. You might use the insights you gained in the previous exercise.

2. What are the underlying, erroneous fear beliefs that you-the-soul are trying to bring to light? For example, if you were frustrated or angry, you might believe the outside world is bigger than you and dominates you, preventing you from expressing your true self. Or if you felt rejected, you might believe you need approval from others to avoid feeling isolated—separate from the Divine and your own soul.

3. Write about how you could turn each underlying, incorrect belief around into a statement of truth. Then imagine how you'd respond to the previous situation differently if that were true. Feel the reality in your body.

4. How could you dissolve the old unconscious reactionary behavior permanently? What methods might you use to notice when your mind has turned negative? How would you change if you didn't backslide and didn't give up your preferred state?

• • • • • • • • • • •

Poet David Whyte, in his book *Consolations*, has an interesting reframing of the idea of hiding. Instead of thinking of it as avoidance coming from fear, he sees it from the compassionate soul's point of view as an important natural function of life and creativity. He says that hiding is a way of holding ourselves until we are ready to come into the Light—and hiding done properly is the internal promise for a proper future emergence.

In a related point, he speaks about how we are overly dissected today—how our thoughts and longings are exposed too early, and how that can result in shallowness. He describes how so often what is real is so deep inside that the left brain, which thinks it knows what's going on, can't possibly fathom it yet. These deep truths need to stay hidden for a while, because they are precious. Knowing a deep truth too early can diminish its life through impatience and lack of respect.

So, hiding, when viewed from fear, might be about self-protection and avoiding attack from an unfriendly outside world (a left-brain perspective), and when viewed from love, might be about the powerful qualities of being still and the patient gestation of healthy, new life and fully formed, mature ideas (a right-brain perspective).

Don't cry because it's over.
Smile because it happened.
Ludwig Jacobowski

When you're speaking with others, you might use reframing to make a point in a peaceful manner. You might say, "We certainly know we can argue well! Perhaps we can do a similar good job at agreeing well." Or "Yes, this idea might seem silly, but it might also be ridiculous to stick with the old way of doing things." Instead of allowing things to be stuck in opposition and polarity, where people face away from each other and stop the Flow, reframing can help re-establish a figure-eight flow, where people face each other again and move toward understanding the other point of view. Instead of using blame talk, which typically begins with "You did (or said) _____," and immediately polarizes people, you can use integrative talk, helping people find communion by combining points of view and opening to include even more perspective.

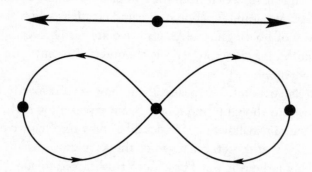

Instead of being stuck in opposition (top), facing away from each other,
turn and flow back toward the other point of view (bottom),
looking for how you also have that idea but perhaps in a different area of life
or looking for how the two views might combine.

Fig. 5-2

The other helpful technique for not falling back into captivity in the opaque reality is *eclipsing the two points in a polarity by taking a third "helicopter viewpoint" above*. You might visualize this as creating an equilateral triangle by adding a third point in space above the linear polarity. This "power of three" creates perspective and a higher dimension, and facilitates integration and stability. There is something harmonious and satisfying, as well as memorable, about the experience of three. We commonly find it in stories and fairy tales—*The Three Stooges, The Three Musketeers, Goldilocks and the Three Bears*—as well as in successful marketing campaigns, graphic design, fine art, and architecture. In consciousness, the third overview point helps you understand the dynamics of the previously opposed ideas; by moving outside the polarity, you see how the two positions are connected and part of a greater reality.

For example, instead of being captive of the polarity of either wrestling with a dominating boss for leadership or letting yourself be victimized, you might leave the company and start your own business. In effect, by eclipsing the polarity, you are increasing your frequency. Spherically speaking, you're expanding your personal ball to a larger diameter, or growing another layer around the onion. With the increase in frequency, you can now see the bigger picture. This way, you allow not just two sides but all aspects of any issue, and the possibility for win-win-*win* solutions. Innovative ideas become effortless in the blink of an eye when inspiration and permission (right-brain perception) and focused, sane boundaries (left-brain perception) combine.

> A group of people coming together in a state of presence generates a collective field of great intensity. It not only raises the degree of presence of each member of the group but also helps to free the collective human consciousness from its current state of mind dominance. This will make the state of presence increasingly more accessible to individuals.
>
> Eckhart Tolle

Communicating in the Bridge Time

If you become more transparent than other people, will they misunderstand or judge you? Or will you be invisible to others and lose friends, colleagues, and opportunities? Communication in the bridge time is complicated by people consciously and unconsciously trying to clear themselves, and others who resist clearing themselves at all. Misinterpretation can be rampant. Most of us are still *partially transparent*, and that means we're not paying full attention to our own self-as-soul. If you don't see your true self, and others don't see theirs, its logical that we won't see each other accurately—that it will be normal to overlook or misjudge each other.

For most of us, the subconscious still holds ideas concerning loss, failure, pain, and danger—thinking these things are true. You may be working to clear those fears, oscillating in and out of clarity, releasing what's false bit by bit as you experience the truth of the new reality. But as long as the ideas still linger, those "mistakes in perception" will surface in your communication and as real experiences, so you can see them and correct and release them permanently. Your beliefs act as inner blueprints that pattern your reality—and other people with matching beliefs show up magically to act out roles in the dramatization.

For instance, if you still think, even a little, that you're alone against the world, you may experience people rejecting you for being too honest, too much ahead of the curve, not ambitious enough, not sensitive enough to their suffering, or too sensitive to their suffering. If you believe you're too empathic, you may find yourself interacting with people who feel they're victims of a big bad world. One way to clear yourself is to notice how what happens to you is also inside you to some degree. *The way you treat yourself is the way the world treats you.*

I had an email from Nancy, who was concerned she had hurt a friend and had apologized, but the friend refused to acknowledge her perception, saying, "Nothing happened." Nancy could still feel the upset in her friend's body, however, and longed to dissolve the tension. She was vaguely aware of a subconscious pattern close to the surface in her friend—a pattern the friend didn't want to see, so the friend pushed her away. Though Nancy was a bit more transparent than her friend, both women were dealing with a similar underlying pattern concerning rejection via criticism, and neither wanted to feel it fully.

As you become clear, you sense and know more of what's happening in the energy realms and in other people's partially hidden underbelly. If you want to help people clear their fear, you can use this information—with compassion—when you communicate. But if you share the same underlying, subconscious issue with the person you're talking to, and don't want to face it in yourself, you might be tempted to project the pattern totally onto the other person, or blurt out an insight in a way that makes it seem like you're smarter or more advanced than they are. You also might inadvertently try to maintain separation, much as the two women did in the previous example, and of course, people may do the same thing with you.

As you communicate with others at this stage, it's important to not take things personally but to neutrally observe what people do and say—they're giving you data about *who* they are and what issue *they* are working on. If you take it personally, you probably share the same underlying issue.

Successful communication in the bridge time is based on a few things. Practice the Golden Rule: How would you feel if someone were saying the same thing to you? What possible misinterpretations might occur if the other person is still quite fear-based? Are you in your home frequency when you speak? Could you say less, or give the insight in smaller segments that are easier to digest and understand? Is it even appropriate to speak about the issue right now? Check to see how honest and vulnerable you're willing to be before you communicate. Are there any double standards at work? Do you have the same issue you're bringing to light?

Might you begin a conversation with a leading question instead of making a strong declarative statement, and let the insight come out in a conversation? Remember that you're dealing with fear in others and in yourself. How can you be more loving in your connection and communication? How can you be like a parent soothing a hurt child, or an animal lover reassuring a frightened dog, cat, or horse? Here are some ways that can help you communicate successfully with others in the bridge time.

1. **Become extra-conscious of your own center, home frequency, and the vibration of your sphere—your preferred state.** When you backslide, have something to return to that realigns and reattunes you to your truth and the universal principles. By recentering often, you learn to live permanently in your own centerpoint and enjoy your own soul's vibration. This is where you find peace, wisdom, and compassion whenever you lose touch. And this frequency is what allows others to understand you easily.

2. **Always start with yourself.** If your left brain tells you that other people need to change, it's just a projection. Change that very thing about yourself first. You set the tone for the way others are allowed to behave in your reality.

3. **Include others inside your sphere and allow them to be at whatever level of transparency they're capable of maintaining.** Maintain your frequency—your transparency—throughout your sphere (which includes your physical self) and let others experience it; don't hide or maintain distance to protect yourself. You can maintain your frequency simply by choosing and remembering it whenever you want, even if other people differ from it greatly. When your field is transparent and you are an example of transparency, you telepathically and kinesthetically influence others inside your field to know the world in a similar way.

4. **See others as souls; understand their vulnerabilities.** When you see people as inside your sphere, they become more intimate to you, like kin. When you put attention on them and identify yourself as your soul, you see them as souls too. It's easier then to penetrate through the crusty outer surface into the beautiful soft centers ("Life is like a box of chocolates!"). When you see others this way, they begin to see themselves this way, and then they see you this way as well. Fear is minimized.

5. **Use intuition and common sense to read people's readiness.** Obviously, not everyone will match your level of transparency. If some are farther along than you, don't beat yourself up—just allow yourself to match their frequency and try on the new feeling state. Be grateful. If others are not as far along as you, don't match their vibration and "bring yourself down." Maintain your clarity, for along with your transparency comes compassion. Just love them.

6. **Adjust your communication and vocabulary to harmonize with other people's readiness.** You may need to find ways to communicate about the new principles and skills of the transparent reality so people with varying levels of sophistication can understand you. Speak of your own process and experience. It's not compassionate to talk over someone's head, or speak to them as if they're five years old when they're fairly experienced. Learn to blend left-brain, analytical descriptions with right-brain, experiential, poetic descriptions. A big part of helping others move from the opaque reality to the transparent reality, without being insulting, is artful communication.

7. **You don't have to please everyone or save people. It's fine to let opportunities that feel like too much work, or that might drain you, slide by.** You don't have to jump through every hoop that comes rolling your way. You can choose what to do based on self-entertainment and deep desire. You can believe in other people's ability to get through to themselves when the time is right.

8. **Resolve not to engage with negativity and not to agree with ignorance.** You can make an agreement with yourself to catch yourself when you start to backslide or feel yourself tilting away from center. Instead of indulging in criticizing, complaining, or avoiding, learn to pause, recenter, reattune to your preferred state, and start again with what you know to be true. Have the courage not to take sides; you don't need to fight. If your intuition indicates it's purposeful for you to speak truth to power, go ahead; it's not the same as backsliding into negativity. Oppositional, two-pointed consciousness can transform into multiple-pointedness when your mind is open and expansive.

9. **Be a thought leader.** Allow yourself to show up and be a unique thinker. Do leading-edge work. How might you take a stand for the soul's new transparent reality? Are you willing to educate people about what's happening? Can you be a peaceful warrior of innovation who pierces the veil with clear vision and action? When events occur that were facilitated by transparency, validate them to yourself and others. Point out the differences between old and new perception. Give people a road map.

> Speak clearly, if you speak at all;
> carve every word before you let it fall.
> Oliver Wendell Holmes

How the Bridge Time Evolves

We begin with the release of the crazy fear thoughts and suppressed traumas from the subconscious mind. These are partial perceptions and misinformation that became stuck and now need to be re-viewed from the perspective of love and unity. Personal and collective anxiety is trying to become conscious so it can be understood and dissolved—so you can live in your home frequency permanently. To move successfully through this phase, you need to return to your center constantly and remember who you really are. Choose deep truth over superficial drama. And choose again, then again. Dedicate yourself to becoming clear until it becomes normal.

Next, join with others of like vibration. You don't have to be alone as you become transparent; there are many other people at the same stage as you, and you can call them forth as friends and colleagues. Ask for your "soul group," or for the people on your wavelength who are coevolutionary with you. By choosing people of like mind, your ability to stabilize your transparency is strengthened. And the frequency of the groups you form attracts more people who are curious about living successfully in this new way.

As more people join in the convening of groups that function according to new perception, it changes the balance of power. Innovations based on the principles of new perception and transparency solve world problems, and people respond because they perceive truth and hope. As a critical mass of people shift into the new reality, it drains life from the old, opaque reality. The opaque reality feels increasingly dysfunctional, slow, and boring. Eventually, the world as we've known it fades and seems like a strange, prehistoric dream.

When a critical mass is reached—and it may not take billions of bodies achieving the same frequency at once, but surprisingly fewer people—a profound change is catalyzed. Think about how rapidly the internet and global interconnectedness became normal, then imagine how fast the new perception can catch on.

New people, from higher frequency soul groups, are incarnating into the physical world continually as it increases its vibration. They bring with them innovations, new technology, and deep knowledge of the power of compassion and what were previously seen as super-human capacities. We will always surpass technology, and we will bring the abilities of the nonphysical realms—like precognition, teleportation, telekinesis, and levitation—into the physical world. The new children are helping ground transparency into the planet.

Remember, too, that the earth's frequency continues to increase. This means you continue to learn more about transparency and so does everyone else. People who couldn't understand transparency and new perception last year, may suddenly "get it" this year. Other people who refuse to change and stubbornly hang on to the familiarity of the opaque reality will suffer increasingly, and may even choose—consciously or unconsciously—to die. Or they'll suddenly wake up and realize they don't have to suffer and that self-sacrifice isn't noble—and they will shift to new perception.

Those who choose to die rather than change will evolve as much as they can in the nonphysical realms, and the absence of their resistance will actually help change the balance of power and consciousness on the planet. No one is lost; everyone eventually evolves to the same high levels of consciousness. Everyone goes "home." The process of transformation has its own compassion, its own pathway. We can trust it.

Transparency

As we are liberated from our own fear,
our presence automatically liberates others.
Marianne Williamson

Just to Recap...

We live in an uncomfortable bridge time between the old, opaque reality and the new, transparent reality. Some people are already very clear and understand the gist of new perception and the Intuition Age. Others seek to understand what's happening, while still others resist change of any kind. We're experiencing various stages of partial opacity and partial transparency. During this time, the subconscious mind empties into the conscious mind, and old fears and wounds reappear and re-enact, causing great upheaval. People are flooded with negativity, their fuse is short, and they are caught in fight-or-flight behaviors. For many, life seems difficult and hopeless, and they may want to give up out of fear. Others fight to maintain control and domination, which is just a cover-up for fear.

You can create a transparent reality in your own life, even if others don't agree or notice what you're doing. It helps to become aware of the stressors in your life that might cause you to backslide into the opaque reality just as you're making headway into transparency. Underneath those triggers are core fear beliefs that want to be understood and dissolved. Notice what you feed with your attention, because what you pay attention to comes alive. Focus on which reality you want and make a clear choice that's permanent. Then practice returning to your home frequency (you as the soul-in-the-personality), saturating your sphere with clarity and compassion, and choosing to cocreate with people on your wavelength.

Keep your eyes and ears open for the negative statements and beliefs of the opaque reality, and learn to reframe them into the soul's positive statements that allow energy-and-consciousness to flow and grow. Be aware of polarities and how they block growth, and eclipse the two opposing positions by moving to a higher vantage point, where you understand how the two positions fit together into something greater. It's also important to learn to communicate with people who are not as far along in the transformation process as you are. You can act as a thought leader, working with the Golden Rule and compassion to assist others in clearing their fear. Resolve to not engage with negativity, and realize you don't have to save everyone.

The bridge time evolves along with the planet as we all evolve personally and collectively. Eventually, a critical-mass point will be reached globally. It's important to realize that transparency starts with you; no one else can do the work of transforming for you. You can join with groups of like-minded others to help stabilize your shift and begin the process of cocreating from the group mind. You can practice trusting other people to make the choices they need to make, no matter what your opinion is. Everyone achieves transparency because they're really already transparent!

Transparency Message
CONFUSION & CHAOS

When things seem to be falling apart, they are really falling into a higher order. Unhook the old connections, allow the ideas to float between meanings: soon, new attractions begin, arising from new perception. When negativity and ugliness fill the air and painful cries are heard around the world, in any moment, just below the surface, there you find peace and clarity, transparency and soul. In this moment, all is well. And in this moment, all is well too. Nature's laws are working, the universe's laws are working, the souls know the truth, the Flow knows where to go next.

Chaos is an in-between kind of order with its own harmony. In chaos, lose the dominance of the left brain: trust the interconnections of the right brain. Trust the Flow to take the old and unfurl the new all at once. Particles are rotating and spiraling out of known resonances and orbits, moving to new positions. What needs to change frequency may fly apart into space and sometimes out of form. New forms appear without linear connection to what was. High frequency and dissonant frequencies cause chaos to begin.

You only call it chaos and confusion in the form world. Under the form, the energy-and-consciousness world is simply moving joyfully into new combinations and creations. This is the attitude you can have, this is the movement you can feel, if you choose. Why suffer? Why label confusion and chaos as "bad"? You are not experiencing destruction, because nothing is ever lost, but recombination. In this time of great transformation, the transformation of eons, all particles are excited and willing. All seek the pathways to higher patterning. The form world experiences deconstruction and the energy-and-consciousness world experiences inspired motivation. What appears to be loss is growth, and the dissolution of security is the return to your home place, the state of being that cannot be damaged, ever, because it is eternally true and real.

When your life becomes chaotic, you may be too superficially involved in it. You may not be loving and trusting enough. Lack of engagement with the Flow can make you feel overwhelmed, while merging with the ten million things in any moment brings simplicity and peace. When you're overwhelmed, you aren't paying attention. When you don't pay attention, you can't find the Sanity. When life becomes chaotic, deep changes are afoot. This is the time to fall into radical trust and allow your particles to be rearranged by the master designers and engineers in the spirit world. This includes you, of course. You are not going to explode into formlessness by expanding into new worlds and new aspects of your true self. You are the ultimate, malleable clay-made-of-Light.

6

Becoming Personally Transparent

*If you want to awaken all of humanity, then awaken all of yourself.
If you want to eliminate the suffering in the world, then eliminate
all that is dark and negative in yourself. Truly, the greatest gift you
have to give is that of your own self-transformation.*

Lao Tzu

Becoming personally transparent is the same as moving through the stages of the transformation process, which I outlined in chapter 1. You might wonder, "What will I look like when I become transformed and transparent?" In my experience, the transparent people are the ones with the least guile and the fewest false notes. They are not holier than thou—instead, when you're with them, you feel better about yourself, as though you can easily match their frequency and know what they know, because they see you as an equal.

When you become transparent, the way you demonstrate clarity, beauty, compassion, and truth comes naturally, without effort; your eyes may sparkle and your skin may glow. There are ironies: you may seem old when you're young, and young when you're old. When someone is nasty, you don't take offense and become nasty too—you realize there are far-reaching effects to even a mundane act, and choose more wisely. Becoming personally transparent doesn't ostracize you from society; you fit right in with everyday life, feeling less different from others and more the "same as you've always been"—deep down, from lifetime to lifetime.

The quality of your life changes, though, to be much more fluid and frictionless, magical and superconscious.

In this chapter, we'll explore some of the key character traits and states of consciousness that facilitate the experience of personal transparency. We'll delve a little more into clearing your clutter and learn to work with liminal space.

A Brief Overview

Understanding the process we go through to become transparent bears a little repeating, so here's a brief summary. You can revisit the material in chapter 1 for the more detailed description.

You first learn to identify and clear your own clutter and live in your home frequency, saturating your body, emotions, thoughts, and personal field (or sphere) with the soul's vibration. As you do this, you realize—and *experience*—that the physical world is the spiritual world, and it responds to love and attention.

You also learn to allow other people to go through their clearing process at their own speed, offering assistance if it feels natural, but you don't try to save them to make yourself feel better. You let people of every vibration have space in your sphere, without affecting your choice to feel the way you like to feel. You learn not to merge with vibrations that are lower than your own home frequency because what you put your attention on becomes real for you, and you can confuse yourself unnecessarily.

After you stabilize the frequency of your sphere at your preferred state and are good at maintaining your center, you gradually let go of your habits, stories, identities, and securities. As you empty yourself of what's old and opaque, for a time you may feel isolated, cold, directionless, disillusioned, purposeless, hollow, vague, unmotivated, or even stupid or crazy. You temporarily become meaningless and allow yourself to be vulnerable.

This is the period of *ego death*, when the left brain reluctantly hands the reins of control over to the right brain, body, field, and soul. There are often some death throes, where the left brain/ego might cause suicidal or violent thoughts, throw you into depression or spurts of hyperactivity, or create panic attacks. Think of these things as surges of random electricity arcing off into the atmosphere like solar flares from the sun. Your system is learning to settle back into the soul's deep, silent peace, and it releases disruptive energy to make space for the new state to emerge, much as you might have fits of worry or flashbacks of the day as you're falling asleep.

Once you're comfortable shifting from the doing-having-knowing part of the brain into the being-experiencing-communion part of the brain, you rest in that stillness for an unknown period; time doesn't exist in that state. This is *liminal space*, and it is akin to the caterpillar-to-butterfly transmutation process. You are rocking out of your form habits and structure into the imaginal realm. This allows the soul to repattern your inner blueprint to relay a new set of instructions that will lead you successfully into your new super-clear self. You may experience this state as captivity and punishment until you learn to know it as peace and reward.

Then at some mysterious point, without understanding the timing or reason, you suddenly rock back in and "reappear" in your life—but with new consciousness and desires. You may feel like a different person, as though you've died and been reborn. Now you are transparent, with your soul radiating clearly through your eyes, skin, words, actions, and accomplishments. You may also have new capacaities, like seeing spirits, reading minds, sensing how current events are materializing, or being able to use your attention to move objects. Now you discover how to live a transparent life, and the dynamics are revealed as you go along.

> He reproduced himself with so much humble objectivity,
> with the unquestioning, matter of fact interest of a dog who sees
> himself in a mirror and thinks: there's another dog.
> Rainer Maria Rilke

It Begins with Honesty

When I feel into the place where honesty arises and ask what it really is, the answer I receive is: simplicity. The motive for honesty comes from the love of the direct path and the real thing. In it, there is a lack of convolution and the absence of distracting, complicating, obscuring tangents. You ask a question and the answer is tagged right on the end of it—right there, waiting. No lag time, no reason why you can't have the just-right response right now. So honesty has something to do with immediacy and being engaged deeply with the moment. Of course, that engagement reveals presence, the energy of Oneness, the power of being. At heart, you are one unified being, simple to perceive. Who else can you be except yourself?

Honesty is related to humility too. Humility is not acting less than you are—that's false humility. Humility is that simple statement of truth about who you are, what you love, what you observe and know, and what you want to do or create in any given moment. So honesty and humility and simplicity and presence and immediacy and truth are intimately interconnected. The word *honest* actually comes from the same root as *honor*—high respect and esteem, adherence to what is right.

When you're honest, your way of being in the world and showing yourself to others is direct, straight ahead, unadorned with secrets or artifice, and real. There is alignment and harmonious resonance between your personality, with its words and deeds, and your soul, with its compassion, higher wisdom, and sane life plan. Honest people are easy to understand and easy to love. You can relax around them. It feels safe to be with them because they don't harbor ill will or derail you with clever manipulation. Being honest is not difficult—it's remembering all your self-protective mechanisms and puffed-up stories that takes energy and effort. *Real honesty is authenticity.*

> I am not bound to win, but I am bound to be true. I am not bound
> to succeed, but I am bound to live up to what light I have.
> **Widely Attributed to (Honest) Abraham Lincoln**

Being honest is a close cousin of being transparent. The connection starts with being yourself—your most true, clear vibration—as much as possible. You don't have to *try to be yourself*; the true self simply *emerges* from your home frequency field of energy-and-consciousness to take authentic shapes and pathways. When you allow yourself to be simple and quiet, in *beginner's mind*, you can experience your core motives—the ones that flow from love and joy, service and freedom, and beauty and appreciation. You learn to like and enjoy your own self. You don't hold back any form of authentic self-expression because it's all interesting and fun, and you don't need cover-ups or lies to protect you because you're fine just as you are. Other people are welcome to see anything about you.

When you interact with other people honestly—especially if they're used to hiding and expressing themselves partially, with caution—you may have flashes of insight about how they feel, what's happening in their life, what might happen for them next, or what they might do to heal a physical problem or emotional wound. This happens because you're open, neutral, and undefended—your own smokescreens aren't in the way of your sensing mechanisms. Respect that they may not want to know, though. You can always ask, directly and tactfully: "I had a thought about what might be causing your upset stomach. Would you like me to share it? You can decide if it's useful." Or "I had a dream about you last night. Would you like to hear it? You might find some meaning in it."

So often, people blurt out their opinions, verbal reactions, or perceptions about other people in a blunt and brutal fashion. They consider it being honest, but the compassion is lacking. *True honesty, which comes from the simplicity of the soul's presence in the personality, always flows from compassion.* Writer Anne Lamott has wisely said that we don't always have to chop with the sword of truth—we can point with it too. Even if you're speaking truth to powerful people, you don't have to yell or beat people over the head.

> All cruel people describe themselves
> as paragons of frankness.
> **Tennessee Williams**

But what if someone has a piercing insight about you? When you're honest with yourself, you remain neutral and consider the idea, feel into its possible connection to issues that might be blocking you, and sense how deep the insight goes. If you have a knee-jerk reaction, it's a good bet that the insight is on the money. (You might refer to Figure 5-1 for a refresher on knee-jerk reactions!) If you become slightly unconscious when hearing the idea, it's probably also true in some way. Being honest with yourself is a huge part of clearing your clutter. If you're honest with yourself, you move forward in alignment with your soul's motives and the Flow. And that means you welcome any opportunity to clear the clutter that's been plaguing you. A piercing insight? Fantastic!

Identifying Your Clutter

Honesty is the precursor to identifying your clutter. If you're 100 percent authentic you can't turn a blind eye to your blockages. Yet when you're seeking greater honesty, it's usually too threatening to see these things in yourself and easier to notice them "over there"—lies, evasions, and secrets *in others* often catch your attention first. It doesn't matter where you see the clutter—inside or outside—because if you notice it, it's yours to clear in your own reality. If you see and feel the pattern in others, you can then recognize your own version of it.

Before you can clear your clutter, you have to know what issues you're dealing with and how deep the debilitating habits go. You also need to acknowledge that the "hell realm" (the opaque reality taken to the nth degree) does exist in human consciousness, and that you can go there and be stuck in any part of it if you give your attention to it—either through agreement or resistance. At the same time, you don't have to live in that kind of torturous captivity if you don't find it somehow titillating or intriguing. To accept being stuck and blocked is the old normal, not the new normal that comes with transparency.

> The trouble with most of us is that we'd rather be
> ruined by praise than saved by criticism.
> **Norman Vincent Peale**

If you feel stuck, you're probably suppressing some experience or knowledge, or holding or contracting your energy. You are actually never stuck; you just perceive that you are because you're focusing on lack and limitation. Something is always happening to evolve your consciousness, though you may not notice it because you're distracted by the "tyranny of the mundane." Stuckness, which so many people complain about these days, is a key to pinpointing underlying clutter; where you're stuck the soul is focusing attention on something that underlies the superficial reason for the snag.

The next section is meant to help bring some of the issues that are blocking you into your conscious mind so you can do something about them. I recommend you work with a journal to record the answers you receive in the following exercises so you can tie back in to the specific issues later to clear them. Here are some reasons you might feel blocked or stuck.

1. **You're out of synch with your natural cycles.** We all move through cycles of creativity, beginning with Be/Spirit, where we merge with a vision in the imaginal realm, then experience natural inspiration, curiosity, and impressionability. Next, we drop the frequency of our fresh vision into Do/Mind. Here the vision crystallizes into a plan that feels real, and we focus on taking action. Finally, the cycle reaches Have/Body, and as the vision becomes a physical reality, we may sense the energy has been used up. It's natural now to stop, let go, appreciate what's been created, and enjoy the fruits of our labor.

   This is where satisfaction and pleasure can return you to the state of simply being with your creation, which returns you to the origin place of Be/Spirit, so the cycle can be renewed and you can find new inspiration. Often, though, you don't want to let go, thinking nothing is ahead and you'll have to confront the Void, or some sort of negation. This is where many people become stuck—in resistance to letting go of form and being attached to the familiarity and security of their creations.

You can also be stuck at the beginning of a creation cycle, not trusting your imagination, or being afraid your ideas are no good. Perhaps you'll be criticized for being stupid or a dreamer, or think there's no point starting because you'll never be able to have what you can imagine. Maybe you don't think you *have* any imagination.

You can be stuck at the point of crystallizing your idea into a plan and making it real by taking focused action, especially if you don't want to leave the dreamy right-brain, idealistic state. You might procrastinate because you rebel against the discipline it takes to focus, or fear you won't do well enough or have the ability to follow through.

You might also create stuckness by jumping ahead of yourself and wanting to be finished with each stage of the process before it's had a chance to ripen and turn gracefully into the next stage. Projecting ahead causes you to use force and willpower to make things work; that's unnatural and blocks the Flow. It means you unconsciously believe that life doesn't support you. Trust that the Flow *is* flowing and it *does* know what to do next, even if you don't yet.

. . . .

Try This!

How Are You Out of Synch with Your Natural Cycles?

1. Where are you in your life right now? Are you resting, gestating, allowing a vision to formulate? Are you beginning an upswing of a new creative phase, finding the feelings of excitement and passion, curiosity and motivation? Are you organizing and creating a plan, beginning to take action while your attention is focused on your dream? Are you seeing your actions take shape? Are you enjoying success and results? You may be in different stages with different projects or areas of your life. Write about these cycles in your journal.

2. Is there any phase of any cycle where you hesitate to engage? If so, why? Drill down and find the underlying anxiety, fear, or negative declarative statement. Write about it.

3. Is there any cycle in your life where you tend to jump ahead of what naturally wants to happen next? If so, why are you so pressured and impatient? What experience are you avoiding? How are you using willpower to force the Flow? What expectations do you have about yourself, how the process should occur, and what the results will be like? Write about it.

. . . .

2. **Something in your life needs to be completed, cherished, integrated, used, communicated, shared, eliminated, or forgiven.** The end of a cycle is a lovely time for pleasure and that deep experience of satisfaction and amazement at how the process of materialization works. We create stuff, then space, then stuff, then space—and each experience is wonderful. However, it's typical that when you've materialized the physical version of your vision, you may gloss over it because you're anxious to go on to the next thing.

The left brain thinks it's facing nothingness and can't compute what right-brain "just being with things" is like, or why it's valuable. So it jumps from stuff to new stuff, skipping the space part of the cycle. Or it jumps to the conclusion that something is wrong. What you just did is now too small, too ignorant, or too . . . *something*. It should be different! Why didn't you see that you weren't doing enough? When you don't fully receive and enjoy the benefit of what you just achieved, it's easy to fall into criticism of yourself and complain about not having the next thing. You may impulsively try to force the next thing into existence before you know what you-the-soul want next.

Part of this is that you may have just learned a life lesson, but your mind has not yet acknowledged or integrated it fully. The lack of integration—making it conscious and meaningful in the left brain—can make you feel stuck. In fact, it can cause you to have to repeat the behaviors that helped you learn the lesson in the first place.

. . . .

Try This!

How Do You Block Yourself at the End of a Cycle?

1. Think about what cycles in your life have recently concluded or are about to end. How are you dealing with the completions? Is there anything that needs to be cherished, enjoyed, used, communicated, shared, eliminated, or forgiven? Are you avoiding any underlying issues that are trying to become conscious now that you have some space?

2. Think back to previous cycles in your life that ended. How did you handle those endings? What underlying issues caused you to be stuck? Write about those times.

3. Think about what you've been learning in any cycle that's currently completing in your life. How are your external achievements also internal lessons? Feel good about it all. Does what you've done still hold your interest? Do you want to continue it? Or are you receiving glimmers of new ideas that feel fascinating? Write about this.

. . . .

3. **You don't use your imagination to begin a new cycle. Instead, you project ideas based on a logical continuity from the past.** When you don't consciously complete a cycle and let go, rest, and allow some gestation time, you can't find the just-right new ideas that will further your life purpose. You don't fully shift from the left to the right brain. When you float in right-brain consciousness, you reconnect with imagination and the magic returns. Ideas drop in out of the blue or pop up in front of your nose, and they aren't always related to what you did before. Or they're things you were interested in as a child that you now understand at a more expanded, sophisticated level, or in a different context.

When you don't let go all the way, your left brain speaks to you in "shoulds"—it tells you what your success *should* look like if you follow the logical trajectory toward popularity, money, and power. The more you adhere to this vision, the more stuck you become. You-the-soul may have a different plan to achieve different end results.

. . . .

Try This!

How Does Your Left Brain Distort New Beginnings?

Write about the following things in your journal:

1. What does your left brain tell you that you should do next? Does it have the ring of truth or does it sound flat and boring? Is it someone else's voice you've internalized? If so, whose?
2. If your life is a linear, logical progression from past to present, what does your left brain say the next phase looks like?
3. Does your left brain want you to start before conditions are truly ready? Why?
4. If your life is a magical occurrence based on the soul's desires, how does it look? What new talents might arise in you? What glimmers of new visions show up? What's most fascinating? Sense the difference of the vibration between old and new.
5. Notice what comments your left brain wants to make about your new, intuitive, possibly illogical desires.
6. How might you sabotage your ability to implement the new ideas, make a plan, and take action?

. . . .

4. **You talk about what isn't and what you're not.** By allowing your left brain to limit your potential experience by making negative declarative statements that seem like ultimate truths, you sabotage yourself. When you tell yourself that you can't do something, be something, or have experiences, you sacrifice yourself. Then how does the soul shine through?

. . . .

Try This!

How Do You Sabotage or Sacrifice Yourself?

List as many answers as you can to the questions below. Write about what the left brain believes is the logical rationale for the behavior and why.

1. What is your self-sabotaging self-talk? Write some of the negative, declarative sentences.
2. What doesn't seem possible to do or have right now?
3. What do you resist that you have now?
4. What negative things do you resist that haven't happened?
5. What justifications do you give for not acting? For not stopping?
6. How do you sacrifice yourself?
7. In what areas do you postpone what you want? Why?
8. In what areas do you not acknowledge that you want something?
9. What excuses do you use to avoid being more of yourself? And in what areas?
10. What do you say to yourself about why you do or don't want to be with other people?

. . . .

5. **You're attached to form, definitions, beliefs, personal identity, or ideas about how life works.** When your mind becomes fixated and you attach special importance to ideas, behaviors, and forms to provide a semblance of security, you inadvertently slow or stop the Flow of energy-and-consciousness. Your creativity and personal growth take a serious hit. You're keeping your attention focused on a limited number of things that aren't allowed to change, and this can make you feel stuck. If you identify yourself too narrowly, the tight boundaries can act like armor or a cage. Hopelessness or depression may result.

. . . .

Try This!

What Are Your Attachments?

List as many answers to the questions below as you can. Write about why.

1. How do you see yourself and define yourself? Write a detailed description. Are there any traits you do not want to include? Why?
2. What parts of your identity did you inherit or adopt from other people? What decisions would you make about these traits now?
3. Because of your identity, what do you do that you don't really love? Because of your identity, what do you not allow yourself to do?
4. What accomplishments or possessions do you cling to for a sense of self?
5. In what ways do you feel better than other people? In what ways do you feel worse (less than)?
6. What has to happen for you to feel secure?
7. What credo, philosophy, worldview, or cosmology do you believe is real? Did you inherit this from someone else?
8. What declarative statements, beliefs, vows, pronouncements, "shoulds," value judgments, opinions, pet peeves, rules, have-tos and can't-evers, and habits/addictions do you adhere to and think are real?
9. How do you believe things come to you? What are your beliefs about the way life works?

. . . .

6. **You hold or contract your energy-and-consciousness.** When you don't trust the Flow and are afraid of negative repercussions, it's as though you inhale and forget to exhale again. Anxiety and worry cause you to contract, and your energy can't move through the logjam you created. Your physical, emotional, and mental health can easily be affected. Your holding patterns become clutter.

. . . .

Try This!

What Are Your Holding Patterns?

List as many answers to the questions below as you can. Write about why you answered them this way.

1. What do you hold back from doing? Saying? Seeing?
2. In what ways do you hide to protect yourself?
3. How do you hold back from being involved with people?
4. What parts of yourself do you hold back from sharing?
5. What are you holding on to for security now?
6. When do you freeze up?
7. How do you hold yourself together? In what ways and in what areas are you afraid you might fall apart?
8. What do you hold out for; are you waiting for something to happen before you'll be more of your true self? What excuses do you always use?
9. How do you hold forth and try to control or influence others?
10. What habits do you keep indulging in?
11. What secrets do you hold back from others?
12. What secrets do you hold back from yourself?
13. What lies do you tell to protect yourself from scrutiny by others?
14. What lies do you not notice in others? What trips you up with people?

. . . .

7. **Your actions stem from soul-blocking behaviors.** There are many behaviors that originate with a fear. Most often they connect to an unconscious drive for survival through fight, flight, or freeze instinctive reactions. These are considered normal human behavior, but to the soul, they are abnormal and a waste of time and life force. When you-the-personality engage in these thinking and behavior patterns, it blocks the wisdom, compassion, and creativity of you-the-soul.

. . . .

Try This!

What Are Your Soul-Blocking Behaviors?

List as many answers to the questions below as you can. Write about why you answered them this way.

1. When do you complain or criticize yourself or others?
2. In what situations do you default into feeling helpless or like a victim?
3. In what situations do you give your power away to others?
4. When do you want to be rescued? When do you want to rescue others?
5. When do you shift into feeling isolated or invisible?
6. When do you tend to feel envy or resentment?
7. What things do you feign ignorance about, or say "I don't know"?
8. In what situations do you focus on lack or loss?
9. When do you become stubborn, rebellious, resistant, or willful?
10. In what situations do you move into opposition, fight mode, or violent reactions?
11. When do you blame yourself or others? Or want to punish yourself or others?
12. What situations cause you to become frustrated or angry? And when might you take it further to retribution or vengeance?
13. When do you postpone or procrastinate? Or avoid knowing certain information or outcomes?
14. What are you addicted to? And what makes you want to indulge in your addiction?
15. In what situations do you become controlling; when do you want to hold on too tightly or hoard?

. . . .

It might feel overwhelming to think about all the ways it's possible to block your own Light, but it's important to bring these shadowy, semiconscious ideas into the open—so you can notice if you're backsliding into one of them. Then you can focus on clearing these outworn habits.

> Honesty and transparency make you vulnerable.
> Be honest and transparent anyway.
> **Mother Teresa**

Vulnerability, Courage & Forgiveness

When contemplating how many fear residues you still have and how daunting it is to free yourself from the behaviors that cover them, your immediate reaction might be to feel ashamed and vulnerable. What if other people knew how messed up you are at a deep level?! If you imagine living without these protective behaviors, you might feel defenseless, helpless, powerless, and susceptible to harm. The root of the word *vulnerable*, after all, is "to wound." And this is where courage comes in. At this point of vulnerability, when your wounds are becoming visible, shift your attitude from avoidance and mousiness to engagement and courage. Be present with it all.

To become transparent, you must risk being out of control and undefended, and make a commitment to love *everything* about yourself, even the insecurities and embarrassing bits. Try on the experience of being vulnerable by choice. One of my favorite stories is about the Japanese monk whose monastery is invaded by warring samurai soldiers. One of the fearsome samurai confronts the monk as he sits meditating. "Get up!" he yells. "Don't you know I can run you through with my sword this very minute?" The totally vulnerable, totally undefended little monk looks up and says, "And don't you know that I can be run through by your sword this very minute?" The samurai bows deeply to the monk and walks away. The courage to be plain and simple and open and present is a powerful thing.

We are all complex, though; we are mixtures of dark and light, conscious and unconscious, visible and invisible, wise and foolish. Perhaps it's that we think we should be just one way that twists us into knots. You have access to every possible way to be human and you can indulge in any or all of them—but just one at a time. The vastness of your opportunities will not overwhelm you. It's OK to accept the fact that you're experiencing kinds of consciousness and actions that don't work, as well as other responses and behaviors that do. It's part of the learning process. The bad habits that block your soul's Light and limit your range of experience are there as primitive medicine—strategies your linear mind implemented so you could temporarily feel good.

Now you know better. Allowing yourself to be vulnerable means that you open all the windows and doors, and even make the walls porous and transparent. You become totally open. You allow people to see whatever they're able to see about you. Their own issues act as filters, so unless they're fully transparent, they won't see all of you—just what matches their own self-image and self-knowledge. If they judge or reject you, they're judging and rejecting a big part of their own potential reality. That's disappointing, but it doesn't prevent you from being yourself. To be consciously vulnerable, allow yourself to not need outside agreement and approval.

> Security is mostly a superstition. It does not exist in nature,
> nor do the children of men as a whole experience it.
> Avoiding danger is no safer in the long run than outright exposure.
> Life is either a daring adventure or nothing.
> Helen Keller

Being vulnerable doesn't mean that you run around naked, broadcasting and flaunting your faults and shortcomings. It's probably not wise to confess you're an alcoholic on the first date, or tell a prospective boss during your interview that you're recovering from major surgery. You can allow others to discover you at their own speed. By removing your self-judgment, you may find that others don't judge you either. All people share the same foibles and flaws, and they do remember what those handicaps are like, even if they've moved past them.

For those who live mainly in the left brain and have rules about how to be successful and popular, being around a vulnerable person is frightening: "Maybe it will rub off and I'll lose my edge. By having this wreck of a person near me, people could think I'm that way too. I need to get them out of my space!" But for those who are centered in their home frequency, the vulnerable person is reassuring; being with them keeps the heart wide open.

I remember a time when I was seeing clients at my hotel in Los Angeles. I had an appointment with a wealthy, powerful executive, and she arrived dressed to the nines in a crisp, perfect, navy-blue business suit, white silk blouse, and high heels. I was dressed casually—neatly but in no way as "put together" as she was. I immediately felt intimidated; she radiated a no-nonsense aura, and I sensed she expected perfection from others. The matter was made more extreme as I looked down at my shirt and noticed I had dribbled coffee on myself at breakfast. There was an unbecoming brown stain right in front.

I began the session, and noticed how stilted and unnatural my voice sounded to me. The two of us were out of synch and my intuition was having a hard time flowing. I kept on, though, as she busily took notes, not making eye contact with me. And then I noticed it—her blouse had come unbuttoned and was open down to her bra. She certainly would have been embarrassed at the impropriety, had she known. But I said nothing and kept on in an easy manner.

From that point, I relaxed and began to like her; she was as flawed as I was. Now my intuition opened and the tone of the session changed and became deep and intimate. She was so much more than her outer presentation had indicated. I never did say anything about her blouse and she didn't say anything about mine, and the acceptance taught me a huge lesson. When vulnerability makes you feel separate, clarity breaks down. When it reveals commonality, the result is authenticity, compassion, and excellence.

> What makes you vulnerable makes you beautiful.
> Brené Brown

Allowing yourself to be vulnerable when you come face to face with fear and shame is one of the first steps in clearing your clutter. If you resist embracing the mistakes in perception you made in the past, when you were innocently ignorant, the mistakes remain in place and cannot be dissolved. But when you allow everything you've done to simply *be*, and see it from the soul's neutral, practical understanding, you can understand how you missed the mark and why you thought the way you did back then. At night, your child-self thought the leafy tree-branch shadows on the wall of your bedroom were monsters, and since then a deep part of you has been leery of dark and shady things, including your present-day, secretive and manipulative boss.

When you're open and vulnerable, your wise, soul-self can penetrate into the pattern represented by your boss and understand how that reaction-contraction originated in your first bedroom. You might suddenly realize how those shadows made you feel invaded by forces you couldn't control. Now you-the-soul can flow in with understanding and sweet love for that child's primitive instinct, and reframe the vision of the shadows as beautiful tree designs given by the tree-beings who were protecting you during sleep. Soon, your boss may not seem so ominous. Compassionate, practical understanding heals all mental and emotional wounds.

So, the early phases of clearing clutter involve *identifying* the clutter—welcoming the previously suppressed subconscious material into your conscious mind. From there, allow yourself to have the courage to be open, nonjudgmental, and vulnerable. Don't hide, just be available as you are. Whatever flies out of Pandora's Box, embrace it warmly and love it. There's a good reason it's been there with its primitive and outdated thinking. Seek to understand—understanding is the true action of the heart. And finally, if any part of your mind is still even slightly ashamed, bitter, or disgusted, seek forgiveness.

If other people were involved in your early decision to protect yourself, accept that they were catalysts for a great life lesson that you yourself were engineering. What were you showing yourself? You may judge yourself severely for not seeing through some illusion, for wasting precious time in your life, or for being stupid. Shift your viewpoint; see it from the soul's wise, tolerant, loving, parental perspective. Forgiveness is about generously letting things be as they are, letting people be the way they were or are, and letting yourself be as clear or unclear as you were and are in the moment. *Forgiveness is really a function of humility, which is a function of truth in the moment.* Once you acknowledge a state of being as it is, releasing resistance or adherence, the energy-and-consciousness that was trapped in it is free to re-enter the Flow and change.

One last thing about vulnerability. It is not only a shift from the left brain to the right brain; it is a powerful choice to move attention out of willpower, control, ego, progress, self-protection, the defined world, and language into stillness, being with, allowing, appreciation, communion, the undefined world, and total acceptance and trust. It makes sense that when you experience vulnerability, you often vibrate and feel shaky, as though your molecules are flying apart. You are deconstructing many foundational aspects of your self-image and life. You are readying yourself, through courage, for transformation. This is good! Whenever you feel vulnerable, you are close to something that's been covering a magnificent part of yourself—a part you *do* want. Dig a little deeper; it's there!

> And that visibility which makes us most vulnerable
> is that which also is the source of our greatest strength.
> Audre Lorde

Clearing Your Clutter

Old fears are really partially experienced experiences. In previous traumatic situations, your mind froze with fear, the left brain locked down around the experience and made a rule that this sort of thing should never happen again, or that it should always be handled a certain way. As the energy on the planet increases, those stuck places want to move, and the energy bottled up in them needs to be freed to re-enter the realm of all possibilities. In effect, subconscious blocks are like lies—part of your mind is pretending the fear is more real than the inherent wisdom of your soul. You need to re-view the experience from the "God's-eye view" of being an eternal soul, full of wisdom and compassion, unable to be damaged.

Look for the vulnerability you had during the original experience, then understand it, accept it, and know there is a bigger picture that can pop the bubble of self-protection. Be like a parent comforting a scared child. Once the love perspective returns, the fear dissolves, you attain understanding (which always contains compassion), and personal ownership of the fear fades. You experience the second part of "forgive and forget." You're left with a strange feeling like, "Did this actually happen to *me*? Or did someone else tell me about *their* experience? Maybe it's something that happens to everyone." Forgetting is the act of the inner blueprint of an idea dissolving back into the unified field. Afterward, you're that much more loving.

Even if you've begun to clear your clutter, there are deeper layers of earlier, similar experiences. Clear one layer and the next one surfaces. You don't have to go digging; when the block is ready, it comes to you. It's important to stay present and embrace what comes, without judgment or commentary. Remember that every time you clear a fear, you become more wise and loving, so you're capable of dealing with the next, perhaps more intense level of fear. That's why they say, "You're never given more than you can handle."

At some point, you realize you're clearing fears you don't personally own all by yourself; they're fears that belong to many people. It doesn't matter, though, because they're still coming through your mind and heart to be realized and healed, one blockage at a time. It's just as easy to clear a collective fear as it is to clear one you thought was yours alone. This continues; as you clear what comes, you spiral down through the history of humankind into the most fundamental ancient origins of our collective, paralyzing terror, oceanic grief, and nuclear rage. Eventually, you find you're doing the transmuting work of the saints, for the sake of the planet. And yet, it's always personal, always about staying present in your home frequency, and not feeding opacity with your attention.

Sunlight is the best disinfectant.
William O. Douglas

When you look at clearing clutter from a linear perception point of view, it looks like a process with sequential steps; this is the traditional therapeutic model. It basically says you must go back into the past, dredge up the emotions tied to traumatic events, and experience the emotions again to release the stuck energy. If you talk it through with a counselor, you can understand how the energy became stuck, how your self-concept developed, and how you don't have to do the same thing anymore, now that the pent-up energy has been released. All this takes time, though, and I'm not sure it goes far enough; it doesn't return you to your home frequency or totally free you from the pattern. When a fear clears, your home frequency must be re-established in every level of your existence, consciously, or the fear-oriented parts of the brain default to the same memory of contraction when the next similar situation occurs.

When you look at clearing clutter from a spherical-holographic perception point of view, there is barely any process involved. The entire experience can happen in an instant, because everything exists in the present moment. Clearing a negative pattern becomes a matter of where you place your attention and how absolutely you merge with the reality you focus on. If you focus on how things go wrong, your reality continues to show you how things can go wrong. If you talk about how you always get mad at other people, you validate that behavior. If, on the other hand, you say, "Things go my way, and everything helps me evolve and grow into more of myself," life starts working in your favor.

When you speak a declarative sentence that's the opposite of the negative clutter, *and feel the truth of how that would be*, your reality changes to match. Even if there are snags or challenges, you don't stop the Flow at those points and fall down the rabbit hole. Instead you see everything as useful data and experiences you need. If you say and feel the truth of the statement, "Other people can't prevent me from being and feeling myself, or doing what I love. They can be themselves and I can be myself; there's plenty of room in my sphere for everyone," you won't work yourself into the level of frustration that causes anger.

Turning a negative pattern around to its opposite and feeling it as though it is real, gives your body the felt sense of a preferable reality.

From that point on, you have a clear choice, a conscious choice. Not placing attention on a negative pattern is different than denial. With denial, you box up the fearful experience, stuff it down in the basement, and refuse to think about it. It takes tremendous willpower and effort. Not placing attention on a fearful experience is simply a preference; there is no resistance or charge. You become almost bored with negativity and it's just easier to pay attention to what's positive, fluid, and evolutionary.

> A belief is nothing more than a chronic pattern of thought, and
> you have the ability. . . to begin a new pattern, to tell a new story,
> to achieve a different vibration.
> Esther Hicks/Abraham

Each time you make the shift from placing your attention on a negative, fear-based pattern to a positive, love- or unity-based pattern, you become clear—in that moment. And that moment is forever, *if you allow it to be.* Here's the rub: Your left brain has made a rule about not experiencing negative patterns, because it believes negativity is dangerous and the default reality. In its experience, the positive always reverts to the negative. So when you reframe a negative belief and let yourself feel the opposite experience, the left brain doesn't believe you—yet.

Its knee-jerk response, based on long-term programming, is to create a new situation that goes wrong, hurts, or upsets you. You have a choice right then: "Where do I want to place my attention? What's my preferred reality? Do I want to think that I'm so disconnected that life doesn't know about me or love me enough to support my growth? Or that there is a big, separate, outside world full of people who can't see who I am and don't support my self-expression? Or do I want real connection, appreciation, respect, and cocreation with others?" You learn to catch yourself right at the moment of backsliding. Then you can suspend placing your attention on the negative reality—which is actually full of false assumptions about the way life *really* works—and focus on the positive experiences.

And once again, in that moment, you are clear. Your body receives a second validation of the more truthful state of being, and yes, it feels better. But the adrenaline rush of the fear-based reality was pretty stimulating and addictive. So your left brain, stubborn little critter that it is, re-creates *another* new situation that goes wrong, hurts, or upsets you. This time, though, it's easier to remember you have a choice, and you don't go as far into the negative pattern. You realize that taking the negative view wastes energy and time when you could be creating what you love. You choose the positive view again. And again, you are clear. Now the positive view is integrating into your reality, your doubt is dissolving, and you have no trouble choosing where to place your attention. You're not at the effect of an outside world anymore.

The more you choose to place your attention on any positive, love- or unity-based reality, the faster your clearing process occurs. Eventually, you realize you only need to choose fully—which means *experience fully*—one time, and that's enough for permanent change. You don't have to go back into the long line of the past to find earlier similar experiences and the original presenting incident and unpack the blocked emotions at those separate points. Instead, as you clear the pattern in any present moment, the image of the original event and all the others show up together as a ghostly composite.

Along with the specific memories, you also understand, all at once, why you blocked them and stopped energy from flowing through them. Just by staying in the present moment, in the centerpoint of your sphere, you receive the hidden messages and deep understanding relating to the entire pattern. The present moment brings the whole picture—and freedom—if you let it. Everything comes to you as you need it.

Always say "yes" to the present moment. What could be more futile, more insane, than to create inner resistance to what already is? What could be more insane than to oppose life itself, which is now and always now?
Eckhart Tolle

Understanding, Releasing, Dissolving, Forgetting

We have an idea that surrender, release, and letting go are difficult actions to take. We wonder, "How does one do it? Do I surrender into *nothing*?" You throw the negativity up in the air, hoping it will blow away, and it falls back down on you. The negative pattern seems to cling to you or return like a boomerang. That is due to the left brain's definition function and its predilection for security.

Simply by placing attention on your preferred state and feeling it as real, you actually *are* letting go and releasing your negative thought and feeling habits. Remember, when you remove attention from a pattern, it dissolves all by itself. Do it often enough and it doesn't try to reappear. As things stand now, it takes a few go-arounds with the left brain to unlearn an old habit and create new learning. As the planet's acceleration continues, one time will soon do the trick.

There is another way to release your fixations, holding patterns, and soul-blocking behaviors: you can imagine how your world might feel and how your life might function without each one. How would you feel and act, and how would your life unfold, if you didn't keep that secret about wanting to explore foreign countries? Or if you didn't lie about not having gone to college? Or if you didn't tell yourself and everyone else that you don't like to deal with money? Use your imagination—it's your friend! What if you stopped telling the story of being physically abused by your uncle? What if you admitted you don't want to climb the corporate ladder to become the CEO? What if you stopped believing that losing weight was impossible? By just imagining the reality, free of restrictions and limitations, your body can feel how to do it. Then it can become real.

Meanings are inexhaustible.
We need to develop our intuitive sense
that allows us to smell out meanings
hidden and dormant in life situations.
Victor Frankl

• • • • • • • • • • •

Try This!

Release & Dissolve Negative Patterns

1. Go back to the previous exercises in the "Identifying Your Clutter" section (page 158) and randomly pick a behavior or habit.
2. Feel yourself engaged with that behavior. Notice any tension, contraction, anxiety, or heaviness. Notice how keeping that behavior causes your life to function in a certain way. Write about it.
3. Imagine you are no longer interested in that behavior, that it's no longer part of your life. Other people may think that way or do it, but not you. The absence of this pattern is not a problem in any way. Write about how it feels to be free of the behavior.
4. Out of the space that had been occupied by that old behavior comes something new, from your soul level. What might that be? When you're free of that particular restriction, where does your natural creative motivation want to go? Write about it.
5. Repeat this exercise with more of the items you listed in the previous exercises. Notice how you feel when openness replaces the clutter; write about it.

• • • • • • • • • • •

There is a courage aspect to both facing and clearing your clutter. Letting go, releasing, surrendering, dissolving, and forgetting can be associated with loss. You are emptying, and the left brain is not at all assured that something new and better will fill the white canvas. If you equate emptiness with the Void, or nonexistence, you'll probably remain in fear. If you equate emptiness with spaciousness and possibilities, you'll open into transparency.

We're used to living with clutter, and even the data we hold in the Information Age can be seen as clutter. We don't quite understand how lovely it feels to be spacious. Sometimes I think of a huge pantry where everything I know or need has a place on a shelf. When I need to use it, I take it off the shelf, use it, then put it back when I'm finished. I don't have to carry the flour and canned tomatoes and chocolate chips with me at all times. Whatever I need is there when I need it. In between uses, I am free and spacious.

When you seriously begin releasing and dissolving your clutter, you may be surprised how deep the clearing process goes. You may find that the values you've lived by aren't sophisticated enough, or your life dream and goals are too shallow, or you really don't know who you are anymore. You might lose possessions you've over-identified with. This happened to me when I distributed my mother's precious belongings, many of which were tied to childhood memories.

My friend Judy had her house burn to the ground, and another friend and his wife got rid of almost everything and traveled around the country for years in a small motor home. There is an element of shock and disillusionment that comes with clearing clutter—and this is a good thing. We really don't need our illusions, which may just be outlived beliefs and meanings. Perhaps you really don't need physical objects to remind you of good times or to tell you who you are. The experiences are all still there, and alive, in the nonphysical realms. Perhaps keeping your dead parents' objects isn't the way to maintain a loving connection with them. Perhaps your lifestyle so far isn't the only lifestyle you might enjoy. Perhaps when you lose everything, you find yourself. When you clear your clutter and let go of attachments, you open to all sorts of possibilities for becoming a new, soul-infused person.

. . . .

Try This!

Dissolve All Your Clutter at Once!

1. Imagine you are sitting in the centerpoint of your sphere and you have a field of your own home-frequency energy all around you, as far as you can see.

2. Review the previous lists of clutter from the "Identifying Your Clutter" section (page 158), and imagine each item—all your contractions, holdings, and fixations—as shadowy spots in your field. Imagine the shadows exist like octaves of music: each piece of clutter exists at the mental frequency, emotional frequency, subtle energy frequency, and physical body frequency; clearing any piece of clutter at any level clears the whole complex.

3. In between the dark, cloudy spots in your field is glossy, transparent, diamond light. The dark spots are only a small proportion of your totality, and they are simply clumped, contracted diamond light. Strike the tone of the diamond light—your soul vibration—as though you're striking a tuning fork, and let it resonate through your entire field.

4. Imagine seeing and feeling that vibration move into the shadowy clumps and raise their frequency, vibrating them into a porous state, then a vaporous state, and let the clumps release the energy-and-consciousness they've been holding. Let your field become empty and transparent, glossy and pure—and deeply restful.

5. Notice that within the diamond light, there are tiny sparkling points of light twinkling throughout. These are ideas, people, objects, and events coming in and going out of form. Relax and just be, knowing the Flow will bring to life whatever you want and need next.

6. If any of the dark spots reappear, let the diamond light soak into them and dissolve them again. The transparent diamond light is stronger than any shadow. Feel how your body is made of the same floating particles of light as your sphere. Feel how your body is now clear of opacity. Take a mental/tactile snapshot of the state of being so you can return to it easily.

7. Repeat this exercise as often as you wish until you realize that you really only have to do it once for it to be real.

Entering Liminal Space

During times when you feel anxious and stuck, and realize you need to clear some clutter, your soul is really redirecting your attention to something simpler and deeper—something only reachable through stillness, something present even in the mundane. You may release and clear some of your contractions and fixations, but to do a complete job of it, you may need to gather all your parts and cocoon for a while. This could be for an hour, a day, a week, a month, or a year—time doesn't exist in this present moment of spaciousness.

I learned from a science documentary that the caterpillar, when it enters the pupa stage, actually liquefies itself before the raw material of its body reformulates as the butterfly. Many of us are doing this internally—melting down. This melting process is a key part of transformation and becoming transparent. It takes you into the experience of *liminal space—liminal* relates to the idea of a threshold—and this calls to mind the space on either side of a threshold. We usually think of what comes before a threshold is reached and not so much about what comes immediately after, before the new form solidifies.

So many of us are in liminal space right now. Perhaps we are about to cross a threshold or have already crossed it but don't realize it, or we are waiting to see how our new self will take shape. We all interpret this experience differently, of course, but you can count on a few things: you feel in-between or in "limbo," that you don't know something important, that the old way is boring or damaging to your body and soul, and that you are out of your comfort zone. You haven't found an answer yet, can't seem to imagine your new life, the Flow seems to have stopped, and you're losing meanings and security.

If you are a left-brain-dominant person, your left brain will go nuts in this undefined state. It wants to know what to do, what to emphasize, what to plan for. It wants to figure something out. It does not tolerate anxiety and ambiguity but wants facts. The left brain may label this as a time of chaos and negativity, or it will throw you into irritability, reactionary behavior, panic, avoidance, addiction, manic activity, numbness, or depression—just to have something to do. It might prefer to fill the liminal space with hyperactivity, drama, trauma, or an accident or illness—anything but nothingness! Many people I talk to identify with these left-brain coping mechanisms, thinking they themselves are crazy, incompetent, unevolved, unworthy, or a failure because "life isn't working."

Transparency

[Liminal space is] when you have left the tried and true but have not
yet been able to replace it with anything else. It is when you are
finally out of the way. If you are not trained in how to hold anxiety,
how to live with ambiguity, how to entrust and wait,
you will run . . . anything to flee this terrible cloud of unknowing.
Richard Rohr

If, on the other hand, you are more practiced in perceiving from your right brain, body, heart, and intuition, you may feel liminal space as a sort of sabbatical or important pause. You trust the Flow and the evolution process, and are more comfortable being with the moment as it is, knowing there is wisdom to be had by paying close attention and feeling into your experience. Waiting doesn't cause impatience. Being quiet doesn't feel like the Void. Feeling spacious and full of potential is downright pleasurable. This is the soul perceiving liminal space.

In liminal space, you are being directed into the nonphysical world to melt down old patterns so you can receive your new set of instructions, new imaginations, and more of your true self. You-the-soul are opening some space so the spiritual can flood into the physical, and you can learn to be soul-directed. In liminal space, you are being asked to occupy the present moment fully, to be still and transparent. Here, you must be comfortable being timeless; you must become the pause.

Liminal space acts like a magnet. Its very openness and peacefulness can catalyze the experience of compassion if you drop into it and be with it purely and innocently. It also clearly points out everything that is not in harmony with spiritual truth and unconditional love. If you choose to trust what emerges in liminal space, you can actually enjoy the dissolving—or in caterpillar terms, the liquefying—that is the pre-threshold experience. You won't make judgments about how what comes is bad or that you're failing somehow.

When I entered liminal space a few years ago, I began to feel like a stranger in my life. "Who is driving this car to the market?" I'd think. "Who needs to buy food and eat? Who is walking this body down the hall?" I began to feel that my story, my history, was not mine and I didn't care to recite it anymore because it felt boring. After all, it could belong to anyone! I wondered, Was I preparing to die? No, my ego was relinquishing control. My identity was no longer about my personality's definitions.

As that stage progressed, I found myself wanting to sleep in the guest room of my house for a month, joking to friends that "I am a guest in my own life." Truthfully, I enjoyed the feeling of visiting this new place and perspective—opening to my up-and-coming life. Perhaps this was my micro-version of a universal process, how we become more of a neutral observer and allow our identity to shift to a higher frequency.

The great thing about liminal space is that it contains the good stuff and it knows what it's doing. Somehow, those melted-down caterpillar particles know how to recombine into the butterfly. It's an amazing sort of intelligence! All you need to do is be willing to *be*. Welcome the surprise of the melting, the threshold crossing, the arising, and the new baby-like state of the fresh self. What shape will your liquefied self be magnetized to take?

> Remembering that you are going to die is the best way I know
> to avoid the trap of thinking you have something to lose. You are
> already naked. There is no reason not to follow your heart.
> Steve Jobs

Reappearing & Trusting the Flow

So! You've released your fears and contractions (at least the first few rounds), and are bored with your story and personal history. You're OK with not knowing, not doing, and not being motivated to achieve great things. The importance of your attachments has faded, along with your value judgments, and you care in a nonattached, nongrasping way.

Though you sense a new kind of self-expression coming, it hasn't quite appeared yet—and that's perfectly fine. You're not worried. You're not letting your left brain tell you there's something wrong with you; you're in the moment, engaged with life. At this point, you realize your quiet time of gestation is crucially important, and the Flow—the combined needs and actions of your soul and all other souls—has the wisdom to know when to move you back into active creativity. You know you'll notice new interests and curiosities, new refinements of thought and behavior, when the time is right.

Toward the end of my fairly prolonged period of being in liminal space, I had just awakened and was lying in bed thinking, "I should get up." Suddenly, a voice in my mind said, "Don't think about that right now." So I let my mind be blank. Then came the thought, "I could clean out that closet today." And the voice said, "Don't think about that right now." So I relaxed. Then before I realized it, my body just sat up and got out of bed. I had the distinct feeling that "the moment was right." My mind had not been involved in deciding, giving orders, or initiating action via willpower. The Flow had moved me. I was in the Flow! In the weeks that followed, I could catch my mind about to give an order for activity or accomplishment, then pause to allow the Flow to take over.

The other thing that happened as I "reappeared" from liminal space was that I naturally moved toward things that excited me and helped increase my frequency. "Shoulds" all but disappeared. Where before, I might have thought, "I should go to the dentist," now I would think, "I feel like going to the dentist." And though I have never been a big complainer, I noticed that I was talking about mundane frustrations in a funny, storytelling way, but I was still giving attention to the snags. It also became clear that I didn't want to waste my breath on what hadn't measured up to some standard of perfection or expectation, and to what had already passed on downriver.

As you reappear, you may find your motives changing as well as the criteria upon which you base your choices. You may not be ambitious in the same way you've always been; you may slow down and stop pushing life, and realize how fast things occur when you just be with them. Or you might find that procrastination and apathy fade as curiosity and desire for creativity take over. What used to be a chore now becomes self-entertainment and cocreation with the Flow. And you may have a much stronger sense of what is appropriate and just right to do next. There is less wasted effort.

There is another powerful symptom of re-emergence—you may lose your small identity and gain a much more expansive sense of self, without feeling overwhelmed. There is a greater sense of presence; you feel your soul as never before and also feel that same self—or presence, or energy-and-consciousness—in everything and everyone. There is a return to the experience of honesty, simplicity, and true humility. You notice when you're "broadcasting" your truth and promoting a self-image versus allowing others to discover you naturally, whenever they're ready. It's ironic that when you stop projecting and the false pressure of willpower lets up—and when presence with constancy takes over—people suddenly seem to see and know you, and find you, with no effort on your part.

> Find out who you are and do it on purpose.
> Dolly Parton

Rita had spent much of her teens and twenties caught in a pattern of needing attention and validation from others in order to feel herself. If someone disagreed with her or didn't understand her, she reacted with anger and caustic remarks. If people ignored her or spent time doing activities she wasn't included in, she abandoned them instantly or hurt herself by cutting or not eating.

As she matured and began to seek her own spiritual growth, she allowed herself to be alone without reactionary behavior, to face the fear of abandonment and lack of self-worth that had plagued her, and to let go of working so hard for approval. She entered liminal space, and when she emerged again, she was much more "in herself." She said she took to heart the Buddhist instruction: "Do no harm." She realized how she had hurt people with her expectations, reactions, and mean words. "Do no harm" became her new mantra and guiding principle, and she applied it to herself as well.

You never know what will emerge with you when you come back from liminal space and step over the threshold into the transparent,

Intuition Age reality. What's clear, though, is that it will be something from you-the-soul—perfect clues about how to be your new self, what wants to happen, or a step-by-step revelation of how your new creation cycle plans on materializing itself.

> May what I do flow from me like a river,
> no forcing and no holding back,
> the way it is with children.
> Rainer Maria Rilke

Just to Recap...

Becoming personally transparent begins with identifying and clearing your clutter and living in your home frequency, at the center of your sphere. You then learn how to deal with the emptiness that occurs when you release old habits, identities, and securities. This is the period of ego death, and it's important to not be carried away by negativity during this time. When you calm down, you enter a period of stillness where you collect yourself, or remember yourself. You may protest about having to face the Void, but really, it's a peaceful time of cocooning, akin to the caterpillar turning into the butterfly. As you emerge, you re-enter the Flow with much more presence and trust.

The whole process begins with honesty, which is connected to simplicity and humility. You allow yourself to show for what you are, and part of what shows up is your clutter. Instead of running away from it, take the opportunity to engage and identify the issues that make you feel stuck, threatened, and afraid. Go into them and discover what's at the core. There are a number of reasons why you may feel stuck. (I outlined seven of them and created exercises to help you identify the clutter related to each.)

After identifying your clutter, it takes courage to allow yourself to feel vulnerable and to forgive others and yourself for participating in the negativity. Actually clearing the clutter can be a simple matter of placing attention on the positive version of the negative habit and imagining how your world might function if the negative version of the habit were no longer present. Old patterns tend to release and dissolve when you compassionately understand how your previous self became stuck in those particular partial perceptions.

After you've cleared a number of old patterns, you are often drawn into the deeply quiet liminal space, or the time before and after the crossing of a threshold from an old reality to a new one. This can feel frightening or deeply peaceful. You may feel blocked or stuck, or abandoned or alone, but this is just your left brain misinterpreting what's happening. In truth, you are allowing your soul to reformulate your personality, and this takes stillness and ease.

During this time, you may detach from old identities, stories, and motivations. You may feel disillusioned in a positive way, and this allows you the space to rediscover and reconnect with purpose and your essential qualities. And then, at some mysterious point that cannot be predicted, you "reappear" in the world, feeling like a new person, with expanded capacity and a new identity that doesn't involve ego.

You trust the Flow, the present moment, and your desire for a higher frequency reality. New ideas are reborn along with you—ideas that fit with your destiny.

Transparency Message
THE CUPPED HANDS

Life is so much simpler than you ever thought, though perhaps similar to the simplicity known by the child when she is fed, sheltered, protected, taught, encouraged, and allowed to explore her own self-expression and creativity. The child moves from meal to sleep to play to exploring her world, fluid as a stream. She makes her needs known without apology. She expresses her joy without artifice. She is totally real in each moment, welcoming the next stimulation, releasing the previous experience freely.

Like the child, you will not exhaust the discoveries, sights, smells, and sounds that can delight you. The difference between you and the child is: she focuses full attention on what appears in the moment, she has no preconceived judgment or expectation to interfere with her experience, she is not split. Do you remember those simple moments of observation without internal dialogue and commentary? Without trying to find meaning? Where the eyes don't yet know there is empty space between you and what you see? Where the senses are inside the big body of the world, revealing it constantly?

Words fly around you peppering your field—swarms and flocks of words. It is easy to be drawn in to their flutter and hum, to look to them for your soul. You've learned to live in them. Let them hover for a while without joining each other. Unclumped, they are symbols yet to take up their work of conveyance of, and looking for an experience to define. Be still and experiences surface from the depths of the field that is you, ready to become real, and the inner blueprints swell and the words gather, almost hungrily, waiting to cloak the experience. Which words are perfect for representation? For elucidation? Which ones together most beautifully convey your truth?

Remain quiet and expectant and the exact words are called forth on the vibration, and they choose each other. Hold out your cupped hands and they settle together, fall into place: the plump baby bluebird blinking its deep orange eyes and fluttering its fuzzy wings now appears from the field, at home in your hands. What created the bluebird? Transparency. Are you the bluebird? Yes. For Now.

Who is the simple, honest, authentic you? Sometimes the bluebird, sometimes the toddler, sometimes the shining star, sometimes the master of ceremonies. Who creates you? Transparency. And the servant-words. You are not fixed in form. New combinations of your field arise constantly and waft out. The soul fixes her full gaze upon these experiences and the words gather, combine, and tumble

Chapter 6: Becoming Personally Transparent

happily into the world, their mission to vibrate and describe. To cloak you so you appear out of the invisible.

You alone are not making yourself. You are not one form but a kaleidoscope of constantly changing forms, falling through transparency. The words are playing with each other to describe you. You appear in the cupped hands of a greater, collective being. We make you, you are We, the field is We, the words are We, the frequency is We, the transparency is We.

Be.   Quiet.   Wait.   And see.   And smile the little smile.

7

When Relationships & Groups
Are Transparent

*I have realized that mystery is what keeps people away, and I've
grown tired of smoke and mirrors. I yearn for the clean, well-lighted
place. So let's peek behind the curtain and hail the others like us.
The open-faced sandwiches who take risks and live big and smile
with all of their teeth. These are the people I want to be around.*

Amy Poehler

Creating a transparent relationship, group, organization, or society begins with you. Transparency is like a benign version of Kurt Vonnegut's concept of ice-nine from *Cat's Cradle*, which acts as a supercooled seed crystal, freezing any normal water it comes in contact with. Just as ice-nine has the power to destroy all of life on earth, spiritually based transparency has the power to enhance all of life on earth. Transparency spreads on contact, melting away fear and building trust, honesty, and authenticity. Your own level of transparency, both horizontal and vertical, affects others.

Your openness encourages others to relax and open up too. When you trust yourself and others, they trust you, and then they trust themselves more. Multiply that out to your personal and business relationships, then to your groups and organizations, then imagine lots of people doing the same thing. The groups overlap, the interconnections grow, and the effect of numerous people being transparent together influences others even more palpably.

In this chapter, we'll look at how transparency affects relationships, small and large groups, and even international relations. The changes in these areas are likely to be dramatically different from what you've known and always expected when getting together with others.

Soul Friends & Mates

Back in the twelfth century, Gampopa, a Tibetan Buddhist philosopher-saint, advised that we be insatiable to gaze at spiritual friends, because it's difficult to behold them, hard for them to appear, and not easy to meet them. Until recently, that was so true! We're more idealistic these days, and that makes sense when you remember that our frequency has increased and thus we have greater memory of spiritual states and higher desires and expectations for our personal relationships. We don't want to be friends and partners with just anyone—we want soul friends and mates! We're functioning at a more optimal level, and naturally, we want to feel the same quality in our connections with others. This is frequency-matching, and it generates a deep, abiding joy.

In addition to the desire to have a life partner with whom to raise a family, we now want a partner on our wavelength, with a similar level of curiosity, interests in the world and in spiritual growth, and a desire to have our work be about who we are. In addition, we're more interconnected via the internet, and though that might not by itself empower the appearing and meeting of soul friends and mates, it influences the subconscious to think that finding people anywhere in the world is possible. Surprisingly, this ease of finding each other is actually beginning to happen. Our higher frequency is causing people of like vibration to increasingly "occur" in each others' fields, and great differences in location or cultural backgrounds don't factor in as much as much as they used to.

However, not too many of us are totally clear yet, so we may still be engaging in partially clear relationships. Our idealism can make us more prone to disappointment and backsliding when we discover that the other person isn't quite who we thought they were. This is all part of the bridge-time dynamics—partnering with people who seem well-suited at first, but at a deeper level don't have the same understanding you do, or they match your subterranean, subconscious blocks more than your innate gifts. When this sort of partial partnering occurs, both of you will likely feel frustrated, even though you're unconsciously helping each other clear your clutter.

So you aim high, sometimes miss the mark, and fall back to earth: splat! This is just part of the normal learning and discerning process, like standing upright and starting to walk. The acceleration of life is on your side, making it gradually more natural to connect with soul friends and family. But during the bridge time, how do you find like-minded others—whether in your personal, intimate life or in business? And why, when you think you've found them, do you often end up disheartened? There are a number of principles at work.

1. **The frequency of your field, or sphere, acts as a filter or set of instructions to the unified field, and your relationships emerge from that.** Your beliefs and deep attitudes determine the kind of people who show up for you; they always match you in some way. If you are partially transparent, you get people who are also partially transparent. If you are partially ready to commit, you get people who are partially able to commit. If you unconsciously expect to not be seen for who you really are, you get people who value superficial qualities or have perfectionistic demands about how you should be. If you feel you must please others to avoid rejection, you may find people who leave when you're "too" nice and helpful, then come back to seduce and please you when you give up on them. And if you think you can change or control others, you get people who control you by being apathetic or a victim. When you're transparent, however, you get transparent people who see and know you immediately. Focus on what you're broadcasting through your personal field.

2. **You've had experiences that helped you feel transparent and high-frequency, but you haven't integrated them fully yet; you're still "testing the waters" to see if the good stuff could be**

true. Hidden doubts and subconscious blocks may be lingering. When you encounter people who are also partially transparent, the yet-to-be-dealt-with opacity in both of you can trip you up. The relationship looks good to begin with—idealism and desire influence you to see the part you want to see—but soon, the leftover fears surface and knock you into doubt and disillusionment. If you thought your partner was on your wavelength then discovered they weren't, you're showing yourself a matching "yes, but" in your own life; it has surfaced to be cleared in you, by you. If you're both on a declared path to clearing clutter, this can go a long way to reducing your mutual doubts and accelerating your mutual growth. If not, the relationship may fall apart, and you'll probably be attracted to another person with the same hidden issues. Just keep a positive attitude; what surfaces is there for a reason, and it contains useful information.

3. **Your left brain thinks about the ideal relationship and quantifies it. It makes a list of must-have qualities, and most people don't measure up.** You never find soul-based relationships when seeing through a filter of "shoulds." Focusing on a list of qualities and behaviors is superficial and can interfere with a compatible person showing up because you're using a subtle form of willpower—and willpower means you believe you have to control the way a process works, that you don't trust enough. Plus, if a person ticks off most of the items on your checklist, you may try to change them so the rest of the requirements are met too. That lack of acceptance and forcefulness always backfires. In contrast, the soul perceives based on core experiences that allow the heart to remain open and soft. The soul likes easy flow, honest communication, people who help you activate parts of yourself you didn't know you had, and right-brain qualities like spontaneity, creativity, and appreciation. Souls know what the personalities need.

4. **Your early childhood programming may have convinced your left brain that you must act a certain way to keep the other person interested.** Souls show up in each other's lives because there is

a purpose to fulfill. Sometimes that purpose is to help each other clear clutter and resolve old karmic issues, and sometimes it's because they just want to spend time together because they enjoy each other. Sometimes it's because the puzzle pieces of their interests and life patterns fall together perfectly to cocreate something for the world.

You don't need to perform to keep another soul interested. If the connection originates from spirit, the souls float in each other's space as long as there is a need. Allow others to use their free will, and trust them to follow their soul's direction to connect or disconnect. Trust yourself to do the same. Allow the right fit to occur naturally. When you're authentic, doing what brings you joy, other people can more easily decide if you're a person they want or need to be with.

5. **You think another person can complete you or provide something you don't have.** If you're caught in linear perception, you see everything as separate from you. That means you can be drawn to someone because they have a quality—over there—that you think you need, or you may be repelled from someone because they have a quality you don't want. With spherical perception, your soul is showing you that you have that quality in yourself—or you wouldn't be able to notice it.

The other person is in your field, and all the qualities you want—and don't want—are in you *and* them. You don't need the attractive person, and you don't need to get rid of the obnoxious person. If you activate the positive quality in yourself, and compassionately understand the negative quality, you can truly enjoy the other person, with no conditions or subtle pressures attached. And that greases the wheels for soul friends to stay.

6. **You think there's a limited supply of people on your wavelength.** If you're surrounded by people who don't match your frequency, you may not have stabilized your home frequency enough, and saturated your mind, emotions, body, and energy field with it. Keep your attention on the frequency you love; feel it and be it. The beauty of moving into transparency is that you show up more easily for who you are

and people at that same level of transparency can find you quickly. Cleared people can "see" or sense each other over great distances. So it's actually *easier* to find more soul friends and mates when you're transparent. There is no limitation in an abundant world.

> People think a soul mate is your perfect fit, and that's what everyone wants. But a true soul mate is a mirror, the person who shows you everything that is holding you back, the person who brings you to your own attention so you can change your life.
> Elizabeth Gilbert

The point here is that most of the reasons why relationships don't work come from ideas based on fear, partial perception, and left-brain dominance. To find like-minded others, first focus on maintaining your home frequency in your thoughts, feelings, body, and all around you in space. Fill your sphere—imagine that there are no holes or gaps—with qualities like compassion, unity, appreciation, and self-entertainment. Choose to feel these things. If you're knocked off-center and backslide, catch yourself as soon as you can, don't beat yourself up, and simply return to center. Substitute a good-quality feeling for the contracted one. As your field saturates with and stabilizes at your home frequency, your self-expression becomes authentic, honest, humble, and courageous.

When you find someone on your wavelength, tell them how happy you are to have met them and how delightful it is to have such an easy exchange with them—in effect, validate the experience for yourself and the other person, without overlaying any expectations. There's something about highlighting the experience for your body so it knows that the feeling state is "the real thing"—this reinforces your ability to repeat the materialization.

In a more practical sense, join groups, take classes, and research companies or volunteer opportunities that resonate with your favorite ideas and the motives close to your heart. If you can't find that sort of thing, start a group of your own or write an interactive blog on a topic you love. When you go out, talk about your insights, or a book that inspired you, or how you're paying attention to living a more conscious life. See who responds. Actions like this act as a trigger or a ceremony of sorts; you're making your desires physical and telling your subconscious—and the whole field of your reality—that you've made a clear choice to have soul friends and mates.

I seem to have loved you in numberless forms, numberless times . . .
In life after life, in age after age, forever.

Tagore

How do you know you've found a soul friend? There is an affinity almost right away. You can talk to them about anything, and they remain open to hear and understand you. They don't have to agree with you, but they don't judge you. If they give feedback, it's constructive or educational, furthering the depth and breadth of the sharing. There is no risk of rejection for being who you are or for thinking or feeling as you do. They realize you are a complex, interesting person. They can be trusted with what you reveal to them; there is no risk of betrayal or gossip.

A soul friend has a predilection to like you, and so they see the best, and the potential, in you. They respect your moods, your process of becoming transparent, your backsliding, and your personal space. If there are misunderstandings, their first priority is to get back to a place where both your hearts are open again. They express gratitude and appreciation easily and often. When you act this way with a soul friend, they act the same way with you, and the relief and pleasure of treating each other so well just keeps increasing.

On top of all this, you may find uncanny parallels and similar interests. You may feel you've known each other in other lives, that you've been through every possible kind of human experience together at some time. You may also discover that your paths are coevolutionary—when one of you hits a growth spurt, the other perks up and wants to grow too (rather than blaming you and finding it cause to separate). The more transparent you become, the easier it is to meet souls who can communicate with you without words, who understand why you are the way you are and help you become more of yourself, and who see how your evolution helps their evolution.

. . . .

Try This!

Open Your Mind to Soul Friends & Mates

Become quiet and drop into your body. Feel and think about each of the following questions in some depth, and write about your responses in your journal.

1. Do you believe it's possible to have soul friends and mates? Is it rare or might it become more normal? Or is it a fantasy based on wishful thinking?
2. If you find soul friends, do you think you'll be hurt more than is normal if they leave? Or would you both understand the reasons and wish each other the best?
3. Do you think soul friends would match all your left brain's criteria? Or might they introduce you to new ways of being? Might they challenge you to become more of yourself?
4. Do you think it's difficult to find soul friends? If so, why? What in you might make it difficult for them to appear in your life?
5. When you have soul friends and mates, write about what you think the core agreements are between you.
6. Have you ever had soul friends or a soul mate? Describe the qualities that made you feel that way. What behaviors did the person call forth from you?
7. Pick any friend or acquaintance and imagine that they could become a soul friend. How would you treat them if they were a soul friend? How would you see yourself if you were a soul friend? Try it and see what happens.

. . . .

Aristotle said that a true friend is one soul in two bodies. It can sometimes feel that way because when you perceive from the soul's perspective, there is little difference between you and another, and this great overwhelming commonality draws you into unity. So Aristotle is right: When you find your soul friends and mates, it can seem like you share a soul because, in a way, you do. Soul wisdom is not divided up among souls but shared equally, since at the soul level, distinctions dissolve and boundaries are unknown.

> A soul mate is an ongoing connection with another individual that the soul picks up again in various times and places over lifetimes. We are attracted to another person at a soul level not because that person is our unique complement, but because by being with that individual, we are somehow provided with an impetus to become whole ourselves.
>
> Edgar Cayce

As you become transparent and experience having transparent relationships, at first there may be the temptation to sexualize the connection. Not all soul friends have the purpose of being lovers or mated as marriage partners on earth. Some want to work and create together, some want to learn and grow together over time. The soul-to-soul connection provides love and evolution in whatever form is required by both people. With transparency, you can see even your coworkers and bosses as soul friends. There is no demarcation line saying these kinds of roles are allowed to be soul friends and these aren't; there is no differentiation between your private life and work life.

Perhaps this idea—the potential for anyone to become a soul friend—is sneaking into our consciousness through *friending* people online who we don't really know but sense have things in common with us. And what about the term that's recently become popular: *frenemies?* Are we finally beginning to understand that our enemies can also be our friends? The Mayans greeted each other with *In Lak'ech*, which means, "I am another yourself." What a lovely way to remember a higher truth and foster soul friends.

Let's not forget about the people who don't frequency-match with you. They are in your sphere too, generating their own vibration, and there is plenty of space for them to exist in you. You are a big situation. You-the-soul accept whatever state they're in, wholeheartedly. You-the-personality, however, may feel frustrated or disappointed when you deal with them, because you feel their soul when they may not. Even so, you can appreciate them and telepathically convey to them your enjoyment of who they really are. When they're ready, they'll jump for the higher reality like they would for a life preserver.

Instead of blocking the flow of life by separating yourself from people at different frequencies, you can take the role of thought leader, healer, or educator and offer insight and stories of personal experience that open others to new possibilities. When you're transparent, you act as if the other person is transparent, and soon, they live up to your vision.

Why Soul Friends Sometimes Separate

One of the hardest things to understand is why soul friends and soul mates sometimes break up or leave each other. It would seem that the ideal nature of the connection would last a lifetime—and it certainly can, depending on the souls' life purposes. I mentioned a few of the reasons souls come together in item four of the list on page 194. Sometimes there's a karmic debt to work out, and even if the original situation occurred with someone else, a soul friend may choose to be a stand-in, patiently and kindly taking the brunt of the negative pattern so their partner can release it. When the pattern is completed, the souls might stay together, becoming creative and celebratory, or they may have other agendas to attend to and need to move on. I've seen many relationships where people stayed together in spite of difficult, semi-abusive conditions, then suddenly parted ways after an arbitrary number of years, for apparently no reason. Suddenly, the karma is complete at the soul level, and no one knows why it took so long.

Leah told me she had been in a relationship that felt ancient, deeply compassionate, and had the potential for being a real soul-mate connection. She recognized the pattern and possibility, but the man was more naïve and involved in the details of his work and family of origin. She had a dream one night in which she was floating on the ceiling, looking down at her body and his, asleep in their bed. Then she looked over and saw that he was floating next to her, also looking down at their sleeping selves.

She realized that he saw her totally and completely at that level, and the love between them was profound. But looking back down to the personalities below, she saw there were twenty or thirty "layers" they would have to go through to bring the knowledge they had on the ceiling back down to the physical reality so it would match up equally for both of them. And she knew intuitively that it would not happen in their current life.

Upon waking, she realized their life purposes were different—she felt destined to travel and explore the world while he was determined to build a successful business locally. She could feel how the two patterns would not evolve well together. She didn't say anything, but in a few months the man began to see another woman, and they separated. She said, after feeling sad, that she thought she had actually separated from him first, in the inner, energy-and-consciousness world.

The more transparent you become, the more trust you have in the comings and goings of the souls in your life. You are able to see more deeply into the purposefulness of all things and understand the compassion in the way the gifts of presence are exchanged. Even if souls come into your life to seemingly stir up trouble or trigger negative patterns, there is compassion behind the occurrence; some clutter must need to be cleared, and the souls have chosen this time to do it. If souls depart, both may need to experience rejuvenation and liminal space. There is always a deeper, harmonious reason for the ebb and flow of relationships.

> You come to love not by finding the perfect person but
> by seeing an imperfect person perfectly.
> Sam Keen

The Convening

What's exciting is that when you and other people become transparent, you're able to find each other via the resonances you have in common, and much more quickly than ever before. It can seem like magic, this synchronicity—you have a thought of something you'd like to do and within days or weeks, a friend connects you with their friend who's in town who knows about that idea, or you a receive a flyer about a workshop that's perfect, or someone gets your name and wants to know if you might speak at a conference in a country you're interested in visiting. People of like mind and like vibration come to the forefront and occur in each other's fields, while those of lower frequency fade into the background. There is less "noise" and distraction from the frequencies you don't need.

This means we're going to see a rapid increase in the forming of like-minded groups—a convergence of cocreators. These congruent groups will then find overlaps with other congruent groups, and they will discover a common purpose or project that suits each group's needs. In this way, there will be a convening of transparent people in transparent groups, and out of this will spring innovations and solutions to global problems. There will be tremendous cross-pollination, and a combination of online, virtual collaboration and in-person, physical collaboration.

> If the group is an art form of the future, then convening groups is an artistry we must cultivate to fully harvest the promise of the future.
> Jacob Needleman

I experienced this many years ago in San Francisco when I joined the Institute for the Study of Conscious Evolution and met another participant, Dr. William H. Kautz, who was involved with SRI International and had just founded the Center for Applied Intuition. As I began to work with Kautz's group, I met Willis Harman and the people involved in the World Business Academy and the Institute of Noetic Sciences, then Jeffrey Mishlove and the members of the Intuition Network, then many of the people involved with the Findhorn Foundation in Scotland.

All these groups began interconnecting with colleges and universities in San Francisco—JFK University, San Francisco State, Stanford, the Institute of Transpersonal Psychology, the Sophia Center at Holy Names University, and California Institute of Integral Studies. Then they interconnected with counseling centers, New Thought churches like Unity and the Church of Religious Science, and spiritual retreat centers like Esalen Institute, Green Gulch Farm Zen Center, and Spirit Rock Meditation Center. Teachers from all these places traveled widely, sharing knowledge and co-leading workshops. It was an amazing convening that had a mushrooming momentum I'd never known before.

I noticed this kind of convening happening again recently when I taught in Chicago for several years in a row. I had worked with George Leonard's and Michael Murphy's Integral Transformative Practice International (ITPI) group in San Francisco, and they connected with Emanuel Kuntzelman's organization, Greenheart International, in Chicago. Out of this came a connection with the Theosophical Society and Barbara Marx Hubbard's group. Subsequently, people from all these organizations began to meet annually to focus on societal transformation. I'm sure this sort of thing is happening increasingly in many arenas, especially where egos don't dominate the group dynamic and a common goal is at the forefront of people's minds. With these kinds of groups partnering and sharing openly and transparently, it seems there really is hope for the world.

With this in mind, we might contemplate what some high-frequency people—the UNDP (United Nations Development Programme)—came up with when they convened to make a plan for "Transforming Our World" and created the "2030 Agenda for Sustainable Development," with seventeen Sustainable Development Goals (SDGs). Each of these goals, achieved, speaks to a quality of transparent groups and organizations expanded out to the level of society. You might browse the list on pages 204–205 (Figure 7-1) and imagine that each of these goals is already met. For each one: How might reality change? How might it affect our internal personal identity, state of being, and connection to the Divine? Imagine how achieving these things might be a normal part of the Intuition Age.

TRANSFORMING OUR WORLD: THE 2030 AGENDA FOR SUSTAINABLE DEVELOPMENT

17 Sustainable Development Goals (SDGs)[1]

Goal 1: No Poverty—End poverty in all its forms everywhere.

Goal 2: Zero Hunger—End hunger, achieve food security and improved nutrition, and promote sustainable agriculture.

Goal 3: Good Health and Well-Being—Ensure healthy lives and promote well-being for all, at all ages.

Goal 4: Quality Education—Ensure inclusive and equitable quality education, and promote lifelong learning opportunities for all.

Goal 5: Gender Equality—Achieve gender equality, and empower all women and girls.

Goal 6: Clean Water and Sanitation—Ensure availability and sustainable management of water and sanitation for all.

Goal 7: Affordable and Clean Energy—Ensure access to affordable, reliable, sustainable, and modern energy for all.

Goal 8: Decent Work and Economic Growth—Promote sustained, inclusive, and sustainable economic growth, full and productive employment, and decent work for all.

Goal 9: Industry, Innovation, and Infrastructure—Build resilient infrastructure, promote inclusive and sustainable industrialization, and foster innovation.

Goal 10: Reduced Inequalities—Reduce inequality within and among countries.

(Continued on next page)

TRANSFORMING OUR WORLD: THE 2030 AGENDA FOR SUSTAINABLE DEVELOPMENT

17 Sustainable Development Goals (SDGs)[1]

Goal 11: Sustainable Cities and Communities—Make cities and human settlements inclusive, safe, resilient, and sustainable.

Goal 12: Responsible Consumption and Production—Ensure sustainable consumption and production patterns.

Goal 13: Climate Action—Take urgent action to combat climate change and its impacts.

Goal 14: Life Below Water—Conserve and sustainably use the oceans, seas, and marine resources for sustainable development.

Goal 15: Life on Land—Protect, restore, and promote sustainable use of terrestrial ecosystems, sustainably manage forests, combat desertification, and halt and reverse land degradation and biodiversity loss.

Goal 16: Peace, Justice, and Strong Institutions—Promote peaceful and inclusive societies for sustainable development, provide access to justice for all, and build effective, accountable, and inclusive institutions at all levels.

Goal 17: Partnerships for the Goals—Strengthen the means of implementation, and revitalize the global partnership for sustainable development.

Fig. 7-1

Relationship & Group Entities

When relationships become transparent, both people practice honesty, compassion, authenticity, and respect. Both of you commit to keeping your heart open and the alignment with the soul intact. If either of you backslide, the other gives a hand to get back to center. That help is not seen as criticism. There is a commitment vertically, within each personality, to stay attuned to spiritual truth and harmony—not necessarily to agree horizontally with the other person. When mutual alignment is present, there is natural understanding and a willingness to find win-win solutions, which occur quickly and satisfyingly.

Eventually, you both realize there is a force greater than either of you—Aristotle's one soul in two bodies—but it's really a *relationship entity* formed by the combination of your soul's total experience and the other person's total experience. It's a kind of *oversoul*, or collective soul, and you might picture it as a much more intense sphere that both of you live within. In this sphere you both have access to the entirety of your collective experience. When one person comes up with an idea or insight, it's not just they who are saying it, it's the relationship entity, and it knows what's coevolutionary for both of you. You might imagine the wise relationship entity is seeding insights to both of you to further your mutual understanding. This way you value the things that come from your partner's mouth—there can be much deeper significance when you consider the source includes your own wisdom as well.

Just as two transparent people create a transparent relationship, more than two transparent people create a transparent group. The same principles apply—the people practice honesty, kindness, authenticity, respect, and patience. There is a collective desire to find win-win-*win* solutions created by the input from all parties. And eventually, there is the realization by all participants that there is a *group entity* composed of the total experience of all the souls involved.

When you feel into that collective oversoul, or pool of knowledge, the resources available are vast and comprehensive. Each person is like a national treasure. When this inclusiveness occurs, compassion and understanding become organizing principles, competition shifts to collaboration, criticism to insightful support, and the potential for genius solutions becomes obvious and easy to access. Several people may take turns acting as leader or facilitator, and the person in that role helps maintain an atmosphere where participants can be heard, express themselves accurately, acknowledge their true responses to input, and find meaning in the process of discovery and cocreation.

> Let us put our heads together and see what life
> we will make for our children.
> **Sitting Bull**

Transparent groups catalyze a sense of community and communion that raises the physical collaboration and communication to a level that invokes an experience of spiritual truth. Barbara Spraker, who works with the Center for Creative Change at Antioch University Seattle, has discovered much about transparent groups by working closely with women's groups. She says that, "Women lead from the inside out, not from the top down," and that a group's commonalities provide a foundation for working together, while their differences expand the resources of the group. She describes how "as each individual listens, with silence and respect, a whole world of understanding opens up within the group," and that it's important to have some silent time after everyone has spoken, for absorption of deeper meaning. And, that "this experience provides an expanded, more holistic awareness."[2]

She emphasizes how important it is for the leader or facilitator to model the ideal outcome; to be like a tuning fork to set a tone; to be genuine, working face to face with the participants; and to be heartfelt, fully present, and accessible at all times. Leaders need to be transparent and not so separate. They need to share more, be more open and intimate, receive more from people at every level of the organization, and lead by the respect placed in them for their visionary capacity, compassion, and courage—not ego and superiority.

In transparent groups, individual participants' peculiarities are not seen as problematic but as helpful data about hidden agendas or information that may have been ignored. The old pattern of participants' ego-based behaviors creating logjams—behaviors like control, aggression, hostility, apathy, pride, and feeling victimized—is not tolerated in transparent groups because it's unnecessary, ineffective, and interrupts the good experience everyone wants to have. Common ground is found, not by eliminating a certain participant's ideas but by combining ideas to find new realities that are just right and uplifting.

We are approaching a time when what works to keep individuals clear and transparent—e.g., focusing on the home frequency, meditating and feeling into the presence inside matter, working with spherical-holographic perception instead of linear perception, and using intuition, empathy, and telepathy—will be integrated into the practical workings of groups and organizations. Groups will meditate, focus on the group entity (or group mind and heart), feel into the possibilities in the imaginal realm, use intuition to access insights that don't necessarily come from the past, and use attention to materialize results without snags or struggle. In the transparent organization, marketing turns into something akin to education and excited conversation, while the profit motive transforms into "I make money if you make money, and if we grow into our higher purpose concurrently."

· · · · · · · · · · · ·

Try This!

Merge with the Relationship Entity or the Group Mind-Heart

1. When you're with another person, even if they're not open to thinking this way, imagine both of your souls' histories and potentials merging together to form a huge, wise sphere that both of you are living in and drawing from. It sources you with the highest motives for coevolution. Decide to trust that it will bring thoughts, words, and actions to you that feel just right and that it will do the same for the other person. What you say and do is what the other person needs, and what they say and do is what you need.

2. Then, simply observe the spontaneous interaction you two have while feeling into the underlying purposefulness of what comes out of you and out of the other person. With an eye toward taking it all positively and making it useful, see the exchange as being sourced from soul. Then compare the experience to other exchanges you've had with other people when you

were skimming the surface, not really listening, jumping to conclusions, secretly criticizing the other, or second-guessing the person before they finished communicating.

3. When you're involved in a group meeting, imagine all the souls' histories and potentials merging together to form a huge, wise sphere that all of you are living in and drawing from. It sources everyone with the highest motives for coevolution. Decide to trust that it will bring thoughts, words, and actions that feel just right and that it will do the same for the others. What you say and do is what the other people need, and what they say and do is what you need.

4. Then, observe the spontaneous interactions of the group members while feeling into the underlying purposefulness of what comes out of you and out of the others. With an eye toward taking it all positively and making it useful, see the exchange as being sourced from soul. Then compare the experience to other exchanges you've had in other groups when you were skimming the surface, not really listening, jumping to conclusions, criticizing others inside your mind, or second-guessing someone before they finished communicating.

· · · · · · · · · · · ·

Working with the Group Entity, or Group Mind-Heart

When I first began developing my intuition, it was in the days of the New Age "channelers," and I never fit that model. No spiritual entity spoke through me—at least none I could identify. Instead, when I meditated, I was "drawn up" to a space above my head (I was probably just increasing my frequency) into a place that contained a large round table. There was an impression of wise beings sitting around the table—I never saw distinct bodies or faces or was told names—and there was always an empty seat for me, which I took. I intuitively "heard" that this was my "council" and that the beings were part of my soul group.

We connected telepathically and somehow all knew what question or issue wanted to be attended to at each meeting. Sometimes it was a question I had about my personal life, sometimes it was societal or esoteric. When I entered the circle, I equalized my consciousness with theirs, to match the council's vibration. When that occurred, a large, crystal sphere appeared, floating slightly above the center of the table. Then two beams of bright light flowed into the sphere from above and below. I sensed this was a connection with higher frequency and lower frequency beings. Next, we each held the question or issue in our minds and hearts and focused our attention into the crystal sphere.

Our council's collective knowledge, and that of the other beings who sent the beams, merged in the crystal sphere and created the highest possible understanding, which was then relayed telepathically back to each of us. Our own individual filters allowed us to grasp the overall pattern in unique ways, and again, telepathically, we communicated the various aspects and angles of understanding to each other. It always left me feeling overly full with a great pattern that would need to be deciphered patiently over time, when I came back to my physical self. It was this meditative experience that helped me understand the power of the group mind and heart, and it became a regular part of my intuitive process.

I worked in Japan annually for twenty-some years, and it was this that taught me the same principle in the real world. I'd be standing on a street corner with a group of people in Tokyo after we'd finished one of my seminars, and we'd be deciding where to go for dinner. I had learned that if I responded with a direct answer when they politely asked what kind of food I liked, the entire group would swing that way, and I'd end up feeling like I'd unfairly dominated the evening. So instead, I would say, "It doesn't matter to me."

What ensued would be a surreal few minutes of rapid-fire Japanese, then suddenly, without a pronouncement of what the answer was, we'd take off like a school of fishes—down the sidewalk, around corners, and end up at, say, a Robata bar. I always sensed that no one had expressed a personal preference, because that would unduly influence the group, but that each person had telepathically arrived at the same answer simultaneously, without any logic.

With transparency, there is a heightened use of intuition and right-brain perception in groups. Eastern cultures, tribal groups, and women are the natural teachers of this. Women's groups and shamanic groups in particular are drawn to work in egalitarian meeting circles, with non-interfering open space in the center. Corporate meetings, on the other hand, often take place around rectangular tables or at individual desks in rows aligned toward a single meeting leader—a more hierarchical structure that separates people from each other.

With the circle format, participants are not blocked and protected by a table or desk but are visible, open, and vulnerable. The chance for honesty and transparency is greater. Meeting circles tend to encourage the emergence of right-brain visions and cohesive wisdom because they facilitate a more sacred sense of space, where members are honored and listened to more closely. With hierarchical structures, the information that emerges may be more left brained, linear, divisive, and partial.

Circles may be convened for the purpose of conversation and exploring topics, building trust, finding discernment about particular issues, and solving problems and making action plans. It's also common in circles to use the method of the talking stick for communication. The talking stick can be any object that is passed from person to person; when one person holds it, they have the floor and the others listen deeply, then acknowledge with a simple nod of the head. This way people don't talk over each other or interrupt a train of thought.

Barbara Spraker, who I mentioned earlier, notes that a few questions can serve to keep people on track. As circles begin, participants can respond to "What phrase or image stands out for you in regard to [the purpose of the meeting]?" Then, "When did you become emotionally engaged? When did you get excited, frustrated, discouraged, energized, etc.?" She reminds us that emotions have as great an impact on our work as thoughts and ideas do. After everyone has shared, it's time to ask, "What does all this mean to us?" And finally, "What action, if any, does this meaning prompt?" If action is required, the group moves on to develop a plan.[3]

I like the fact that attention is given, at first, to the intuitive, feeling nature of each person so the symbols and feelings can be interpreted intuitively before being passed to the left brain to find meaning. Once meaning—so closely tied to purpose—has been delineated, an action plan can be found, again by using intuition first, then crystallizing it into form using the left brain's analytical, logical expertise. This way, the group stays aligned with a higher, more cohesive process and end result.

> We need a collective intelligence of a kind that may not have characterized the human species in the past; but we see no reason to believe that a whole population cannot reach a stage of mature self-consciousness much as an individual does.
> Paul Hawken, James A. Ogilvy, and Peter Schwartz

Let's imagine we're taking part in a group, and the purpose of the gathering is to access a vision for a new product, method, or service that solves a major national or global problem—let's say, water distribution. We begin by meeting in a circle. We introduce ourselves and share about our emotional engagement with the issue, perhaps sharing an image that comes to mind. Then we close our eyes and are led by a facilitator into a quiet state below the yackety-yak of the inner voice, the left brain's "shoulds," and ideas based on the logical progression from what's worked in the past.

When we are centered, we expand our sphere to include each of the other people in the group. Each person's bubble includes everyone, and a unified group mind coalesces as the entire history and knowledge base of each person merges to be shared by all. Then we focus on how our hearts open to include the other people's hearts. We focus on the feeling of relaxation, appreciation, and belonging that occurs when hearts are open.

Next, we visualize the crystal ball floating in the center of the circle, connect it to higher and lower frequencies of the collective consciousness, and focus our minds and hearts into the spherical center of our group entity with the issue of water distribution in mind. Remaining relaxed and neutral, we wait for an idea or pattern to return to us, allow it to emerge in our consciousness, and bring it to the surface to describe it. We open our eyes and go around the circle, one by one, sharing the insights we accessed. The facilitator helps meld our ideas together, then we shift to the left brain to find a holistic win-win-win solution, how it might be implemented, what things need to happen for it to be effective, and how long it might last. At the end, we bring our full attention back into our own center again, gather our energy, thank the others, and separate.

I've just sketched a rather simplistic recipe for working with the group entity, but it's a place to start contemplating how transparency-enhancing values like respect, deep listening, honesty with compassion, and the use of intuitive visioning skills could reduce the distortion and frustration common to most groups today. If you'd like to help catalyze a better group experience, you might take people out of their normal context or habitat into a more informal setting, since minds so often match their environment and routine. Give participants a little logical explanation of how they'll be experimenting with intuition, energy, and the balanced left and right brain, then lead them through the experience I've described. Make sure they know there's no right or wrong way to do it, or just implement one section of the process at a time, to see how it goes.

When Group Transparency Is Partially Perceived

In this bridge time, many people have yet to do the important clearing work, and there is bound to be resistance to being open and intuitive. After all, most people are still living in their head, looking for logical left-brain answers that provide security and proof. Anything intangible is generally thought of as unreliable or useless. When the idea of transparency is seen as only horizontal, that is, just in the physical world and relating to information, solutions tend to be shallow and filtered through left-brain analytical thought.

I spoke with two clients recently who were trying to bring greater depth and balanced left-right brain perception to their teaching, training, and counseling work within traditional organizational settings. One was teaching performance enhancement, resilience, and metacognition to a branch of the military. Her topics were ripe for a huge injection of right-brain perception, and she wanted to take the experiences she was facilitating much further, but she was working inside a box with rigid walls, limited to strict standards based on past structures, and everything she did had to be "duplicatable." Still, she was looking for ways to poke holes in the box.

My other client had been working with counseling in a university setting and had risen to a high position where she was now training dozens of other counselors. She herself was opening into an expanded capacity based on her intuitive and spiritual growth, but was restricted to a conservative protocol called "data-driven counseling," which was almost entirely left-brained and didn't touch the deep causes of clients' issues. She was looking for ways to stretch her students' subjective experience.

So many of us face similar organizational consciousness these days—a consciousness that only understands the tiniest percentage of the potential for real transparency.

I recently read Dave Eggers's book *The Circle*, which drives home the point about how an organization's perception of transparency can become skewed and go to extremes; its dystopian vision actually made me shudder. The book chronicles the fictional progress of a young woman who climbs the corporate ladder at a mega-company (The Circle) involved with everything internet-related. The company demands horizontal transparency of all its employees and in all its practices. To achieve that, people are required to have a constant presence on social networks, give up their anonymity and privacy, and reveal their every move, past history, and health records.

At The Circle, everything is recorded and nothing is ever deleted. The company invents cameras that can be placed everywhere around the world, so there are virtually no places where people cannot be observed. And to become *really* transparent, people agree to wear tiny cameras on their bodies, broadcasting everything they see, do, and say to millions of online followers. The fact that they're under constant surveillance seems not to matter, so hypnotized are they by corporate propaganda. In fact, several of the company's mottos are: Sharing Is Caring, Privacy Is Theft, and Secrets Are Lies. The tyranny of this out-of-control horizontal transparency is trying, even for the naïve, young woman with her seemingly endless energy and capacity for pleasing the company. She revels in displaying herself, besting others, and devouring data at breakneck speed.

> Under the guise of having every voice heard, you create mob rule,
> a filterless society where secrets are crimes.
> **Dave Eggers**

At one point, the last remaining sane person in the company tries to broadcast "The Rights of Humans in a Digital Age" to all the "watchers" around the world. In it he says, "We must all have the right to anonymity. Not every human activity can be measured. The ceaseless pursuit of data to quantify the value of any endeavor is catastrophic to true understanding. The barrier between public and private must remain unbreachable. And: we must all have the right to disappear."[4] Of course, the watchers no longer understand this ethic.

The Surveillance Society

Related to this frightening tale of the dark side of horizontal transparency is the reality we are experiencing today with our "surveillance society." I mentioned earlier that as the planet increases in frequency and transparency, secrets are no longer viable. But clearing the withholding of secrets is a complex can of worms. People are greedy for personal, private information about each other, celebrities, and leaders, while business and government want to profile us for profit and so-called security purposes. We want to reveal ourselves but don't want to be invaded forcefully. And of course, we don't want to lose our individuality, which we associate with our privacy and, ultimately, our security.

We don't want to be lied to; we want to make the invisible visible, unless it applies to our own vulnerabilities. Governments, police, and corporations maintain secrets partly as a way to keep society under control and partly to hide illegal behavior. That means hackers and whistleblowers are highly motivated to penetrate through encryption into these organizational superstructures. And the superstructures are highly motivated to spy on the populace, justifying their surveillance due to possible "suspicious activity."

James Bamford, author of *The Shadow Factory*, says that as of 2015, the US National Security Agency processed information at the level of the yottabyte—that's 10^{24} bytes. This would equal one septillion—one trillion trillion—pages of text! But surveillance encompasses personal data collection and profiling of individuals for commercial reasons as well. Evidently, Americans surrender more private information to service providers and social networks than anything the NSA has so far accomplished, and sales of data gathered about customers from cell phones alone are estimated to be in the billions of dollars.

As horizontal transparency grows, it may be that the loves, opinions, habits, and philosophies of each person will be known by everyone. It will take the development of vertical transparency—the integration of the spiritual realm into the physical—to change our perception, and especially our ethics, so we can trust being known and be trusted knowing so much. In the spiritual realm, after all, everything is already known, but life in those realms is governed by harmonious, compassionate, unity-based universal principles, which we are just beginning to integrate into our lives on earth.

> I think the currency of leadership is transparency. You've got to be truthful. I don't think you should be vulnerable every day, but there are moments where you've got to share your soul and conscience with people and show them who you are, and not be afraid of it.
> Howard Schultz

Creating Healthier Transparency in Organizations

The idea that transparency is taking a foothold, even horizontally, in the physical world and in the information realm is good news. It's a place to start. The fact that 71 percent of employees feel managers don't explain goals well enough, and 50 percent of these people say that a lack of transparency is what's holding their company back,[5] are signs that people are responding to the acceleration of energy-and-consciousness on the planet and in themselves. We don't want to tolerate gaps in knowledge, hidden agendas interfering with the Flow, misalignment between purpose and results, and outright lies and manipulation.

It's become widely recognized that transparency helps people engage in the workplace, and that's crucial when, according to a 2013 Gallup poll, 87 percent of employees are mentally checked out on the job.[6] Employees want to know what's happening in their organization, what the company's goals are, how well the company is doing, and what the company's major challenges are. We want to be connected to what's "real." When a company holds back this kind of core information, people don't trust management.

Just working for a wage isn't enough anymore; people want their work to have meaning both personally and societally—again, a sign of the spiritual realms interpenetrating the physical. So secrecy undermines trust, and mistrustful employees quit. When employee turnover can cost 50 to 60 percent of an employee's salary, lost engagement is estimated by Gallup to cost the economy $550 billion a year.[7]

It's probably no accident that the current trend in interior design is toward open floor plans, where functions can easily connect and people can be seen and heard throughout a space. Just as homes are adopting this design, so are some offices. It's a move toward unity. Open office floor plans foster transparency by making it easy to see what everyone is working on and easy to collaborate on projects. Some companies send meeting notes—even from board meetings—to the entire workforce, some have an open email policy where every email is internally searchable, while others publish the criteria for calculating salaries to all workers.

Zappos, the online shoe and clothing store, went so far as to abolish titles and management positions to create a "holacracy," with self-governing teams organized in circles. Many employees did not adapt well to the new self-management style, however, and 14 percent decided to leave, according to *Forbes.com*.[8] It may have been a bit too impulsive a move, but facilitating shared leadership among executives and recognizing team members for their contributions—not their titles—does improve creativity and performance. Many corporations, about 20 percent, now offer some form of empathy training, and experts expect that number to double in the next ten years. In fact, the 2015 Global Empathy Index revealed that empathy pays—the top ten most empathic businesses generated 50 percent more income than the bottom ten firms.

We definitely need to focus on the ethical issues related to horizontal transparency so the trend toward transparency doesn't tip toward the dystopic, Big Brother vision presented in *The Circle*. We need to introduce the concept of vertical transparency to round out the experience. Vertical transparency, with its focus on spiritual truth and universal principles, automatically solves many of the more unhealthy tendencies of an exclusively horizontal focus. If you think about it, it saves time and headaches down the road as the dysfunctional solutions must be rethought and redesigned to fit the Intuition Age reality.

To keep things on the up and up, companies should probably keep their efforts aimed at productivity, employees' need for both social and private time, and training employees in spherical-holographic perception. Tracking progress, helping make corporate decisions, suggesting innovations and good ideas, and having transparency applied equally across the board are great ways to build trust and participation.

Customers appreciate transparency as well. When you buy something online and don't know what it will cost and how much shipping will be until you give up all your financial information and get to the last page—how infuriating is that? Being manipulated and ambushed doesn't sit well with anyone. To increase ethical transparency in groups and organizations (this applies to families as well), see Figure 7-2.

> Nothing truly valuable can be achieved except by
> the unselfish cooperation of many individuals.
> Albert Einstein

CREATING HEALTHY TRANSPARENCY IN GROUPS

- Tell the truth, be honest, keep it simple.

- It's OK and necessary to speak truth to power figures, even if it's difficult.

- Increase the frequency and candor of communications. Share information openly.

- Use the word *we* more often than *I*.

- Demonstrate a clear concern for others.

- Ask more questions.

- Really listen to people's answers.

- Admit your mistakes; see them as learning opportunities. It's OK to say, "I don't know."

- Be sure your actions support your words.

- Make it clear that transparency applies to everyone, and that it's a two-way street.

- Feedback can include a critique, but also make suggestions; find the important points in others' arguments.

- Challenge people to think creatively; reward unusual thinkers and risk taking.

- Gather information from diverse sources for a multifaceted understanding.

- Make the group's vision, goals, and information available to everyone.

- Make yourself available, face to face; be responsive.

- Share compliments and positive feedback; don't gossip.

(Continued on next page)

CREATING HEALTHY TRANSPARENCY IN GROUPS

- Don't let your role interfere with your relationships.

- Underpromise and overdeliver.

- Give a voice to people; encourage open-door policies, internal blogs, suggestion boards, and whistleblowers.

- Promote intuition training, empathy training, and right-brain perception to encourage whole-brain and whole-body perception.

- Have the group dynamic reflect the values behind the brand.

- Be present, compassionate, appreciative, and patient. The fastest solutions come in the present moment.

Fig. 7-2

Just to Recap...

As you become transparent, you increasingly want to connect with other transparent people who are on your wavelength—people you might call soul friends or soul mates. Because we're still moving through the bridge-time transition, the people we connect with may be partially transparent, like us. We may see through to the soul but miss some of the hidden clutter that will surface in the presence of both people's transparency, and that can cause the relationship to end.

There are a variety of reasons why soul-friend connections may be limited, but if you stabilize your home frequency as the tone of your sphere, your relationships will soon frequency-match that vibration. You might think the clearer you become, the more difficult it will be to find a partner, but it's just the opposite—transparent people can sense each other across great distances because there's no clutter in the way.

Chapter 7: When Relationships & Groups Are Transparent

When people are transparent, there is a convening of like-minded souls who show up in each other's fields without any searching or attempt at attraction. They form congruent groups that come together to cocreate and enjoy each other; then there is an overlapping of these groups and more cocreating at a larger level. It is these kinds of high-frequency, transparent groups that will solve pressing world problems.

> [My] body has become transparent, almost nonexistent. . . .
> It doesn't oppose the vibrations: all vibrations pass through it freely.
> It feels spread out in everything it does, in everything around, in all
> circumstances, in people, movements, feelings.
> **Mirra Alfassa, The Mother**

Transparent relationships and groups become aware of a merged oversoul—a relationship entity or group entity composed of the combined history and knowledge of both or all the participating souls. That entity acts as a teacher, guide, and engineer for the evolution of all involved. When a partner or group member speaks, it's important to remember that your higher consciousness is also speaking through them. Groups can choose to work consciously with the group entity in meetings to help balance left- and right-brain input and perception. Circles particularly lend themselves to accessing intuitive, right-brain information.

Transparent relationships and groups are becoming more common, but we still chafe at the limitations of opaque relationships and groups. We hate secrets but want privacy. We want to reveal ourselves but don't want to be invaded and hacked. The push for horizontal transparency in the information realm is great today, and it's a start. But we need to integrate vertical transparency as well, to develop the ethics that will help us trust being so totally known and be trusted knowing so much.

Meanwhile, organizations are working to instill transparency in their operations, because it has been shown that transparency pays off financially. Still, corporations and governments must walk a fine line between revealing information to facilitate trust and engagement, and becoming Big Brother, spying on the people who belong to the organizations.

Transparency Message
TWO VIEWS OF RELATING

As you enter the time of transparency, relating becomes easier, though it might seem more difficult: Are you now so overloaded with information and insight and feelings and interconnections that you cannot feel yourself? Will your dutiful, beautiful mind shut down from too many choices, too much wisdom, too much fear, too much to love? This is the old view, seen by the isolated and isolating left-brain mind: it is too tight to comprehend simultaneous knowledge, too protective to allow communion. It gives you a shady perspective on relating: difficulty and negativity are constantly in the making, and loss is the inevitable outcome of creation.

It teaches that you are alone, so relationships seem like salvation. Then loss rears its ugly head and grins at you, and you expect misalignment, emotional pain, abandonment, and death of your loved ones. It programs your heart to close. With groups of people, this view looks for conflict and opposition, the draining of energy by dominators and victims, wasted time, and frustration based on the dissonance of frequencies caught in ego. These are ideas you assume are normal.

Seen from the soul, though, people are part of one great energy-and-consciousness, flowing harmoniously, evolving constantly, moving ever into increased wisdom and love. Relationship is normal, isolation is unreal. From this view, any gathering of souls-in-bodies, be it two or three or more, is the potential for a merging of sources, an amplification of spiritual truth and memory. Since souls know how interconnected they already are, the sense of personal self is not based on isolation but mutual inclusion with all others. Identity involves belonging. There is no fear of loss when everyone is always there, intimately connected with you and inside you. Souls know anything easily, understanding comes telepathically, and all points of view form a simple yet intricate whole. There are never-ending results with pause points for recognizing love. The heart is not programmed at all, it is free to do what it loves and that is: stay soft, open, and expanded. It becomes the field you live within. It becomes the field that sponsors your engagement with other souls-in-bodies and souls-without-bodies.

When you become transparent and see the soul's view, all that seemed terminal, dark, depressing, fragmenting, frustrating, and frightening turns into its opposite: ongoing, light, uplifting, unifying, freeing, and reassuring. Relationships expand in potential and creativity. Soul friends occur easily and are not the rare occurrences they were when fear dominated your mind. Now, anyone might be a soul friend if you pay attention. Group interactions move from a tangled knot to the feeling of each person's puzzle piece dropping smoothly into place with the others, revealing a surprising, delightful picture. Arguing is old and boring. Discovery via harmony is engaging and stimulating.

Soul groups intuitively feel and respect each stage of the creation cycle: emergence, inspiration, motivation, vision, organization, present-moment plan, tasks, actions, satisfaction, results, more satisfaction, relaxing, letting go, being with, appreciating, rejuvenation, and re-emergence. There is simultaneous sensitivity to the value of the individual and collective vision and experience, to the particle and the field, to form and imagination. When people need space, the group mind provides it, when they need action or physical results, it comes as the next natural thing. There is a time for the overview, a time for the detail. Open hearts create clear minds and sensitivity aligns with the Flow. With trans-parency what is needed by all is appreciated by each.

8

No Walls, No Secrets: Seeing Through & Being Seen

We can see through others only
when we see through ourselves.
Eric Hoffer

You're becoming transparent! You no longer want to live within labels and definitions, or be limited by the story of your personal history, as entertaining as it may be. Your attachment to beliefs and fixed identity, ego and accomplishments, and righteousness and control feels like a waste of energy and attention. And yet you can play with definitions, ideas, identities, stories, and accomplishments—lightly, for fun, and to teach and create with others. You can remain open yet also "draw the line" wherever you please, noticing what it does to your energy-and-consciousness.

You have faced your defense mechanisms and now understand how they helped the old you avoid pain. With love, those locked doors opened magically and you walked through, bringing your Light with you; the walls and fears melted away, leaving fresh air and space to create anew. Your emotional self has healed, the way your scraped knee or broken arm healed—as a natural function of energy seeking harmony.

Now you live inside the Flow and trust it, you feel intimately connected with all other souls, and you know it's normal to be supported and able to create anything you can imagine. You have practiced living inside your sphere at your home frequency, knowing there is no outside world, knowing everything is in you and familiar. Self-protection, striving, and struggle are old, silly games. As your transparency increased, your restrictive boundaries dissolved. Now you can be yourself without defenses. Now nothing separates your body from the earth, your mind from the consciousness of machines and objects, or your emotions from the spiritual realm. You are capable of feeling anything at any frequency, and in spite of the vastness of the unified field's content, you are not overwhelmed but know what you need to know whenever you need to know it. What you need comes to you, and what you don't need fades back into the field of energy-and-consciousness.

You think back to the time when you held yourself rigid and apart from others, kept secrets, told lies, and projected an inflated or camouflaged image of yourself to the world. You remember what distrust did to you and what a relief it was to trust. You remember the difference between ignorant, gullible vulnerability and wise, compassionate vulnerability. Remembering how contracted you used to be, you have to laugh a little at the need you had then to maintain all those subterfuges. It's so much easier now.

In this chapter, we'll explore the power of being seen—for everything you are—by your own self and others, and the power of seeing through surface presentations, ideas, and limitations to find the truth and harmony at the core of everything.

• • • • • • • • • • •

Try This!

Feel the Rhythm of the True Self

1. Sit with your back supported, breathe evenly, bring your attention inside your skin, and be centered.
2. Imagine that every cell inside your body is relaxing, softening its walls, and allowing the membranes to be more porous, transferring energy in and out

easily. Now imagine the same porous quality in your skin so that what's outside can flow in and what's inside can flow out.

3. Imagine that everything you've been holding can now flow from you into the field around you to dissolve. Let yourself feel empty and spacious. Feel into what's left to sense the presence that remains.

4. Now imagine that anything you need can flow into you easily from the field of your greater, collective self. Let yourself feel comfortably full. Feel into the fullness to sense the presence in everything.

5. As you breathe out, say and feel: "I am nothing." As you breathe in, say and feel: "I am everything." Repeat for five minutes or more. All the while, feel the steady presence within both states.

. . . .

See Thyself, Know Thyself, Revel in Thyself

With transparency comes the willingness to be seen and known by your own self, by other people, and by beings in the nonphysical realms. It's fine to be seen for your mistakes and flaws as much as for your gifts and talents, because you know you have everything in common with everyone. The need to hide dissolves with the release of self-judgment and clutter; with open space all around, visibility is normal and "no big deal."

There is a moment, though, when you realize you're becoming truly transparent, and it can stop you in your tracks, mouth agape. An element of awe—a stunning, mind-blowing quality—takes you over. You may have had all sorts of good ideas about who you are as a personality, but now you notice your vast, underlying, nonphysical self, the quiet one who's been riding in the back seat all this time. That You has been doing the backseat driving patiently, without nagging or yelling, just by using gentle, telepathic suggestion or by activating rapid, intuitive reflexes you didn't know you had. Now this You moves up front and takes the wheel, and your personality comes into perfect alignment with it. Now you-the-soul integrates fully with you-the-personality and there is just one unified You.

Transparency

Your attention focuses on simply being your honest, integrated self in each moment, and enjoying whatever aspect arises. You're not concerned with how others see you. Granting yourself permission to be any of the billions of ways humans can be, grants permission for others to do the same. That lack of pressure frees our collective good nature and goodwill.

As this revelation dawns, life unveils its previously hidden glory and magic, and you feel yourself as a beautiful—astoundingly beautiful—person with fathomless depths and kaleidoscopic light and color radiating constantly from your core. It's like becoming a narcissist but in the most positive, innocent, beneficial sense of that word. You may exclaim, "I just love myself!!" And you may be delighted to bask in your own energy. This is not ego, but the child being "full of it" and full of herself.

A SONG OF ME

I am hopelessly in love with myself!
I am hopelessly in love with myself!
I'm in love with myself
There's no hope, it's no joke
I'm in love, I'm in love, with myself!

There are others in my self besides myself!
There are others in my self besides myself!
There are others in my self besides myself!

Penney Peirce

When you are willing to be seen, you become acutely self-aware. The workings of the new integrated You become obvious. You notice what you notice and why you're noticing it. You observe yourself, see how you respond to situations, and decide if you want to improve the way you perceive life by filtering your observations through your home frequency. Self-observation helps you clear any last remnants of opacity and validate what enhances greater transparency. You increase your presence and engagement in each moment, giving your undivided attention to whatever or whoever is at hand.

Being Authentic

The more you show up, the more authentic you become. The more courageous you are about being visible, the more authentic you become. *Authenticity* is really the pure, honest, compassionate radiance of the soul from its home within the personality, which is composed of the physical body, the subtle-energy body, the emotions, and the mind. The more spirit-infused all these parts are, the more authentic and transparent you become. But how do you "know thyself" as the soul—especially when you're jettisoning your story and identity definitions, not listing your accomplishments and possessions, and breaking old habits? Where is the soul in the resulting empty space?

Finding you-the-soul in the vast openness of the unified field is perhaps a bit like discovering a hitherto invisible planet by tracking its effects on gravity, photons, and the behavior of known planets. To drill down through your outer crust to find the symptoms of your soul's presence, you might try any of the following.

1. **Look deeply into your core motivations.** Why do you do what you do? There are probably some universal, uplifting values that have been gently guiding you. To make money might seem a superficial motive, but underneath, it might be about understanding the materialization process, or learning to feel supported by and supportive of others. A burning desire to have children might be a way to make amends to people you abandoned in other lifetimes, or to develop a deeper experience of unconditional love. These are soul—not ego—goals.

    Sometimes these deeper motives are based on values or virtues that are inherent in your makeup and have been with you in many lifetimes; teachers and priests often having a "calling," for example, that's been with them since birth. We all know people who were born to make others laugh, or to bring beauty to the forefront of ordinary life, or to lead courageously, or to comfort and heal the deepest wounds. Our core motives are from the soul, and fear has no influence upon them.

2. **Make a list of things you always like to talk about and always like to do. What engages you so much that you lose track of time?** When does your enthusiasm bubble of its own accord? You probably liked to engage in these activities as a child and throughout your early years. See how these fascinations have evolved over time into more sophisticated forms. The repairman who fixed the complex parts in my broken refrigerator the other day told me he liked to rip old bicycles apart and rebuild wild new forms of vehicles when he was eight or nine, then he evolved to rebuild mainframe computers later on.

I was fascinated by assembly lines when I was six, created one in my bedroom to manufacture ornaments for a big tree branch I brought inside, and later became a corporate art director, managing dozens of design projects in varying stages of completion. The attraction to certain ideas and activities reveals a part of the creation cycle that gives you joy. Those ideas and actions bring forth key aspects of your core self. When you want to share ideas with others, the content is always close to your heart.

3. **Notice what bores you and what grabs your attention. When do you prick up your ears?** What themes are surfacing into your consciousness? What dreams have been floating around you? What visions of potential projects or creations? Strong attraction and strong aversion both point to character traits that are of key importance to you. If you notice something appalling, like a news clip of elephants being killed for their tusks, you may be directing your attention to your innate compassion and love of animals. If computers bore you, you may be directing your attention to your adventurous or artistic nature. Consider following those loves. The flow of your attention is a form of guidance from your soul that reveals more of who you are.

4. **Be alert to the balance and flow of your life experiences.** Let the personal feed the impersonal and the spiritual feed the physical. Notice when you need rest, action, concentration, staring-into-space time, social activity, alone time, more or less stimulation, or more or less left-brain or right-brain focus. Notice when your attention naturally moves from one interesting activity to another. You are wildly multifaceted! Communicate your needs to the people around you; they may benefit from helping you. Know your deal-breakers, yet question and revise them often. Your authenticity emerges when you flow in a constantly rebalancing way among the discrete areas of your life, so you feel connected and well-rounded.

5. **What does your home frequency feel like? What qualities does it exude?** When you're happy with yourself, proud of yourself, enjoying the moment, and open to surprise, what images, scenes, or memories come to mind? How would you describe the feeling state, sensations, and symbols connected with your preferred state? Does it feel innocent, sincere, cheerful, enthusiastic, sublime, or pure? Does it feel like silk, velvet, cool water, fresh air, effervescent bubbles, or soft fur? Does it seem like a triangle, circle, spiral, figure eight or a candle, crystal, white bird, or redwood tree? Tuning in to the feeling state of your home frequency allows you to access every part of your authentic self.

6. **Be totally quiet and still. Stop the internal dialogue. Be with the energy-and-consciousness inside you and around you.** Don't label or describe it, just fall in and merge with it. Allow yourself to feel the essential quality that's present. Stay with it beyond the point where your mind becomes restless or unconscious. Feel into the presence. You don't have to do anything with what you experience. You don't have to quantify it. If your mind jumps away, the state will be there, waiting, when you are quiet and still again. Saturate with presence.

7. **Make a list of qualities and traits you don't think you have. Imagine you do have them and feel what you'd be like then.** You might start by noticing things you envy or admire about other people. Or go the other direction: What irritates, bothers, or disturbs you to the

point of blame, anger, or retaliation? Either way, you may need these qualities to balance yourself and become more complete.

A mild-mannered, super-polite client of mine dreamed she looked in a mirror and the pop singer Madonna looked back at her. The nose was sharp, the eyebrows black, the lips fire-engine red, the eyes penetrating. Then she saw herself onstage in a brash, gold lamé bustier, prancing around, having a great time singing loudly into a microphone. Imagining Madonna's audacious character as part of herself immediately increased her confidence and willingness to show more of her unpredictable, creative side to others.

I think I'm most myself when I am writing a song because I'm trying to be honest with what's happening. I'm open. There would be times when I'd be struggling and when I'd get out of the way, the song would be there. In neon lights. Right in front of me.
John Denver

Being Seen & Known by Others

Most of us think no one can see us. When we're in a group or in public, the herd mentality focuses on the most dominating personality—the way lionesses prefer lions with black manes—whether that person has real character or is simply loud, abrasive, and outrageous. The rest of us, in comparison, might fade more into the background—and that fits with the idea many of us have that if we're too visible, too much will be expected of us, we might be in danger of losing our freedom, or we'll be put on the spot, humiliated, and rejected. So while becoming unnoticeable does meet certain fear-based needs, we still secretly want to be recognized.

When I changed from working corporate jobs in my twenties to "coming out" as an intuitive counselor and spiritual teacher, I was being truly authentic but many people, including my family, thought I was foolish or crazy, throwing away all the progress I'd made. For a number of years, my path forward was fraught with anxiety caused by feeling too visible in the wrong way. I wrote these little poems then.

Chapter 8: No Walls, No Secrets

when first I came into the open
I thought I was so naked the
very thought was cover all the cover
I had the thought was cover all the
cover I had the thought

• • •

be aware, the flight of bees the
swarming over all the
fields the
open skies the
neverending view of the
summer sun
Penney Peirce

When other people are transparent, however, they see and understand you—right off the bat—accurately, usefully, and in a way that allows your perfect self-expression. Around that same time period, I attended a weekend workshop by Robert Gass about self-expression, and as we lined up to leave the group space, he said something to each person. When it was my turn, he looked in my eyes and commented about how I looked so innocent but had deep wisdom (or some such thing), and I said, "Wow! I didn't realize anyone could see things like that about me." And he said, "Did it ever occur to you that you're very easy to see?" That simple sentence had an enormous impact on me; it helped me come out of my shell and dispelled my feelings of both invisibility and hypervisibility.

The more authentic you become, the more you like who you are, and the more you're willing to be seen and known by others. After you've seen your authentic, integrated self, unfiltered and undistorted, it turns out others can see you more easily as well. You allow this because there's nothing to hide—no worries, cover-ups, or projections to maintain. When you are transparent, you are tuned to truth; you can see and feel the authentic heart of anything—the most-real, ideal bird, daisy, song, horse, windowpane, cupcake, fighter jet, movie star, diamond, or wrinkled bag lady. Now you can simultaneously see the authentic, unified self in others too. Authenticity begets authenticity.

. . . .

Try This!
Write About Being Seen & Known

1. Imagine that others see your potential and encourage it, that they want you to be the best you can be. Feel how it might be if others supported you in expressing yourself fully and stretching beyond your comfort zone, if they didn't undermine or negate you. What if people see all the way to your soul and your innate talents and motives? Sit in that imagined reality and soak it up.

2. How might your present reality shift if this were the case? What new directions might you take? What new work and play routines might you try on? How might it change your relationships? Your energy level? What you think is possible?

3. Describe this new potential reality in your journal.

. . . .

Try This!
See & Be Seen

First try this with a partner. The person listening and being seen can take notes in a journal. After the exercise is finished, give your partner some feedback; you may be surprised by how much you actually do know about the other. Then exchange roles. You can also do the exercise as a meditation by imagining that you're the soul, and you're seeing into your personality, who is sitting across from you in a chair. Then exchange roles so you are the personality seeing and describing your soul.

1. Focus on the other person's energy-and-consciousness; feel it filling the space in front of you.
2. Describe three qualities of what their personal energy feels like on the outside as it radiates from them.
3. Describe three qualities of what their personal energy feels like deep inside them.
4. Describe three of their soul motivations in life.
5. Describe three hidden talents they have yet to discover and develop.
6. Give them three specific compliments they would love to receive.
7. Describe their true energy with sense words: color, music/sound, textures, odors, taste, etc.

. . . .

The Plus Side of Exposure

In To the Reader, I recounted the experience I had when I moved from California to Florida, to an area where I didn't seem to fit in. My mind was making the best of it, thinking I could expand my work more easily along the East Coast and in Europe, when my inner voice chimed in loudly, saying, "It's not about expansion, it's about exposure!" That statement popped a bubble of illusion for me. I saw I'd been indulging in the ideas—shared by so many—that life is difficult, that I am alone in the world and the world can be against me, that I need to practice caution and covert behavior to be safe, and that I need to use willpower to succeed.

In California, life had been fluid and effortless because there was so much agreement. But in Florida, it felt slightly "dangerous" to be known in my entirety. In spite of this, my inner guidance told me to relax and let myself be seen. Remove all the unconscious psychic shields and veils of invisibility. Show up for who I am. Be simple, don't promote myself, radiate my home frequency, keep my heart open, enjoy the people and the new culture, and be a clear space of calm and good humor.

As I practiced this, I saw how the lack of anxiety allowed my personal field to become like a star in the night sky. It was just shiny, just being itself—without being pushy or forceful. Without the "trying," my field could stand out without irritating or confronting anyone. And the calmness allowed my energy-and-consciousness to permeate through the "ethers" and reach far, without effort. Those of like vibration could easily find me. Those who didn't need me, wouldn't notice me. It was a more refined version of something I had done when I began my work as a spiritual teacher.

Before I went to sleep, I used to imagine a lighthouse up above my bed, penetrating into the higher realms. Its beacon revolved around and around, letting people know where I was and what I was offering. I used to set it in motion and let it run continuously—but now I realized that the frequency of my authenticity and transparency would do all the work. If I felt like creating new venues or networking, fine; it was just another fun thing to do. I noticed that opportunities were now coming to me more readily, emerging straight from the field around me, and seemingly without a cause in the physical world.

One result of allowing yourself to be seen, or exposed, is that the way you achieve what you want changes. As I described above, marketing and promotion transform. You no longer need to try to make yourself attractive via clever use of description and convincing claims, or amp yourself up with a positive charge. When you allow yourself to be available and undefended, you don't need to use willpower and intention to be successful. Instead, connections to what you desire are taken care of by the unified field, the Flow, and the natural inclination of all souls in the collective consciousness to receive and give what's needed. It doesn't mean you don't make phone calls, take out an ad, make a great website, write a super resumé, or share with others in social conversations. Those things are ceremonial acts that validate the reality you're imagining and ground it into reality. It's "stuff to do"—but with full enjoyment—that's in alignment with your vision.

The power of exposure begins in the nonphysical realms as a state of being entirely open, and it translates into a tactile feeling of presence that your body recognizes as deep comfort and that other people sense as real, confident, and competent. What makes you noticeable is not adolescent hijinks or me-me-me behavior, but alignment and coherence between your personality and soul—that quiet merger that results in an integrated self. All this occurs without willpower by simply asking, revealing, enjoying action, and focusing your attention.

> Art lies in the moment of encounter: we meet our truth and we meet ourselves; we meet ourselves and we meet our self-expression. We become original because we become something specific . . . As we gain—or regain—our creative identity, we lose the false self we were sustaining.
>
> Julia Cameron

Another effect of being exposed is that your creativity increases. Seeing your integrated self, without negative self-concepts and judgments, reveals the unlimited nature of creativity and the vastness of the imaginal realm—because your soul lives in the imaginal realm; this is its element. Your integrated self (your soul merged with your earthly personality) brings this knowledge into the physical world and allows the soul's motive to surface and flow as it wishes; the soul loves, loves, loves to translate nonphysical combinations of variables and ideas into their form version.

What will the inner blueprint look like when it materializes? Here is the joy, the fascination with the magic of incarnation—having a lifetime on earth is not about suffering! And it's just as fascinating to create space and emptiness, watching form dissolve once again into energy-and-consciousness to become the raw material for new creations. When you realize how much you adore creativity, you see everything in life as a creative act and are always ready to jump in.

When you allow others to see your forms of creativity, the people who resonate to your sensibility and find beauty and meaning in what you create can locate you and use your creations. Or they can emerge from the field to cocreate with you. My friend Carol Adrienne had written several books on numerology and had ghostwritten a few other books when her agent contacted her about another project. It was Carol's ability to tell good stories and organize material clearly and fluidly that made her agent think of her when she needed someone to cowrite the experiential guide for James Redfield's blockbuster, *The Celestine Prophecy*. Carol met with Redfield and proceeded to write that experiential guide with him—and the next one too. Her confidence increased and she felt empowered to draw on more of her own wisdom to write *The Purpose of Your Life* and several more of her own books over the next few years. And that brought her to the attention of Oprah Winfrey, who invited her to be a guest on her television show.

I was amazed at how Carol's process unfolded so effortlessly, yet it was in large part because she was so authentic, positive, in the Flow, and willing to be seen. In her book *When Life Changes or You Wish It Would*, she says, "Writing had never been on my list of things to do with my life, but I was following my intuition, and the universe was responding. Today I can see how each change of circumstance was forcing me to grow—even when all I wanted was to stay safe. Your inner state of being is always working to fulfill your destiny, and you have the best chance to receive new ideas and a broader perspective when you are relaxed, open, and empowered by the belief that your life can and will change for the better."[1]

> If you do not tell the truth about yourself
> you cannot tell it about other people.
> Virginia Woolf

Seeing & Being Seen in the Bridge Time

We must remember how ultrasensitive and telepathic we all are, and how we feel into each other constantly to read each other and to sense what's safe or dangerous. The more transparent you are, the more conscious the process and the more comprehensive the insights. The less transparent, the more unconscious the process and the more narrow the bandwidth. When you become practiced in the ways of the transparent reality and can allow yourself to be seen and to see others accurately, yet are still living and working with people who aren't there yet, some challenging situations can arise. It helps to be prepared.

1. **You have less in common with others, at least for a while.** When you're transparent and clear of clutter, you can see the soul in others, but they often don't see you accurately because of the clutter they still hold. You notice you don't have much in common with them because they're still focusing on the clutter, not what's beyond the clutter. You can't relate to commiserating about how bad things are. You don't agree with all the good reasons people limit themselves, or with the assumptions they hold about how results will occur, or how long it takes to change or heal, or how certain things are impossible. It takes patience and consistency to hold others "in the Light," see the soul's view, and convey that to them telepathically and kinesthetically.

2. **People may think you're naïve and looking through rose-colored glasses.** When partially transparent people see you when you allow yourself to be exposed, they may think you're powerless, insignificant, and ridiculous because you don't project ego, which they associate with confidence and capability. If you don't stimulate their adrenaline response, they may not respect you. If you don't take sides, they may think you're wishy-washy instead of wise. And where there is a more extreme contrast in frequency between you and others, they may not be able to see you at all. This requires full presence from you, so that in each situation you can sense what might be said, whether something is worth pursuing or not, and if there is a potential teaching moment at hand. Always, with misinterpretation or partial perception, patience, kindness, and simple, clear communication are your best friends.

3. **People may attack, reject, or abandon you.** When you are exposed and transparent, you're holding nothing in particular in your space. You're not broadcasting opinions and beliefs, nor are you trying to sell people on your value to them. They feel into you but don't find what they expect to find. They're looking for that familiar

interplay of resonances—matching frequencies, validation of beliefs, or commiseration—where they can feel safe because you match their clutter.

If there's nothing to match, they become confused, even frantic. They don't know how to know you. Encountering openness is frightening to them and when there is no agreement, the left brain switches into fight-or-flight mode. They may react by feeling rejected because you're not meeting them halfway, or think you're making them "wrong," or that you're hiding something, or are dangerous in some mysterious way. Then it's easy for them to distance themselves—by attacking or belittling you, or rejecting and abandoning you. If possible, you can explain your point of view in a non-oppositional framework, and look for those teaching moments.

4. **People project their own clutter issues onto you.** When you allow yourself to be seen for who you are, with no defenses, holding no beliefs or fixed ideas about identity, some people who still hold this sort of clutter may see a distorted version of you—one that matches their own limited perception of themselves and the way life works. Their clutter is what they pay attention to—it's a filter that stands between them and the larger world, coloring their view. It's their first line of identity and just as looking through blue-tinted sunglasses gives the world a blue hue, so a lack of self-worth, for example, can make the world seem critical, uncaring, or just plain mean.

It's easy, then, for the other person to assign their clutter to you. As water flows downhill, so clutter flows into the empty space. They don't want to own it, so it must be yours! They may blame you for something they themselves are struggling with and assume that *you are their own negativity.* You can serve them by allowing it all to be, and not reacting or validating the misperception, so they can eventually see it, allow it, and clear it. If you react and contract, it just makes them hold more tightly to their contractions. But take away resistance, and opposition becomes silly and useless.

5. **If you're still clearing some of your own clutter but are mostly clear, other people's reactions can stall you.** You may remember that it often takes three times of centering into your home frequency to clear a subconscious block and convince the body that contraction is not normal. The third time grappling with the issue is often a test, where the last remnants of your doubt are called forth by someone who challenges you. They act out the very behavior and belief you're in the process of clearing, as if to say, "See? This really is the way it is. Are you sure you want to change things?" You must remember what you're doing, complete the recentering, and avoid investing attention in the challenge.

   Also, when you allow your "flaws" to be seen—negativity, dark secrets, embarrassing mistakes, spinach in your teeth, and all—some people will validate that about you. They'll point out what you're doing wrong, accuse you of misdeeds, and reinforce any old, self-effacing beliefs. They may be jealous that you're getting rid of your clutter and getting ahead of them, and they don't want to be abandoned. They want you to remain weak or wounded so they can feel comfortable being weak and wounded too. Or they want to feel above it all: "You have problems and I don't." If you believe them, it stalls your growth. Continue being vulnerable and letting go of what's not true about you.

6. **If you allow yourself to be seen for your good stuff, people may try to sabotage you.** Part of being exposed and transparent is allowing people to see both your imperfections *and* your talents. In the bridge time, people who are caught in lack of self-worth and separated from their beautiful soul may feel jealous or frightened when they see soul and excellence embodying and expressing in someone else. They may not be able to sense the difference between simple, joyful, overflowing self-expression and ego-expression that wants attention, specialness, and power over others. When we're blocked or stuck, we're caught in ego—whether we feel we're more than or less than others. Then it's hard to see talent as something everyone

has, and the left brain moves into polarized better-or-worse mode, which can lead to attack mode.

. . . .

Try This!

How Do You Deal with Being Seen?

1. In your journal, write about times you've felt inhibited, shy, or overly self-conscious and bottled up. What were the underlying worries? What were the underlying negative self-judgments or self-doubts? What did you not want others to see about you? Go deeper and look back to see where those doubts or judgments came from: Who influenced you? What were their limiting beliefs and self-judgments?

2. Imagine dissolving your underlying hesitations and contractions. Just let all that go and be neutral; you don't have to be any certain way. Imagine that when people can see you, it doesn't call forth the old worries, doubts, or judgments. Imagine basking in the attention, allowing spontaneous self-expression to come from both the seer and you.

3. Now write about times you've been dramatic, a show-off, audacious, funny, onstage, or bigger than life. Certainly some of these times were spontaneous, but other times you may have acted as a way to distract or please people. What were your underlying motivations? What did you want others to see, or not see, about you? Was there a compulsion to act? Was there a devil-may-care attitude?

4. Imagine dissolving the need to be seen in a certain way and the motive to dominate the space. When you allow yourself to be seen for who you really are, you can be self-expressive in any number of ways. Go deeper and find the origins of your motives: Who or what influenced you? Imagine that when you allow yourself to be seen, it doesn't call up the need to perform. How would you express yourself if you didn't have to do it a certain way?

. . . .

Chapter 8: No Walls, No Secrets

I was speaking with a friend recently about what authenticity and transparency really mean. She brought up the notion that some public and political figures espouse ideas that come from a core place of fear, embodying states like anger, control, domination, isolation, or aggression, but those ideas seem to be in keeping with their personalities. Does that mean they're authentic? When public figures and celebrities "show up" on the national and international scene, they are supposedly allowing themselves to be seen and exposed. Does that make them transparent?

My take on these questions is that when someone's words align with their personality, they are expressing themselves honestly to the level of their current consciousness, but they may still be steeped in the opaque reality, disconnected from soul. That makes them authentic narcissists, perhaps, but not truly authentic, because true authenticity is the soul shining forth from within the personality, driving the car from the front seat. People who are also steeped in the opaque reality will sense these public figures as authentic because there's agreement, or frequency-matching, among them all.

These same people, when seeing public figures open themselves to scrutiny and watching their secrets surface and their flaws be exaggerated or downplayed, may either vilify them or put them up on a pedestal, depending on their own polarized opinions. The celebrities have not cleared their clutter and are probably gritting their teeth to get through the exposure period, using public-relations people to spin their image. So, no—they are not transparent. People who have cleared themselves and are truly authentic and transparent—His Holiness the Dalai Lama comes to mind—are seen by most people accurately, without a positive or negative charge.

Another thing we talked about was the idea that when you get rid of your clutter—say, your personal story or fixed opinions—are you just an empty shell? Can people recognize you? Do they see you as boring? Do you hesitate to have opinions from that point on, or to talk about your personal history, or to have talents that you call your own? My sense of this is that *clearing clutter is about releasing attachments to ideas and behaviors, not getting rid of the ideas and behaviors.* When you don't need something for identity or safety, you can have it or not have it, whichever is most useful.

You are free to be any way you like, to think any thought, act any way, speak about anything—without needing to attach your consciousness permanently to any pattern. You don't need to define your identity; your identity forms itself moment to moment by what arises from the Flow and passes through you. You engage, materialize, or dematerialize some form, then be, then create again. The Flow guides what comes to and through you. You don't need to nail it down or preserve anything, since everything is always available.

So, no, you're not empty, or boring, or afraid to think certain thoughts or take certain actions. Instead, you're playful. A spontaneous flow of new creative content arises constantly. You can tell your story for entertainment purposes and have your talents for the joy of soul-based creativity. It's the attachment that creates the clutter. It's releasing and allowing everything to be that creates transparency.

> For now we see through a glass, darkly; but then face-to-face:
> now I know in part; but then shall I know even as also I am known.
> The Bible, I Corinthians 13:12

The Power of Seeing Through

It's so interesting how transparency works. Not only can you see yourself when you open, relax, show up fully, and allow vulnerability to be natural, but that empowers others to see more of you—and of themselves. On the other hand, when you're open, exposed, and undefended without even trying, you can see through layers of interference or illusions of opacity in people and situations that used to stop you. You have Superman's X-ray vision!

If another person is hiding behind a wall of clutter, you can still see their soul, their deep life motivations, how their wounds and contractions formed, why they're caught in fear, how they might clear their fear, and what their potential is. You can see whether someone will be able to frequency-match you or if they'll be stuck in resistance. You can see through the lies and subterfuges because they stand out like neon at night.

Even now, when most of us are still partially transparent, if we relax and soften our eyes and hearts, we do see through—information about others or various situations appears mysteriously from the background. We suddenly "just have a feeling" or our little voice says, "This is a con man," or "This is someone with an authentic connection to the truth," or "This situation will drain my energy." Even now, we know things we don't have a logical reason to know. With full transparency, when your X-ray vision activates, seeing through to important information is much more matter-of-fact, because you accept that you have access to all knowledge. You're able to know more, and that becomes natural—but do you feel overwhelmed by too much data? No!

Transparency allows your perception to be precise; you know that the present moment regulates the scope of your zoom lens and need directs the flow of attention. Your perception is more efficient; it goes to the heart of what's most appropriate. You don't miss the important insights about relationships and creative endeavors, and you penetrate into the just-right way of acting. You see more holistically because you're integrated within yourself.

You might think, too, that if you can see through other people's clutter, you might disturb them by stirring up their fears and self-protective behaviors—just by the act of touching those ideas with your attention. Of course, when you're transparent, you're touching everything you see with compassion and understanding, so seeing through someone's clutter isn't uncomfortable to them or dangerous to you—if you do it without judgment. In fact, it can help them accept themselves. Transparency facilitates telepathy, empathy, clairvoyance, and clairsentience, so when someone places loving attention on your foibles, you get the idea—via a kind of osmosis—that you can love these parts too. Seeing through someone this way, with the soul's vision, can facilitate rapid transformation.

*If you begin to understand what you are without trying to change it,
then what you are undergoes a transformation.*
Jiddu Krishnamurti

Seeing Through Defense Mechanisms

I spoke with a psychologist recently who had been working to help people see through their defense mechanisms and clear them. He said people needed to see past their automatic, unconscious, reactionary behavior to isolate the defense mechanism, then see it as a friend, that the defense mechanism had been helping them in some way. When they could befriend their habitual reaction instead of resisting it, they could then see through to what was underneath.

A man who flew into rages at his wife and family first needed to acknowledge that rage was his defense mechanism; he had been seeing it as a normal part of his personality that he'd inherited from his family, a logical response to ignorant behaviors by others. By seeing through that, he discovered that rage had helped him by distracting him from a painful belief that he was not good enough for them. Penetrating further, he saw that under the belief was a feeling of terror, that if his family saw who he really was, they'd abandon him.

By seeing rage as a protective mechanism instead of vilifying or rationalizing it, he was able to move into the deeper experience of the anticipated experiences of terror and abandonment. As he went through these realities in his imagination, he found that being alone wasn't frightening; on the contrary, it brought him back to himself in a neutral way so he could feel his own goodness. After that, when he imagined his family seeing who he really was, he felt comfortable. He could allow them to have their responses and their own experiences without trying to distance or manipulate them with his rage. And he realized, finally, that they had no desire to leave him. The rage no longer had a purpose, so it dissolved.

Another client, a woman, had been suicidal for many years. Penetrating into the defense mechanism—the threat of suicide—she discovered it had been her friend because it acted as a pressure-release valve. As long as she felt she had a way out, she didn't have to really kill herself, and she could face her current difficulties for a time. Seeing through the suicidal thoughts, she penetrated into a belief that she was inadequate and unprepared for life on earth. As she saw through that belief, she found a terror that revolved around paralysis and helplessness. By not making the suicidal motive into a monster, she could let it go and move into the deeper experience of finding presence and competence inside herself. She could feel how it would be to trust her own common sense, take appropriate actions, and break her addiction to being overwhelmed.

> In the stone that waits the turning
> Of some curious hand, from sight
> Fiery atoms may be burning,
> That would fill the world with light.
> Alice Cary

What Can You See Through *To*?

When we talk about seeing through and penetrating into, let's pay attention to what we're seeing through *to*. What's the end result? When you see through a defense mechanism, you don't stop at the intimidating behavior but go right on into the underlying misperception about life and through that to the path back to harmony. When you see through people's fear-based actions, motives, and secrets, you're really aiming for their sweet vulnerability, inner beauty, and magnificence—and you find their soul. When you see through a flower, you move into the form, and even the color and scent, to experience the sensual exposure of how the flower offers itself freely to the world. It reminds you of a way to be.

Seeing through is intimately connected to "feeling into" and "merging with"—it's a function of a desire for universal truth. To do it, you maintain your attention on what you're observing a little bit longer, then a little bit longer. The more thoroughly you pay attention, without willfully "pressing into" what you're being with, the more is revealed and the closer you get to the deep truth inside. The end of seeing through anything is the reconnection with essence—the recognition of kinship and the One Self in everything—along with the lovely feeling of resting in the elegant workings of the universal principles.

Seeing through and feeling into is not a habit many people have yet. In the opaque reality, it seems impossible, unwise, exhausting, and even dangerous to try to see through the density. Our attention keeps stopping at the limitations, negative emotions, excuses, distractions, misperceptions, wounds, and shocks. If we go further, it seems we'll either lose control and go crazy, or someone will attack us.

Many people who work with intuition, for example, only notice the emergence of the insight (surprise!) as it comes into left-brain territory and becomes mental—they don't go all the way into the imaginal realm to merge with the right-brain process of how an idea moves forward from the background and what the insight knows at its deepest level. Instead, they grab the descriptive words and don't "become" the insight—thus they miss the direct experience of the many hidden nuances contained in the pattern that underlies the idea. But with transparency, you focus on seeing through—all the way. This connects you to an expanded experience of trust in the Flow. You can see through many superficial things to find the deeper knowledge. Here are some possibilities.

1. **You can see through ignorance.** Underneath "I don't know" is the sense that "Somewhere inside me, I do know; some part of me already knows." When you see ignorance, you create a block and focus on what you can't know or haven't learned. Focusing on ignorance keeps you ignorant; seeing through and beyond ignorance helps dissolve it. You choose an attitude that says, "All knowledge is available to me in the Now. When I want or need it, it comes to me and I engage with it. I know what I need to know right when I need to know it. If I don't know something right now, I can when I want to. Knowledge is natural to me, and what I choose to create in the physical world will pull the exact right amount of knowledge to and through me. In fact, I am capable of genius."

2. **You can see through problems.** Just stopping at the problem and wrestling with it keeps it as a barrier. Seeing through a problem is about discovering why you stopped your attention at this particular point in the creation cycle. What is the real question or issue underneath the problem? If your car needs new tires, you may be dealing with the issue of safely and smoothly moving forward in some aspect of your life. What has been holding you back? Seeing through that hesitation returns you to the Flow and opens new creativity. Perhaps you realize you want to move to a new city to find a better job and that—big revelation!—you don't have to stay put to take care of your parents, who aren't really having any problems. Suddenly, making a big change seems totally doable. Seeing through the problem took you to fluidity and innovation.

3. **You can see through illusions, like death and suffering.** Paying attention, feeling into, and seeing through the experience of death reveals a whole different understanding. Just stopping at the idea of death as an ending keeps you opaque. With transparency, death becomes a transformational experience of freedom and joy, a return to full memory of your soul's path and the workings of the universe.

   Stopping at the idea of suffering creates and reinforces the experience of pain. But seeing through it reveals how fearful attachment and contraction create suffering, and how agreement with suffering maintains it. Seeing through these insights reveals deeper understanding—suffering is not normal to the soul, it doesn't exist at higher frequencies, and you don't need to engage with it.

4. **You can see through the present reality.** When you look only at what exists, you may forget that what you have is a result of what you asked for previously. You may forget how easy it is to change things, and that reality is not set in stone. Seeing through present circumstances frees you to fall headlong into the imaginal realm, the world of all possibilities. Seeing through what you have lets you create something even more original and authentic; it reminds you how fluid life is and how multifaceted you are. Seeing through

your present reality allows the effortless emergence of innate talents you've yet to realize you have.

> One eye sees, the other feels.
> **Paul Klee**

5. **You can see through your life story and goals.** Living your life story and pursuing logical goals may not be enough. Seeing through this outer layer reveals the wisdom of your soul's path. You've been learning what you needed to learn and now you're ready for more. Under the events and accomplishments of your life are the experiences that taught you about the power and usefulness of both sides of life's many polarities, like balance and imbalance, conflict and harmony, self-awareness and other-awareness, generosity and support, and self-development and self-sacrifice. You see the fine-line distinctions between hoarding and receiving, dissolving and destruction, abandonment and moving on, and seduction and resonance.

   You feel the soul's goals, the wisdom and purposefulness of each noticing and choice. Instead of stopping at the struggles, failures, and successes, you see through to the more impactful lessons you set up for yourself. You see through your "mistakes" to the soul's ability to trick you into learning more, and through your "flaws" to the soul's wisdom in temporarily restraining certain character traits to emphasize others.

6. **You can see through matter.** If you only see matter, you're limited to the opaque reality. When you see through solidity, you enter the realm of energy, where everything vibrates at its own frequency in a sea of vibration. You experience the principles of resonance, attunement, dissonance, frequency-matching, oscillation, and flow. You enter the realm of consciousness, where every frequency is a kind of knowledge and a reality. You experience the end of boundaries and separation, the reality of expanding your scope to include more energy-and-consciousness, and you see that at every level, you are

what you include and bring attention to. Seeing through all that, you find a stillness filled with what love really is. And you know it's you and that it's the true identity of every *one* and every *thing*.

7. **You can see through time and space.** When you practice spherical-holographic perception, you see through the illusion that time is fragmented into past, present, and future. You expand to a state beyond that linear construct, where both past and future are contained inside your sphere and are a current part of you. There are infinite realities in unified time—all at different frequencies. Match your consciousness totally to any of those frequencies and you can slide into that reality.

When you see through time to its unlimited nature, you also see through space—because they are flip sides of the same coin, just as energy and consciousness are. All space is contained within you, and the way space materializes into place is also related to frequencies. As you learn to materialize realities, they automatically include time, space, and place. From your earthly viewpoint within your current reality, when you're transparent, your clairvoyant abilities skyrocket, and you can see into other places at great distances.

> Dig within. Within is the wellspring of Good; and it is always ready to bubble up, if you just dig.
> Marcus Aurelius

The Ethics of Seeing Through

At first, being seen and seeing through bring tremendous levels of vulnerability for both you and others in this challenging bridge time. Seeing what you haven't wanted to see, either in yourself or others, is a confrontation that has typically resulted in fight or flight. Becoming transparent and facing your fears and flaws in a calm way takes courage, consistency, commitment, and compassion. If you react to fear with fear, you perpetuate fear. If you assign the cause of disturbing energy to another person, you perpetuate disturbances. If you resign yourself to living in the cesspool, you perpetuate the cesspool.

I believe the positive way to clear the clutter that relates to being seen and seeing through is what is really meant by *ethics*. Ethics are not about the left brain's right-or-wrong morality; they're about what aligns with universal principles to bring increased harmony, love, and wisdom. When you want to see through a person or situation ethically, but encounter blockages and disturbances in the Flow, practice any of the following.

1. **Don't stop at the blockages. See through to the soul and the truer vision.** You can always come back later to deal with the clutter; don't get stuck in it on your way to the truth. It's important to see the bigger picture first so you have the correct context for seeing the real purpose of the blockage or current challenging situation. You know when you hit clutter because it will likely activate one of your own defense mechanisms. Your mind might blank out, or you might feel antsy, slightly nauseous, or tight through the stomach, chest, or throat. Notice what's happening, stay present, and keep seeing through, feeling into, and looking for the Light inside—find the peaceful insight that indicates heart and soul. .

2. **Stay out of accusation.** When you see through to fear, it's easy to become captive of either-or thinking. Your worldview can shrink down to the gunslinger mentality: "This town ain't big enough for the both of us!" If you're in either-or thinking, you can project the problem you've encountered onto the situation or another person and indulge in inequality and conflict perception. You move into right or wrong, safe or dangerous, good or bad, better or worse. With your attention absorbed in this useless, energy-draining, polarity consciousness, you temporarily backslide into the opaque reality.

3. **Remember the relationship entity!** If you're seeing through a person, situation, or problem, there are always at least two of you participating—you and another person, you and a problem, or you and a whole situation. Your reality blends with the other, forming a unified body of knowledge containing both the shared fear-based issues and the *shared* soul-based wisdom. You can more easily shift into both-and

thinking when you realize: "You're afraid of being too visible in one way, and I'm afraid of exposure in another way. You're impatient for results, and I'm ahead of myself, wanting something beyond what I have now. You don't understand me, and I haven't taken time to really understand you. We are occurring in each other's reality because we're alike!" If it's a situation or a process, you might realize: "It's snagged because I'm allowing myself to be fragmented. It's chaotic and over-whelming because I'm not focusing on what's important, and I've lost my center. It's not completing successfully because I'm bored with the involvement; it's not on purpose for me."

When you can see through the commonly held clutter without blaming or taking on blame, you reach the shared soul-based wis-dom: "Aha! There's something about you and me that fits together to create a greater experience or result than either of us might find alone. We are making some key insights conscious that we both need. The situation (or problem) and I are actually helping each other."

4. **Fix whatever you see—in yourself first.** When you clear your share of the clutter and create transparency in yourself, you can see through to the soul or heart of the matter. And the other person sharing the blockages may suddenly become aware of their version of the clutter and clear it. Or it may seem overwhelming to them—too much for one person to bear. They may try to project it all onto you but if you don't receive it, they have to own it. They'll have to choose which reality they want. To stick their head in the sand, make you wrong, and realize the clutter keeps following them around? Or drop the clutter and match you in a higher state?

You don't have to try to change the other person at all. Remove your own version of the shared blockages, hold the other person inside your clear field, and they can choose clearly. If they're ready, they'll shift gently, and sometimes rapidly, into a more optimal expression.

5. **Visualize and feel the soul and the spiritually based reality.** When you see through the clutter and arrive at the open, fluid, inspired,

soul-based experience of a person (or situation), stop a moment and feel deeply into it. Merge with it, let yourself become it, and it become you. Know it intimately. Feel the innate consciousness and purpose, and from that feeling state allow a vision to arise that represents the ideal expression of what wants to happen. In that vision is information about what, why, and how. Gently hold the vision and feeling state, and offer it telepathically to the other or others.

6. **Describe, represent, or communicate what you've seen through to.** Go ahead—say it out loud! Or draw a picture, create a design, arrange flowers, write a poem, or facilitate a celebratory gathering. Make your deep dive into the truth real and physical in some way. When you share something, it becomes more real for you, and it attracts the attention of others. And remember, attention is the force that materializes results. Remember, too, that your word is law in your universe, and what you describe in declarative sentences acts as an invocation with solidifying power.

7. **Always use empathy and compassion.** When seeing through anything, keep your frequency at the level of compassion. *Compassion is the new evolutionary force, the driver of expanded understanding, the connection to miracles.* Compassion sees not the mistakes we make but the sincerity and vulnerability behind the mistakes. It focuses on innocence and innate goodness, the ease of healing, the inevitability of genius, the heart-melting beauty, and the ecstasy of creating from and with spirit.

With transparency, it's OK to know both the surface and the depths of other people; we see with compassion, understanding, and acceptance. There is no need for shame or guilt, secrets or lies. When everything is seen, there is acceptance and acknowledgment of the possibility for every kind of human experience and creation, whether contracted or expanded. There is no right or wrong, just what works elegantly and joyfully and what doesn't. We see the good reasons for underlying pain and for how we "medicate" ourselves with behaviors to heal. There is a simple preference for what aligns with universal principles because this is the soul's delight.

Chapter 8: No Walls, No Secrets

The Universe should be deemed an immense Being, always
living, always moved, and always moving in an eternal activity
inherent in itself, and which, subordinate to no foreign cause, is
communicated to all its parts, connects them together, and makes
the world of things a complete and perfect whole.
Albert Pike

Just to Recap...

When you become transparent, you can see yourself from your soul's point
of view. You accept your flaws as temporary—as simple mistakes of perception—and the negative charge goes away. You see your beauty, talent,
latent talents, and innate wisdom. You *love* yourself, but it's not about ego;
it's the way a child behaves when she's "full of herself" and naturally joyful. You enjoy spending time with yourself. You become truly authentic.
When this occurs, you allow others to see you as you are, without shame
or embarrassment. You also become self-aware to a heightened degree,
observing why and how you think, act, and interact. This helps you show
up even more as your soul-in-your-personality—your integrated self. Since
it's not easy to sense exactly what "soul" is, there are a number of ways you
can tune in to find the "symptoms of soul" when you lose touch.

Seeing into yourself allows others to see you. When you decide it's
OK to be "exposed," you allow others to have their own responses and
to understand what you're all about. If people are transparent, they "get
you" right away—all the way to the soul level. If other people are partially
transparent, they may have a distorted view of you and project their own
clutter onto you. There are challenges for you to face in this, but there are
also ways to maintain your clarity without offending or hurting others.
You discover that, with transparency, others can find you more easily,
without the effort of promoting yourself with willpower, cleverness, and
overly positive hype. Your creativity increases, as you open to include the
entire imaginal realm.

When you allow yourself to be seen, you can see through the illusions, subterfuges, and inaccuracies in other people and situations. You

develop Superman's X-ray vision! You can see through to the underlying, fear-based clutter, understand how it got there and how it can be cleared, and see further into the true core of a person's (or situation's) potential and purpose. It's important not to stop at the clutter and be sucked into the negativity; if you do, you just re-create the opaque reality for yourself. You need to pay attention to what's possible to see through *to*. Keep penetrating and you arrive at an amazing, visionary understanding of the ideal state of everything. You learn to practice a kind of ethics when seeing through; there are a number of practices that promote alignment with universal principles, harmony, and wisdom, and minimize misunderstanding.

Transparency Message
WHAT'S EVIDENT

Being transparent, what shows up? Everything and nothing. You shimmer with your ideas, where your attention goes, your field lights to reveal it. You can be as bright as igniting magnesium and as deep and dark as the purple-black, new-moon night sky. As cool as an Arctic lake, as warm as a bundled baby. Shift your gaze and the light goes from one place to another, particles dissociate and reconvene, forms dissolve and reappear, morphed by new frequencies, pliable as liquid clay. The forms follow your desire, just to please you, to serve you. And you: you can be invisible or visible depending on how much attention you place on and in yourself.

Watch your world arising and subsiding as you walk along. You are not simply passing some objects, they are changing in partnership with your imagination. This world is about companionship. If you show up, you can play. Showing

Chapter 8: No Walls, No Secrets

up, bringing full presence into time and space, is about your love of the experiment of three dimensions, your love of earth as your sponsor and teacher.

What's evident when you are transparent? Your love, your commitment to fullness, your willingness to engage with the Flow, with the collective Soul in cocreation. You show for your own long history that's entirely alive in the Now, and in that history are the gifts you gave and the mistakes you allowed your mind to make so you could have particular kinds of experiences and watch how the effects of your creativity cascaded through groups, across space, and through evolution. You see the births and deaths of all your personalities and how you lost memory or retained it by your focus on separation or unity. All the personalities you created are still alive, interconnected, and learning from each other. And all the beings you've known—family, friends, and enemies—are interconnected in a great ball of yarn.

You can love the outer show and see it for what it is: the faithful servant of your imagination. Form manifests for you and dematerializes for you. You can live in it without being captive of it. You can light up matter from within, giving it a glow, making it supremely happy. When you love matter, it loves you back and comes and goes with your internal breezes. When you leave matter, thank it. When you rejoin matter, greet it as a long lost friend. The truth is, it's You you thank and welcome.

Being transparent: you understand honor and respect for all beings, all frequencies, all realities. You play, you create joyfully, and you are serious, not heavy, but fully attentive to your choice to live in a physical, emotional, mental world. You notice emptiness and become it, and notice fullness and become that. One day you will have had enough and you will move on into total union and Awareness. You will lose everything and gain everything in the permanent heart. And you will know you've always been there.

9

The New Normal:
Being Transparent in a Transparent World

On our planet and perhaps simultaneously in many parts of our galaxy and beyond, consciousness is awakening from the dream of form. This does not mean all forms (the world) are going to dissolve, although quite a few most certainly will. It means consciousness can now begin to create form without losing itself in it.

Eckhart Tolle

Imagine you're standing in a doorway. You've just left a big space you know well and are about to take that first step into a totally new place. You turn and face sideways so the old space is to your left and the new territory is to the right. You pause a long moment to consider, allowing yourself the luxury of feeling unbiased and neutral. If you lean to the left you can feel the familiar old reality. You remember how slow it is; how linear, logical, opaque, and sticky with negative emotional energy; how much misunderstanding there is; how much pain and suffering; how much competition and one-upsmanship. Time there is fragmented and seems to change with personal will. You're used to it, though, even if it *is* difficult and full of stress. Even if remembering who you really are is nearly impossible over there.

If you lean to the right, you can begin to feel the new reality. It's an unusual feeling—clear, like mountain air. At first, you can't see anything. There is no resistance, yet there are currents of energy spiraling about, whooshing and falling into lulls, jumping into action, and relaxing into satisfaction. There are patterns of light forming and unforming, as easily as clouds. And those patterns quickly materialize into their parallel physical forms and dematerialize again, always at the right moment. There's an odd sense of welcome over here, a comfortable feeling of safety and encouragement, of freedom and readily offered service. There is no sacrifice, just a sense that every action fits perfectly with a higher vision. The people here are relaxed in their experience of being themselves and liking themselves; there is no need for hiding, creating lies, or protecting secrets. Everything can be known, and that's fine.

You center yourself in the doorway again. Then you lean to the left and recall the feeling of that old, familiar reality. And back to the neutral center. Then you lean right and dip back into the new, transparent, frictionless reality. It's unfamiliar to your body yet deeply familiar to who you really are. It's not magical; it actually seems like it could be normal. Your skeptical mind isn't quite sure it could be real, though. Then back to the neutral center. *Hmmm.* Which direction do you choose? Back to what's difficult but familiar? Or on to what's yet to be discovered—the place where fluidity, trust, exposure, and harmony feel like the order of the day?

Try on the idea of *deciding* to move into the new, transparent reality. Turn and face the new world. As you prepare to step over the threshold, allow your mind to present you with any fears, hesitations, or "yes, buts" about the change. What might they be? Are you afraid you might not know how to act when you get there? Like you have to be perfect before you take on something like this? Perhaps this new world is a kind of death! What might happen to you? Are you worried you could never go back? Or are you worried about the people you'd leave behind? If your loved ones aren't ready to go with you, will you lose them forever? Are there enough people in the new reality? Will you be all alone?

For now, let these concerns go and trust your sense that the core experience of the new reality is a huge relief. Let your intuition be accurate about what's better and trust that answers will come when you get there. Then step beyond the threshold into the transparent reality.

Take a moment to acclimate; let your body and sensitivity adjust. Turn around to look back through the door. Surprise! The door is no longer there, and neither is the wall separating you from the old reality. The new, transparent reality has expanded to include the old one. All your loved ones are now in the new reality with you; you can still connect with them, no matter what their frequency is. And lo and behold, there are many other people on your wavelength in the new reality—they've been waiting for you! You haven't lost anyone or anything. What's different is you realize you don't have to frequency-match a vibration that's lower than you prefer, but you can allow people of every vibration to exist in your world.

In this chapter, we'll look at living in a transparent world—what might it be like? What stages might you go through as your transparency stabilizes? And where is transparency taking you? Into what kind of expanded capacity? How will things you take for granted shift into their new Intuition Age expression? Finally, we'll look at how transparency can lead you into enlightenment.

> You simply have to turn your back on a culture that
> has gone sterile and dead and get with the program
> of a living world and the imagination.
> Terence McKenna

The "Yes, Buts"

As you let the transparency settle in, answers come to you as telepathic insights. The field of this place knows your reservations and questions and gives you completion before you can worry. A voice speaks inside your mind . . .

1. **Will I know how to act now that I'm here? Do I have to be perfect?** Accept that you are already perfect at your core. Perfection isn't about knowing a certain amount or being able to act in an optimal way. It's about you-the-soul and you-the-personality becoming one integrated self. From this one source of consciousness, without the numbing and distorting clutter, you clearly see exactly what you need. You act exactly as you need to act. The transparent state teaches you about living in the new reality, simply as you go along.

You don't need to memorize a text ahead of time. With transparency, you realize you and the world you live in are one. Of course you know how it works!

2. **Is this new world a kind of death? Will I lose myself? Will I ever be able to go back?** The only death in the transparent reality is ego death. You temporarily lose your definitions and story, yet you still have them, along with many other possible definitions and stories, because these declarative statements help you-the-soul sculpt and resculpt the personality you use to play in the world of form. You can play with your identity now and not be limited by it. This reality is supremely efficient—you only lose those things that are useless. You gain everything that makes you real and true. You do not need to go back to the opaque reality; it's inside you at a lower frequency of your totality. You can visit it if you want, but you'll likely be so bored with it that it becomes an old, faded dream.

3. **Will my loved ones come into the new reality with me? Will I lose them forever?** The only thing separating you from others is negative thinking and fear. Your loved ones are with you always because all beings live in the field of love. You know they are with you, though they may not fully realize it yet. They will eventually awaken. All souls respond to attention; it's the basic connecting force. When you place attention on them, including them in your world, they feel you and think of you. Undivided attention facilitates communion and telepathy. Your compassion, attention, and telepathy assist others in waking up to themselves and transparency.

4. **Are there enough people in the new reality? Will I be alone?** There are many beings in the new reality with you. You have not seen them because you were paying attention to the opaque, fear-based people in the old reality, and were preoccupied with how to navigate the tricky dark alleys. Now you know both physical and nonphysical beings, from every time period and place, and interact with them all equally. You continue to interact with partially opaque people, offering the amount of yourself that their minds can process without panic. In the new reality, you have more soul friends and soul family than ever before.

5. **If I'm transparent, is there anything for people to recognize? Does my uniqueness disappear?** When you are transparent, there is actually *more* for other people to recognize. You're still unique, because your body still acts as a filter of consciousness, allowing selected soul desires to translate into thought, action, and form. And yet, you're not limited to one pattern of soul desires for your whole life, as people so often are in the opaque reality. Whenever you feel fully satisfied with a particular pattern, you-the-soul will "shift the beam" to focus through other facets of your totality. You may have dissolved attachments to specific identities and accomplishments, freeing your potential, but you may retain the deep interests and tendencies you've used as your life purpose in numerous lifetimes. These things are consistent because they are truly "of the soul."

When others see you and you see them, since there is no longer any clutter to match, the idea of relationship based on matching becomes less meaningful or common. Instead, there is a playful interacting of miscellaneous variables—as if both people took a handful of their own experiences, talents, interests, and potentials and tossed them up in the air like fairy dust, allowing the variables to find their own magical, unusual interconnections. It's stream of consciousness; we're all just playing in the Flow.

6. **If there are no secrets, what creates excitement in my life? Or motivation?** In the opaque reality, secrets trigger interest because you instinctively sense the contracted, withheld energy-and-consciousness. Your left brain is curious about withheld information and energy for superficial reasons that come from intrigue and adrenaline addiction, but you-the-soul simply do not like frozen energy and blocked consciousness. You-the-soul want to free the force locked up in fear-based contractions.

When there are no secrets, the soul is harmonious and the Flow can function. There is no need for fight-or-flight responses; instead, excitement comes from the pleasure of cocreating and entertaining each other with perception. It's the "impromptu dance" that absorbs attention. Motivation comes from diving consciously into the fluidity of evolution, the pursuit of infinity. Instead of secrets, you adore the mystery of what's next. There is no concept of boredom; now there is the interesting turn at every phase of the creation cycle. Action turns to surprising results, then to letting go into the gratifying experience of stillness, then to the new vision, and the bubbling desire to create and do comes again.

7. **If I can see through the surface, will I be depressed by what I see?** In the opaque reality, remember how seeing through a carefully crafted, projected self-image usually reveals a hidden, shameful secret? The popular celebrity is a drug addict who abuses his wife, the humanitarian nonprofit organization has a CEO who makes an enormous salary, the sustainable, green corporation partners with suppliers that pollute rivers. With transparency, though, the people who were influenced by fear to act from ego have cleared themselves. Shame and guilt are gone. Now there is coherence between the unlimited, nonphysical, inner reality and the physical, outer one; results are lit up with the surprise of "just rightness." Depression and feeling "let down" are artifacts of an old world where it was common to frequency-match realities lower than your own.

8. **Does being transparent mean I become dangerously vulnerable? Or brutally honest?** Without secrets—without needing to lie and then be caught in the lies, humiliated, injured, or imprisoned—the old meaning of vulnerability goes away. Vulnerability, instead of being about the openness to being wounded, becomes something akin to innocence, the simple openness to expanded experience. You don't expect pain anymore, and being wounded goes away. Woundedness comes from experiencing pain and resisting it—contracting the body, which contracts the emotions and mind. When you identify as the soul, nothing contracts that doesn't release in the next second.

Contraction becomes focus. Pain becomes the interruption of the natural flow, the distraction of perception from harmony. The soul does not recognize these untruths, and so it returns the mind and feelings immediately to "the way it really is." As for being brutally honest, transparency carries with it the context of compassion.

Honesty sees the compassionate truth and expresses this truth in a way that acknowledges soul, fairness, and wisdom. Verbal brutality in any form has no basis for existence.

9. **Might I not want to be on earth anymore? Might I ascend, never again to incarnate?** With transparency, you can feel into your own evolutionary path. You become conscious of what is still incomplete and unintegrated. You might understand the concept of something, like forgiveness, yet still not have experienced the way forgiveness affects your body, heart, and the frequency of your personal field. You might have experienced the nuances of creating an illness or a good marriage partner but might still be curious about what goes into creating a fortune or making an important contribution to worldwide evolution. For reasons like this, you may remain on earth to refine your knowledge. You also might choose to continue incarnating— even if you don't need to—just because you love creating form, or because you love serving others and the planet.

It's equally possible that you might feel totally complete with the experiment of three-dimensional life on earth—or that the transparent world in which you're now living is so much like the spiritual realms that there's no big difference anyway. You're not caught in resistance to the physical world, or in suffering, so you may want to move on to higher frequency realms.

Sinking into Transparency

As you stabilize your new consciousness and move into the part of the transformation process that comes after you've cleared the bulk of your clutter, you rise from the ashes as the golden phoenix. You're a "new human," yet ironically, you feel more like yourself than ever before. The new reality feels so familiar—it's almost casual while feeling ecstatic at the same time. And yet, there is more to do. You are still acclimating and integrating. These last phases of transformation bring some dramatic challenges.

You may now face the deeply buried last remnants of your fear-based beliefs—and these are the whoppers at the bottom of the bucket shared by all of humanity. How do you maintain your center when facing terror, oceanic grief, and nuclear rage? Perhaps, you've cleared your own personal blockages, but now societally shared blockages affect you, reminding you of your own clutter, so recently gone, and perhaps this triggers you to backslide. How do you handle these collective levels of negativity?

As you allow yourself to include more people and global situations in your sphere, you may once again feel the familiar contractions—but now the fears belong to the rest of the world. Even so, it doesn't matter; the work of dissolving societal blockages is the same work you did with your own wounds and frozen places. In effect, you're slowly realizing that you are simultaneously both an individual consciousness and the collective consciousness of all beings.

So! Don't invest attention in the fears, but don't deny or resist them. You don't possess blockages, they just pass through you and try to attract your attention. Be neutral and you won't be triggered. When you identify yourself as the soul and feel the soul's vibration in your personality and personal field, *that alone dissolves blockages.* Soul presence disperses clutter instantly—whether it's yours or ours—because the soul doesn't recognize fear. And it doesn't recognize private ownership of suffering.

Now you are normalizing transparency, understanding it thoroughly, living in it, and exploring the new world. How does transparency feel as a new way of being? How do the rules of life change when you're practicing spherical-holographic perception? Let's have a look at how you're doing so far.

· · · · · · · · · · ·

Try This!
Take Your "Transparency Temperature"

1. Be quiet, and center yourself in your body and home frequency. In the clear space in front of you, imagine a thermometer with percentage markings from 0–100. As you focus on the following questions, notice the reading on the thermometer and note it in your journal. Trust what percentages you get.

2. How much do you live in the present moment, centered in your body?
3. How much do you project into the past? Into the future? Into other locations? Into fantasies? Into other people's lives?
4. How much do you trust the Flow to bring what you need?
5. How much do you focus on the soul in people versus what's wrong with them?
6. How much do you focus on situations as problems? How much do you see problems as opportunities and data?
7. How much do you see how other people and events are part of your bigger self and not separate from you?
8. How much do you hold back from others?
9. How much do you lie?
10. How exposed are you?
11. How much do you experience yourself as your soul? How much do you experience yourself as your left-brain thinking patterns? As your emotions? As your body?
12. Go back through each of the previous questions and write about how you might improve each situation.

. . . .

A Real Story of Opening to Transparency

Leisa began writing to me several years ago, sharing the unusual experiences she was having. She was concerned that she might be going crazy and wondered if I knew of anyone else who had had similar changes. Here is a brief synopsis of our conversation.

Leisa: I experienced something last night that was odd but wonderful. I was watching a TV show when suddenly something shifted—physically, emotionally, and spiritually. It was as though I was transported from somewhere else and placed in my home. I physically felt my body being "placed," and there was a feeling of alignment. I missed parts of the show.

Penney: It feels like an exaggerated blinking-out-and-back experience. We all rock in and out of form constantly, but this feels like you energetically stayed out longer, allowed yourself to align with a higher frequency pattern, then snapped back to your "normal" reality. It feels like you slowed the whole thing down so you could be more conscious of the re-formation part of your process—so you experienced it as being "placed." Watch for subtle changes in the way things work over the next few weeks, as the new, higher frequency pattern begins to function.

L: Ever since that "blink," I hear the prayers of the world and the heartbeat of the earth. I "know things"—it's like walking through a sleeping planet. I am filled with an extreme love, and I cry over this feeling. I know what it was like before humans manifested everything that we have today and polluted our spirits. Please tell me I'm not the only one experiencing this!

P: I would say you had a conscious experience of being in the spiritual realm and the body simultaneously. I like your idea of walking through a sleeping planet—I often feel like other people are moving in slow motion or speaking a language that's in an ancient dialect, with old phraseology. Or there is a sort of suspended animation with some people and a very heightened action with others on higher frequencies. At the same time, it's like walking through love; the love is like slippery, shiny air. I can notice it or forget to notice it, and the world changes in an instant, depending on which thing I pay attention to. Similarly, where ambition used to be, there is simply a feeling of enjoyment and excitement. There are no "shoulds" left. I sense everything is "just right" and that it will become ever more "just right." I don't need the same things I used to need and am happier with what I have and with what comes.

L: I no longer feel as though I'm a spiritual being in a human body but that this body is becoming spiritual. Almost an interweaving of the two. The physical body no longer holds the limitations of boundaries. I trust you will understand this. Next: Words that would normally upset me seem to have no emotions attached to them. They are just words. When something starts to align with a frequency lower than what my higher self desires, there's like an "automatic correct" that activates to adjust my thoughts.

P: Yes, I feel like the field is my body and vice versa. I think this is part of us moving beyond old perceptual patterns. People who react with anger, meanness, or pettiness just seem boring anymore, or I feel drawn to give them a blessing. Part of this is a lack of interest in the news; I don't want to add attention to the negativity. The old patterns of taking offense seem to be a waste of time and energy. Better things to do!

L: I'm more aware now that the two worlds don't exist separately. Things I used to hear and see using "spiritual gifts" are now just appearing! For example, sounds that are so clear that everyone should hear them, but they don't. People and objects appear from nowhere—such as someone walking down the street, or a random object appearing on the table I just cleared off. Coincidences that I know are not!

P: Exactly! I find a synchromesh sort of occurrence of the answers to my sometimes idle thoughts. It happens with timing for appointments, and how and when I answer emails. Clients say sentences that are the perfect answer to something I was thinking about. Everything seems coordinated by a higher force.

L: I hardly know who I was just a short time ago. I know that everything I desire is already here, and I desire nothing. Everything seems, for lack of a better word, "perfect"—in a universal way. This has all happened so quickly but without the experience of time.

P: As to "my" history and "my" story—I continue to hold my history as a way to be real to others, to have something in common with others, and though I can project my attention back into the memories and feel all the sensations associated with the experiences, I can feel how I'm not at all invested in them or in the meanings I may have attached to them previously. I feel a deep sense of satisfaction, really, with remembering, gradually, the fullness of all the lives I've lived and who I really am.

L: Here's a new one: I wake up and have to literally get out of bed and stretch my spine. And I'm not talking about a little stretch! My spine feels like it's getting longer. I feel—*grander* is the word I'm given. Also, my body is tired but then I want to take a walk. I don't feel like doing anything but then I feel I need to be doing something, and this carries some urgency with it.

P: I also have been conscious of getting the kinks out of my spine; I seem to do it every few hours, all day long, and especially first thing in the morning, when I do lots of stretching. Perhaps we are sensitive to blocked flows of energy now—wanting the body's information without having it jam up.

And finally, Leisa sums it all up with a clear experience of transparency.

L: Recently I began to notice big things in the world had seemed to have suddenly appeared or disappeared. There are homes on my block (I've lived here 6 years) that weren't here before—not new homes! Or a street crew that was blocking the entrance to my coffee shop was absolutely gone when I came back out to the car. Reality has become so fluid! Is it all about my perception? How solid is our reality anyway?

One morning during meditation, I started to cry. I was shown and told that this was the end of my journey as I have known it so far. I was given a pen and paper to continue to write my own destiny. It was as though I was saying good-bye to the person lying there at the altar—me! I was shown the entire world. Nothing is impossible any longer. Now I find it easy to remain in my "light body" for extended periods, and everything seems new and amazing. I merge with energies and feel into objects! Everything has blended together, and it seems as natural as breath.

I feel like whatever keeps us from seeing the truth has been removed. Manifesting has become effortless. Knowing has become, not second-nature, but just the way it is. Everything happens at exactly the right time. Then, when I was lying in bed one night, I saw my cells lighting up like little fireworks. I also felt I had no physical boundaries, that my spirit or energy was not contained in a body.

I love Leisa's honesty, humor, and fresh innocence about welcoming every new shift in her perception. She models the process of integration for us so genuinely. She moved from having her intuition open wide, to high levels of empathic sensitivity, to mystical and mediumistic experiences, and on to many more subtle symptoms of transparency. You might relate to a number of the things she experienced. The point is that each person's path into transparency is unique in its timing and insights, yet so many of the core experiences are universal. There are states of being that come upon us, and by being with those states—becoming those states—the energy-and-consciousness within teaches us. In a moment, we just "know."

> What happens to entities as they evolve? We become more intelligent. We become more capable of higher level emotions, so we become more loving. We become more creative. We become more beautiful. And so we're actually moving exponentially to have greater levels of the very properties we ascribe to God without limit.
>
> Ray Kurzweil

KEY ELEMENTS OF PERSONAL TRANSPARENCY

- You're comfortable being seen for who you really are, flaws and talents included. You can see, feel, and know your true self and understand your mistakes, so you live with full acceptance.

- You don't need to keep secrets, tell lies, hide, or project an inflated or deflated image of yourself. Embarrassment, shame, deception, and guilt are things of the past.

- You don't hold fixated energy or consciousness; no withheld information or action, hoarding, or holding forth. You can focus, define, then release; you can contract from pain or shock, then release; you free yourself from habits and addictions.

- You have no ego but a strong sense of yourself as the soul; your soul infuses your personality and directs you; you can play with your personal history and story and not be bound by them.

- You live in your home frequency, at the center of your expandable spherical field, working with spherical-holographic perception instead of linear perception. You are inclusive of everything in the universe.

- You live in the present moment, accessing frequencies (realities) with your attention; you interact with the imaginal realm constantly. You can easily shift back and forth between your left and right brain, and different foci of consciousness.

- You live in the Flow and trust its sanity. You trust the ideas that come to you from within and from other people. You allow collective evolution.

- You occupy yourself fully; you love your body as part of your mind; you penetrate into gaps to find the self; you can feel full as well as spacious.

- You don't perceive separation but, instead, feel the underlying unity of all beings and things. You do not perceive an outside world but can place boundaries wherever you want to see how those lines affect your consciousness.

(Continued on next page)

KEY ELEMENTS OF PERSONAL TRANSPARENCY

- You experience the nonphysical world inside the physical. Your inner blueprint is evolving—forming you, changing you—and you are immediately responsive to it. There is no "other side" or "heaven" beyond you; you can connect with nonphysical beings as easily as you can with embodied people.

- You do not engage in opposition and conflict but eclipse it to find the unifying view. You understand how both poles relate to a single issue.

- You are comfortable seeing through surface distractions and disturbances to the core truth in others and situations. You can share insights with others honestly and without brutality.

- You are motivated by compassion and the desire to understand others and all of life, deeply and truly.

- You are connected to others and the experience of wisdom telepathically and kinesthetically; clairvoyance, clairaudience, clairsentience, and other expanded human capacities are normal to you.

Fig. 9-1

Our New Permeability

When transparency occurs, there is a feeling that brings a tactile sense of porousness of the body. You might feel you're breathing in and out through your skin, that the skin is not a barrier but a collection of particles vibrating at a slightly different speed than those of the air or the table that's right next to your skin, allowing a slight interpenetration and natural familiarity. You might sense that your cells are drawing nourishment directly from the unified field. You might feel a normal environmental sound moving through your stomach or throat or up your spine, setting off a subtle, pleasant—or irritating or alarming—sensation in your entire being. Or the sound of the cicadas on a summer night might sound like a choir singing Gregorian chants.

You might experience *synesthesia*, where your senses begin to combine and overlap. You might hear colors or see sounds. You might see certain letters or numbers coded in particular colors or located closer or farther away from you in space. You might hear a word and feel a corresponding impression in a specific body part. Perhaps you feel a physical tingling in your legs, for example, when you smell an orange. Or you are left with an astringent taste in your mouth after you see the color chartreuse.

Higher tactile senses can be activated—for example, you might feel real "impressions" in your body concerning abstract things. You think of a possible reality—a vacation to visit the sacred standing-stone sites throughout the British Isles—and immediately feel the trip has been taken and completed. You have a strong sense of how everything felt—the high and low points of the journey, what you learned, even a sense of having had a past life there that causes your body now to contract with anxiety. Or you might have physical impressions of someone when you think of them, like a headache or deep tiredness, and find out they've been having the same symptoms. This is a form of *clairsentience*, or direct feeling. When you place attention on someone else, or on anything in particular, you can merge into its inner blueprint and feel the person, object, or situation as if it's your own body of knowledge. What was impersonal becomes personal.

Not only are you becoming ultrasensitive in this time of acceleration, you are becoming permeable as well. You don't need to hold yourself together anymore, as though your skin pulls you in and keeps you recognizable. As though, if it weren't for the density of your flesh, you'd simply expand and eventually dissolve in the unified field. When you relax the act of holding yourself in form, you don't just drift off—you find your natural "shape." That true shape continues to materialize without you "trying" to maintain it. When you're permeable, you might stop "holding" excess weight, or your posture and physical energy level might change. You might find dramatically increased tolerance for things that have bothered you in daily life: disruptive children in public places, bad grammar, commuting, utility bills that increase every month, constantly breaking machines, and so on.

We're already seeing another of the symptoms of this permeability—the ease with which we can read each other's thoughts and emotions without verbal communication. You're with a friend and your mind drifts to thoughts of your father, who recently died. She says, "Have you had any dreams about your father since he passed?" Telepathy is really a heightened sense of impressionability, and it's becoming much more normal. You think of someone for a week and finally call them, and find out that they've been thinking of calling *you*.

With transparency and permeability, you live in the nonphysical reality concurrently with the physical, and communication can come instantly—even across great distances—because it's actually surfacing from the inner world, where time and space are not separate. Everything is in the here-and-now. The realms have no dividing lines. Every time you rock out of form, you receive messages from the unified field. When you come back to your physical life, it seems the information appears, as if by magic.

In *The Archaic Revival*, Terence McKenna, who experimented with the perception generated by hallucinogenic plants and came into great mystical wisdom in his life, said, "I believe that the totemic image for the future is the octopus. This is because the cephalopods, the squids and octopi, have perfected a form of communication that is both psychedelic and telepathic—an inspiring model for the human communications of the future. The octopus does not transmit its linguistic intent, it becomes its linguistic intent. Like the octopus, our destiny is to become what we think, to have our thoughts become our bodies and our bodies become our thoughts. In the not-too-distant future, men and women may shed the monkey body to become virtual octopi swimming in a silicon sea."[1]

This might conjure up some pretty wild images of us becoming shape-shifters who change more quickly than Dr. Jekyll and Mr. Hyde, but aren't we already a bit like this? Certainly some people can hide their feelings behind a stone-faced mask, but body language, the light in our eyes, the constriction or fluidity of our voice, the energy radiating from us, and the way we move, already pattern and reveal us according to the inner blueprint of our thought and feeling.

• • • • • • • • • • •

Try This!

Read Other People's Thoughts & Emotions

1. Notice who comes into your mind this week and make note of it. Wait. See if they return to your mind. If they do, notice your body, and see if there is a particular sensation, in a particular place, or a mood that comes along with them. Play with the idea that if the thought of them occurs, they're actually coming into your attention field energetically. This can happen with both physical and nonphysical people. You might take it further; imagine having a telepathic conversation with them. You might write it in your journal, using direct writing. Finally, if you can, contact the person physically and see how they are.

2. When you meet or are physically close to another person this week, let yourself be still and receptive, neutral and impressionable. Place your attention gently on them, and bring them inside your attention field. Feel into them, or allow their inner energy blueprint to merge with yours and "impress" you with certain information. Do you sense a particular emotion? Do you feel they are fixated in their left brain or spaced out in their right brain? You may receive the impressions kinesthetically through your body or you may just "know" telepathically. You may receive a complex knowledge pattern that includes their problems, the causes, and the solutions. If you know the person, share some of what you notice, tactfully and kindly. Or open a conversation with something like, "I sense you're feeling a bit preoccupied right now. Anything important on your mind?"

3. You might keep a section of your journal for telepathic and kinesthetic impressions or messages you receive about others in meditation or in dreams. Read back over it and see if you feel an urge to follow up with certain items.

• • • • • • • • • • •

Where Is Transparency Taking Us?

The day science begins to study nonphysical phenomena,
it will make more progress in one decade than in all
the previous centuries of its existence.
Nikola Tesla

It's fascinating, encouraging, uplifting, and sometimes frightening to track the new innovations coming in the various arenas of life. So many wonderful ideas for healing the planet and humanity's wounds originate from people who are now becoming both horizontally and vertically transparent. And yet there are also many projected trends in technology and the Information Age coming from people who are focusing mostly on horizontal transparency, using old perception.

Looking at the news from the tech world, I read headlines about the artificial-intelligence revolution or how synthetic biology and "biohacking" are taking the human body's experience "beyond what nature intended" (as if that's a really great thing and we can know "nature's intent"). I'm reading about how the next wearable technology could be your skin, that there are computer chips made of live brain cells, and about how sending nano-robots into the brain will provide full-immersion virtual reality from within the nervous system, connecting our neocortex to the Cloud. Whew!

Many developments raise ethical concerns since the right brain-heart-unified field connection found with vertical transparency seems to be lacking. Here are a few of these ideas. A technology known as "gene drive," which gives humans the power to alter or perhaps eliminate entire populations of organisms in the wild, aims at invasive rodents and disease-carrying insects. But how far could it go, and what side effects would it have? Scientists are working to create synthetic human genomes that would make it possible to grow human organs for transplant—but might it eventually result in creating children with no biological parents?

New small, robotic killing machines, called lethal autonomous weapons, or LAWs, would have a military mission to seek out, identify, and kill a human target independent of human control. In some sort of parallelism, perhaps, the U.S. Navy announced an "office for unmanned warfare systems." Extreme miniaturization of sensors, cameras, antennas, and even computing equipment—known as "smart dust"—can now be combined into information-gathering devices at a micro-scale. What happens when these devices are scattered to the winds in the trillions to measure the world in ultraclear detail?

It's interesting that science and technology visionaries seem to be tapping into the advanced human abilities that will become normal in the Intuition Age, but they're pursuing them in a literal, physical way. They speak of "intelligence" not wisdom, intuition, compassion, or soul. They speak of "exponential growth," which is still linear—not the kind of total transformation that vertical transparency and spherical-holographic perception would generate.

Researchers at Duke University have created a project called Brainet that experiments with wiring rats' and monkeys' brains together, and rewards them for synchronizing their brain output to accomplish basic tasks. What about teaching people to develop telepathy and group mind as part of their own nonphysical skill sets—without the aid of computers?

Scientists at Tel Aviv University are experimenting with "quantum levitation"—coating a thin superconductor layer on a sapphire wafer and penetrating it with flux tubes so the wafer floats. Though these terms sound super sci-fi, it could be that the era of levitating cars or building another great pyramid is closer than we think. On the other hand, Michael Murphy, director of Esalen Institute's think tank, the Center for Theory & Research, and author of *The Future of the Body*, has begun a special project to study human levitation *directly*.

With horizontal transparency, technology brings us cell phones with video interface and texting, which introduces us subliminally to the idea of interconnected collective consciousness, immediate global communication, and knowing others intimately in just a few moments.

Chapter 9: The New Normal

Is the addiction to having machines do the work for us causing our own telepathic and clairvoyant abilities to atrophy? Can we learn to heal ourselves with our innate perceptual power, or do we just have a new body part 3-D printed and installed?

Peter Diamandis of Singularity University says, "We're going to look at your genome and all of your body's systems and identify what's likely to kill you and find it before it does. So stopping you from dying is the first bit. And the second is replenishing your stem cell population so you have a restored regenerative engine throughout your life."[2] I wonder: Is there a sensitivity anywhere in this to the soul's purpose in dying in a particular way at a particular time, or in using an illness as a healing and learning device?

The idea of extending life and minimizing aging is noble and worthwhile, but do scientists understand that, in the Intuition Age, death is seen as a different frequency of life, and the big work is in experiencing all the stages of consciousness as we transition from form to pure energy-and-consciousness—so the shift seems normal and doesn't negatively affect our memory and continuity? And that when we do this, reducing the fear of death, we may extend our lifespan naturally? Only vertical transparency reveals these things.

Kevin Kelly in his book, *The Inevitable*, describes twelve technological forces shaping the future. Among them are words I recognize as relating to transformation and personal transparency—like becoming, flowing, accessing, sharing, interacting, tracking, and questioning. But Kelly uses them to describe phenomena relating to the Information Age. For example, from the old-perception view, focused only in the physical realm, "dematerialization" relates to the trend of making better products by using fewer and lighter materials, while from the new-perception view, dematerialization integrates the nonphysical *with* the physical, relating to the shift from form to energy-and-consciousness. Again, I see a gifted visionary thinker touching on vertical transparency but not really integrating it yet into the fabric of the vision. Please don't get me wrong—visionary books of this caliber are stimulating and important in their own right. I'm just saying they are partial.

Kelly has an interesting view on what may be happening as we head toward the end of the Information Age. He says information has been growing at 66 percent per year, which is the same as doubling every eighteen months. He also says that in the next few decades, we will knit together all the books in the world into a single networked literature, aided by algorithms. He's describing a reality limited by physical, logistical dynamics—a horizontally transparent view rooted in the Information Age—yet I sense he's touching a higher vision that includes both horizontal and vertical transparency, one that would enable us to merge directly into the universal mind and know anything.

He says, "We'll come to understand that no work, no idea stands alone, but that all good, true, and beautiful things are ecosystems of intertwined parts and related entities, past and present."[3] As this physical melding of literary works occurs—and I suspect it will—I wonder: What becomes of the passion for unique, individual creativity? How do leading-edge works stand out enough to make an impact?

Understanding vertical transparency and including this view in our vision and imagination for innovations to come would balance the needs of both the collective and individual realities simultaneously. It would allow compassion, wisdom, and deep understanding of universal principles to be the guiding forces for new developments—not just cleverness-without-conscience or the left brain's short-term linear solutions that don't feel into potentially damaging repercussions.

> Some kind of dialog is now going on between
> individual human beings and the sum total of
> human knowledge and nothing can stop it.
> Terence McKenna

How Transparency Will Transform Reality

When you develop both horizontal and vertical transparency and merge the two views, the result is a comprehensive "holistic" transparency—a state that both creates and is created by spherical-holographic perception.

This is what I'm really talking about in this book. With this perspective, you can penetrate any illusion and open into the fullness of a true evolutionary view, which shows the potential of everything to transform into its higher nature. In a transparent world, then, what happens to our experience of such things as technology, ethics, time, healing, freedom, emotions, learning, birth, humor, business, entertainment, marriage and family, or innovation?

When things are seen through a filter of the fear and separation inherent in old, linear perception, life looks physical and dense and behaves a certain way. From this view, we use willpower and cleverness to deal with the acceleration and the transformation process. As we become fully transparent, however, we see through another filter that brings everything into the present moment, reveals unity, and works easily with the inner blueprint of the physical to facilitate change. From this view, we are aligned with universal laws and flow in concert with transformation.

Let's imagine how things we currently take for granted might transform in a transparent world—how each thing might be reframed so it shifts to its more ideal, high-frequency expression. I've summarized some of these things in previous chapters, but let's pull the vision together here.

1. **Time and Space:** When you move from linear to spherical-holographic perception, there is no more past and future; there are simply different frequencies of potential realities in your vast present moment. You can match any of them with your attention, and when you do, the reality you imagine occurs physically. The more fully you match the reality's vibration, the faster it materializes. So what you think, feel, and radiate is what occurs in your life. It's not hard to know things in other locations because everything is inside your sphere. You travel this inner world via your attention. As you become truly transparent, you may be able to time travel, bilocate, or teleport yourself or objects across space. You may clairvoyantly see the whole of your lifetime or the history of the earth, and yet still live it lovingly, moment by moment.

Transparency

If you surrendered to the air, you could ride it.
Toni Morrison

2. **Body and Matter:** In a transparent reality, form still exists. Gravity still works. Objects are still solid, and bodies appear as real as they do now. The difference is that your body and matter itself are more porous energetically, and are lifted in vibration by the Light within. You are ultrasensitive to subtle frequency variations. You know for sure that you have an energy body inside your physical body and that you can make changes to your inner blueprint and your body will shift to match. You have expanded perception of auras and the energy radiating from and surrounding people, places, and things, and you read these fields consciously when you interact. By shifting your own energy field, you can easily heal, lose or gain weight, look older or younger, or seem invisible or super-visible. Since you don't think of matter as being so heavy or dense, phenomena like psycho-kinesis, apportation, teleportation, and levitation occur more often.

3. **Emotion and Thought:** The more transparent you become, the more emotion and thought blend—a thought is a feeling, a feeling is a thought. As your feelings merge with your understanding, you move past negative emotion and see it as a waste of time and attention. Your thoughts take on feeling tones, and emotions rise in vibration to become pure sensation experienced as color, texture, flavor, odor, sound, or numbers. You prefer expanded, heightened experiences and don't choose contraction and fixation anymore. Eventually, the combination of thought and emotion refines into a high-level ultrasensitivity and empathy, producing direct knowing of the vast potential of humanity. Ideas carry with them the whole blueprint of how they can become physical, how their reality will feel, what lessons are contained within, and what they might evolve into next.

4. **Creativity and Innovation:** With transparency, you no longer feel you must stretch to find new ideas or struggle to go beyond what is known. Instead, you're in touch with the entire unified field and

imaginal realm, and there are gazillions of ideas waiting for you—every possible combination of an infinite number of variables. The ideas you need come to *you*, guided by you-the-soul and the collective consciousness of all souls, and the process of creating is ecstatic and soul-nourishing. You realize all creation is cocreation, and your part in the experience is as vital and interesting as everyone else's. Originality is respected as much as the collective source of the ideas. You learn that creativity is about materializing and dematerializing form, and that these actions are a function of *attention* in the present moment—not *intention* focused on the future—since there is no future anymore. You also know that innovation is tied to the frequency of the planet's current evolutionary stage.

5. **Planning and Flow:** In a transparent world, you still plan, but those plans are extremely fluid. You interact with the inner blueprint of a project or end result continually, allowing it to evolve as you and the world evolve. It's a waste of energy to plan too far ahead, because the result isn't in the future; it's in the present at a new frequency. More attention goes into achieving and maintaining the energy-and-consciousness state that matches the final result—which catalyzes the result into materialization. The cocreators of a project may come and go as their inner purpose dictates, and this flux of cocreators is always perfect for the optimal end result.

6. **Work and Play:** Transparency reduces the survival pressure associated with "having to" work. Work and play become synonymous, both being about the authentic expression of soul. There is no resistance to work, nor is there a need to escape into wildness or addictions as "play." Self-entertainment at a deep level, through creativity and service, becomes a strong motivation. Competition transforms into mutually supportive cocreation and collaboration—to the joy in what can come from aligned minds and spirits. Personal effort changes to full-on involvement and delight in expanding the sphere of what can be known and accomplished. Humor is seen as a high-frequency state that opens creativity and productivity and restores the Flow.

7. **Money and Possessions:** With transparency, there is no greed. Poverty and astronomical wealth become functions of the old, opaque reality, and neither extreme works optimally. Too much or too little of anything is seen as ineffective, and possessiveness is seen as a form of ego. There is a knowing that every part of creation is supported by a greater, life-giving force. What you need comes to you, depending on the frequency of your attention. What others need may more easily inspire you to spend or donate some of what you have. There will continue to be a function for currency that allows giving and receiving to be tracked in the physical realm, and symbolizes the ebb and flow of energy-and-consciousness around the world. It may take the form of physical money, bitcoin or barter, or something entirely new.

8. **Learning and Memory:** With transparency, learning is remembering. Knowing is direct experience. Revelations and insights are brought to you by the soul and the collective consciousness at just the right moment, as a function of need. Curiosity is also a function of need—your attention goes where you and "we" need it to go. All knowledge exists at once, and your attention to it allows it to become conscious. When you're finished using the knowledge, it goes back into the field until the next time you need it.

   Memorizing with willpower is replaced by merging with the information and allowing it to pattern your energy body and physical body until it emerges in your left brain as a description and definition. Education is deeply intimate. Memory spreads out so that what was personal and individual becomes impersonal and collective, and vice versa. You realize you don't own memories but share them with all beings.

The body represents the gap between the little bit of mind you call your own and all the rest of what is really yours.
A Course in Miracles

9. **Communication and Communion:** Verbal communication is backed by telepathic communication; internal images and subtle, underlying

feeling states are aligned with the words. Since everyone is so sensitive, empathic, and telepathic, a lie or partially felt communication is immediately questioned. Reading the thoughts in the space of a relationship or group is common, so people may say, "What I'm picking up on right now is this," or "I sense an undercurrent of this in the space," or "Joe, did you have a concern or idea you wanted to share out loud?"

There may be times where the parties involved concurrently "know" what to do, and an excitement fills the air like a racehorse at the starting gate. Everyone wants to bring the concept into language and ground the vision! A high priority is placed on the act of moving into communion with an idea, person, or object. "Becoming one with" something and having direct knowing reveals important information about the final form, the possible snags and changes of direction the form might take, the length of materialization, and the evolution of the core concept.

10. **Relationships and Family:** With transparency, you more easily find people who resonate with your level of energy-and-consciousness and can evolve along with you. You have more soul friends and soul family—people you've known in other lifetimes or who are on parallel developmental paths. You are aware of being part of a relationship entity or group entity that contains everything both or all of you know and that guides the growth and self-expression of both or all of you. You are aware that other people are inside your sphere, so you can relax into feeling that you already know them at some level, and they you. You have an expanded sense that the members of your family of origin are not your only family; everyone is a potential best friend or family member. Marriage becomes a focus for spiritual growth, not just a space for raising children or finding financial security.

> Home interprets heaven. Home is heaven for beginners.
> Rev. Charles H. Parkhurst

11. **Attractiveness and Sex:** When you and others are transparent, you see through any residues of fear-based beliefs, emotional defenses,

or sabotaging actions—to the vulnerability and beauty inside. The quality of a person's heart becomes the attractor, as well as the Light coming from the eyes and skin. The quality of individual creativity and self-expression reveals the soul's beauty. Sexual passion and intensity come from the states of consciousness the partners reach together, not just the physical pleasure, and it is more a state of ecstasy than lust. Attraction is high when partners are able to play creatively, cocreate surprising realities, and contribute to others in unique ways.

There is less jealousy, because each partner respects the connections the other makes with other people and trusts the integrity of the connection they have together. Having a variety of partners teaches one kind of spiritual openness, and committing to one partner brings a depth and teaching of another kind. People realize there can be a need for both kinds of experience in a lifetime. Disloyalty and betrayal are old ideas, because you can see each other's true needs and act appropriately from the very start. As relationships evolve, honesty keeps the inner blueprint aligned with the outer form—even when partners separate to move on to a new phase of life.

12. **Freedom and Commitment:** When you're transparent, you know yourself. You know you're free to create any reality you want, commit to any experience, and flow where the great Flow takes you. When you are free to be anything, you learn that creating experiences that go against universal principles causes blockage and pain, both for others and yourself. You recognize the difference between captivity and limitation (opaque reality ideas) and how the Flow naturally pauses and focuses. You understand that commitment is not a loss of freedom but an experiment in focus and attention, so resistance goes away. What you choose to do with your freedom is: create beauty and useful contributions to others, serve others in realizing their full potential, and celebrate existence.

13. **Ethics and Morality:** With transparency comes the Golden Rule. You are so aware of your interconnectedness with others that even to project fear, doubt, and beliefs onto them is to be unfair, to handicap

them. To not believe in someone is to make their life more difficult. To try to rescue or heal someone who needs their problem to be able to evolve, blocks their path instead of clearing it. To be sarcastic is to belittle the gift of life, and to entertain certain states—like jealousy, guilt, false humility, self-sacrifice, or victimhood—prevents both you and others from shining brightly.

During the bridge time, ethics are imposed on you by external laws, but in a transparent world, ethics are inherent and based on the soul's natural tendencies; they don't need to be enforced. Compassion is the first criteria, and win-win-win is the next. It's no longer either-or, but both-and perception. Justice grows from the core truth about the way the universe and energy-and-consciousness actually function.

> Thinking is learning all over again how to see, directing one's consciousness, making of every image a privileged place.
> Albert Camus

14. **Religion and Spirituality:** In a transparent reality, fear diminishes, as well as the perceived separation between you and your soul, you and the collective consciousness, and you and the Divine. You don't need priests to act as connectors and interpreters of the Divine since you are directly merged with higher realms. You don't need dogma to keep you in line since you're highly sensitive to any misalignment with the universal laws and the Flow. You keep yourself in alignment because it feels good. Grounded metaphysics and physics combined with mysticism and art are closer to the new spirituality—a blend of knowledge about how the universe and consciousness function, and the direct experience of love, appreciation, beauty, trust, and the perception of life's perfection.

You're open to the ancient history of the planet, understanding that intergalactic beings with high levels of knowledge have regularly visited the earth, contributing to evolution. You know that the advanced souls who became our master teachers throughout history all had connections to intergalactic, cosmic wisdom. With transparency, the main form of spiritual practice is the undiluted expression of the soul and the Divine through the personality, and we understand this to be the doorway to enlightenment.

15. **Birth and Death:** When we're transparent, parents see the souls of their children-to-be long before gestation and birth. They understand the purposes that draw them together as family. The birth process itself is not felt to be sacrificial or painful to the soul of the baby, as it is in the opaque reality, but more of a shaping process. Medical developments ease the pain and danger of complications in childbirth for the mother, and birth by a mother is seen as preferable to birth in a laboratory. It does seem that there is a choice, and the souls who choose a nonorganic birth are likely from soul groups we'd now consider extraterrestrial, where consciousness is highly impersonal; this kind of birth suits their life purpose. There is a greater recognition of different types of soul groups just as there is recognition of racial types.

    Death becomes a simple process of transition between frequencies, and Centers for Continuing Consciousness use advanced technology to assist people who don't have skill in adjusting their frequency, to gradually shift their vibration beyond that of the body so they can experience a conscious passing. Many of the after-death experiences, like the life review, are accomplished while still in the physical realm. Disease and violence are greatly reduced, so the time and manner of one's death is much more of a choice. And there is more focus placed on the successful accomplishing of life lessons.

16. **Healing and Longevity:** In a transparent reality, healing is seen as returning to the memory of who you really are—to unity and innate harmony. Most healing is accomplished through meditative states and powerful, guided visualizations to shift brainwaves, along with assistance from technology that adjusts the vibration of the body, emotions, and thought to the home frequency and love. Sound, light, and other high- and low-frequency waves do much of the mechanical work of healing.

Raising the frequency of the body and emotions beyond the vibration of cancer or viruses, for example, doesn't permit the existence of the disharmony. There are many ways to rejuvenate cells and organs, and people easily live another fifty years or more without great handicap in old age. Some people may choose to go through an experience of medically induced death and resuscitation, or a conscious near-death experience, to bring memory of higher states into the body.

17. **Danger and Safety:** In the opaque reality, you perceive life to be separated into an inside and an outside world. This creates the possibility for danger and the belief that something can prevent you from being your totality. In the transparent reality, negative emotions, secrets, defensiveness, and separation dissolve. You realize that you and what used to be a source of danger are familiar with each other, and there is no need for attack or avoidance. You also know you can be at the exact spot where a flower pot falls off a tenth floor balcony and hits you in the head, or you can be there five minutes later. You know that if you carry a sense of unfairness, criticism, or blame in your field, someone or some situation that matches that state will emerge to play out the oppositional scene with you—and that it's unnecessary. You can be safe or you can experiment with danger.

> Science does not know its debt to imagination.
> Ralph Waldo Emerson

18. **Science and Technology:** As transparency increases, scientists and intellectuals—people who have been predominantly left-brained and operating in the physical world—naturally shift into intuition and right-brain perception. They open their hearts and apply that perspective to innovation. They join together in groups where they can align their consciousness to higher frequencies and receive visions of important new technologies, machines, and processes to heal the earth and assist evolution. Physics and metaphysics merge.

Science learns to be sacred. Expanded human capacities fall into the realm of the new supra-science. Like the left brain, machines are used as they were intended—to serve right-brain perception, the soul, and the collective consciousness.

19. **Business, Government, and Organizations:** The pyramidal hierarchical structure of organizations shifts to a flatter, more networked structure, with small self-managing teams, or circles, interconnected with other circles in a holographic way. Leaders are catalysts and facilitators, known for their intuition and balanced left brain–right brain agility, and they join together in peer-group circles to keep each other aligned and inspired. They aren't so removed from the action and aren't treated as highly paid celebrities. The purpose and work of the organization evolves constantly, with contributions made equally from all participants.

  Organizations network and overlap with other organizations, the art and science of interconnecting rises in prominence as duplication is reduced, and progress naturally accelerates via collaboration. It is an advantage to share information and goals; competition changes to cooperation and collaboration—instead of one-upmanship—and new forms of profit occur based on these new values. Employees might work for a number of organizations simultaneously. Government moves more toward the council structure, away from just two opposing parties.

20. **Confidentiality and Privacy:** In the bridge time, there is much fear and upset about identity theft, and loss of privacy and anonymity. Originality and copyrights don't count for much, as personal works are pirated and distributed for free. Spying robs people of their experience of sacrosanct personal space. The motives behind hacking, pirating, identity theft, and surveillance come from ego, envy, lack of self-experience, and the need for control. Once again, the opaque physical reality is acting out a healthier process occurring in the nonphysical realms but with a huge dose of fear, distorting the results. The higher, healthier process pertains to ego death, exposure, and the dissolution of secrets and lies.

When you're truly transparent, everything about you can be known, but that knowledge is not misused, because compassion and understanding are an integral part of transparency. When you're transparent, what you create is freely shared with others, yet the creations and the creator are both deeply respected. When you can know anything, anytime, about anyone, the craving to spy, hack, and blow the whistle fades. You trust the Flow to bring the knowledge you need, whether it be about a situation or the inner workings of another person. When each person is connected to the source of unlimited supply, their own creativity takes precedence over stealing and intentionally damaging others.

21. **Stories and Mythology:** When you're transparent, you've moved beyond linear perception. That means the plots and storylines we're so used to—with a beginning, middle, end, and turning points—aren't as interesting. The primary mythology of the hero's journey to the underworld becomes a thing of the past. You've already set off on your quest for clarity and truth; you've faced your challenges, demons, swamps, and tests of character. You've emerged from the journey and come home, like the prodigal daughter or son. You don't need to hear about it all again.

Now you may be more interested in stories about the transformation of relationships, groups, and nations. Or you might want to hear stories about developing extraordinary human abilities that aren't framed as good and evil superheroes fighting in bizarre ways. You might want to hear stories about past and parallel lives and how souls function. And with spherical-holographic perception, new ways of telling stories emerge. Perhaps a series of stories or scenes is tossed into a space at the same time, and readers make connections between them according to their own filters, with each person finding their own story in what is presented.

I've touched briefly on a smattering of life's components and how they may shift as you become transparent and live in a transparent world. Even though that time is still in the process of landing, I encourage you to feel into how things might function differently without fear, self-protection, fight-or-flight responses, and negative thought and emotion. Anticipating and imagining the transparent reality will do much to birth it.

Globally and culturally, we are undergoing an initiation.
We are moving out of the journey of the hero and the heroine—
that process of individuation. An archetypal shift is occurring where
we are moving into the journey of partnership or the tribe.
[This] requires the spirit of cooperation and collaboration,
that we learn about collective leadership
and collective wisdom.

Angeles Arrien

The True Possibility of Enlightenment

Being transparent is a state that prepares you for enlightenment. It is your doorway into that higher state called Awareness, nirvana, or satori. Zen Buddhism has a saying: "The mind does not halt; if it halts, it is Enlightenment." With transparency, we're still intimately connected with the mind and still focused as individuals. We're preparing to return to the supreme Oneness—the self-that-isn't-self.

With transparency, you understand involution—how you moved from the unified field to become the particle—and this allows you to know the consciousness of individuality. Now you're remembering evolution—how you expand beyond the personal self, to the collective self, and back to your original state that is the entire unified field of energy-and-consciousness. You live harmoniously, surrendered to the laws of the universe, trusting the innate wisdom of the Flow to bring you into form and lift you back out again. That surrender is the relief of a mind that knows how to be quiet, the relief of belonging in the Flow and to the Field.

There is no desire to hold on to anything because you realize it's a waste of mind. Finite thoughts and materializations come and go without your mind locking them down in time and space. You are honest about experiencing. You know life and soul directly—without an agenda or having to interpret and make meaning. And yet, of course, you can make things meaningful if you want to play that way.

You can fall into what you notice, and if you stay present, you fall through all the layers of insights and noticings into an open state of pure being. With transparency, nothing is totally solid, even though the world of form still exists; you experience it as energy, responsive to thought and feeling. You see that we are made of Light—that we are the Light. You allow the Light to shine through and out of you. You see the Light everywhere, in every particle of matter.

You've learned to merge with life by investing attention, so you experience no separation between seeing and what is seen, between feeling and what is felt. As you meet each layer within anything you observe, and know it by becoming it, you find the "knowing" was already there and that it rose to join *you*! You find yourself everywhere, and your sense of self changes drastically—the individuality you've known dissolves to become a much more comprehensive, impersonally personal unified consciousness or integrated self. This state is not the absence of life as you've known it but the opening of your attention to everything simultaneously. You're simply not that interested in the idea of "myself" anymore.

> What, then, was the commencement of the whole matter?
> Existence that multiplied itself for sheer delight of being and
> plunged into numberless trillions of forms so that it might
> find itself innumerably.
> Sri Aurobindo

Buddhism teaches that there is state called the "original mind" that is complete within itself because it includes everything in itself. You might think of it as the unified field. It is different from a closed or biased mind—it's more like an empty and ready mind. It is often referred to as *beginner's mind*, which has no thoughts, is open to all possibilities, and is rooted in compassion. In contrast, any self-centered thought immediately limits the vast, original mind because it creates a contraction. Seng

Ts'an, who lived in the late sixth century, wrote in his long poem called "On Trust in the Mind," "View the ten thousand phenomena as equal / and all will revert to naturalness. / The very basis of their being wiped out, / impossible to rate one above another."[4]

With transparency, you can watch the behavior of your mind and see the patterns that have ruled your life. You can see how everything is exposed, how nothing can be hidden. And so, you clearly see how your left-brain perception gives certain ideas preferential treatment (it is especially fascinated with the drama of its own suffering, for example). You recognize how it feeds on dislike, guilt, and self-sacrifice and how the idea of being blocked becomes the main block. You see how your original mind has been blocked by a small ego consciousness that wants to analyze itself ad infinitum and only hears what it wants to hear, so it can be "right."

With enlightenment, the sense of a separate self dissolves. There is no interpretation of events, just the direct experience. There are no highlighted extraordinary experiences, just the simple being in the doing of something. Chop wood, carry water. You are talking, you are eating, you are making money, you are daydreaming. There is nothing special because everything is special.

> I regard consciousness as fundamental.
> I regard matter as derivative from consciousness.
> We cannot get behind consciousness.
> **Max Planck**

Bernadette Roberts, a Catholic nun and the author of *The Experience of No-Self*, writes about her journey of several years into the falling away of everything she had called her "self." She observes that there were a few stages she went through, beginning with a movement toward the self's union with the Divine, that parallel the psychological process of integration—what I've been describing here as the clearing of clutter and the merging of the soul and personality. This stage is marked by trials and dark nights, after which the self moves into a permanent experience of the Divine as the stillpoint and axis of its being.

Chapter 9: The New Normal

As the integrated self functions from its innermost center, it then experiences a variety of trials that test its unity. As it builds certainty about its true nature, oneness is revealed in all things. It discovers intense wonder and beauty, what wholeness means, and how it works in daily life. It compares the old life where it could be easily fragmented, to the new reality where it does not divide or move from its center.

A state is eventually reached where the self is completely aligned with the stillpoint and cannot be moved at all. It can no longer be tested, and a revelation occurs: The self is no longer necessary—it has outworn its function. Then we learn to live without the experience of self-consciousness, which allows us to discover what is beyond the self. As this happens, the mind exists totally in the Now, and experiences leave no wake. In effect, we learn to live without a past.

Other people have described enlightenment as a simple neurobiological event that can happen in an instant, at any time. It has nothing to do with how long you've been on a spiritual path, how good you are, or even whether you believe in God or the soul. It has nothing to do with the content of your mind. In fact, they say enlightenment cannot be achieved through your own efforts; it occurs through grace when you have recognized and released your illusions (clutter). If you think you can make it happen via your own willpower, you stall it. And ironically, at the moment of enlightenment, you realize you've always been enlightened—that it is your natural state. It's home!

. . . .

Try This!

Write About Your Transparent World

Use the following questions as triggers to prompt some direct writing; imagine your soul-consciousness is doing the writing.

1. What makes you (or allows you to) expand your boundaries without willpower or difficulty?

295

2. What takes you beyond worry?
3. How do you know who you are before you're defined by society?
4. What parts of you are not in your official story?
5. What are you actually sharing with other people over time?
6. What is your transcendent, universal self like?
7. What's the next phase of your consciousness like?
8. What things that usually preoccupy you would you like to not have to think about again?
9. What is beautiful to you? What does the pure experience of beauty do to your perception and to your experience of yourself?

• • • • • • • • • • •

Imagination and Invocation

The goal of becoming transparent is not to become enlightened, though that may occur spontaneously as you're cooking dinner one night, taking out the trash, or sitting at a stop sign. Becoming transparent makes your reality function in a smooth, synchromesh way and compassion takes over as the evolutionary force. As you practice the things in this book, you will strengthen and stabilize your ability to be transparent. Thoughts will come through the transparency: "What amount of myself do I want to embody? Who am I meant to be? What do I want to create? How can I help? What is my next courageous, authentic act?"

I remember before I wrote *Frequency*, I was meditating one day and had placed my attention on my father, who had recently died. I was having a conversation with him in my imagination and taking dictation in my journal. My father had been successful as a leader in his life, and I was asking him how I could move forward. What did I need to do to fulfill my destiny? He said, quite clearly: "Penney, everything up here is all set up for you. What you want already exists. You are not asking for enough. Widen the bottom of the funnel." And I saw an image of a huge funnel with a narrow spout suddenly widening and a vast amount of new "stuff" falling through into materialization. No effort, no will, no struggle. I didn't need to put in any more dues, or prove myself, or be "worthy." I just had to ask for more and make a path for it to flow in upon.

In my imagination, I saw and *felt* the funnel widen—and I *knew* I had merged with and internalized the experience of that widening. Then I experienced the feeling of things that were rightfully mine, and that other beings wanted me to have, falling through from the higher dimensions into my life. The following year, I wrote *Frequency*, and it became a bestseller around the world. With the expansiveness of that book's international welcome, I began to feel that I was also more expansive, and there was more that wanted to fall through me. This has continued to be true.

I share this story because you are probably also at a stage where you're ready for an expanded sense of self—for that experience of letting your full spiritual blueprint fall through and into you, to live in you, to guide you, to free you. And yet, as my father reminded me in my imaginal-realm conversation, it's all waiting for you but you must call it in.

This is the old art of *invocation*, which originally was the act of calling upon the gods for help. Thus, the use of an invocation as the prelude to prayer: "Our Father, who art in Heaven," or "Hail Mary, full of grace, the Lord is with Thee, blessed are Thou amongst women," or "O Mahadevi, sitting on a pink lotus, thank you for letting us see Your beauty, elegance, exquisiteness, perfection." As you become transparent, it is fitting for you to invoke, or call in, the next part of your life. Call in your next courageous act, the next level of your expanded sphere. Call in those who want to cocreate with you and act in a mutually serving way.

When you invoke the next part of your development, you don't need to know fully, or in detail, what it is. You only need to attune yourself to your home frequency and feel the absolute comfort of that centeredness, then imagine your home frequency intensifying and expanding, radiating to fill a larger space. The purity of your "tone" magnetizes your desire for greater truth and capacity, and souls everywhere smile and bring you the gift. So from your space of widening the bottom of your funnel and allowing the gifts to fall into your hands, I invite you to think and write about the following ideas.

1. **What do you want to be involved with?** A certain segment of the population? A particular arena, like nurturing the environment, educating all children, feeding the hungry, inventing new technologies, being a great performer, or creating inspiring art?

2. **What skills do you want to develop that you feel have been ignored?** How might you need these skills to balance yourself?

3. **What new activities do you see yourself doing?** These may be things that are slightly intimidating. Perhaps your left brain tells you they might be boring, beneath you, or beyond your reach—but you want to experience them anyway.

4. **Who do you admire?** How do their accomplishments relate to what you are trying to tell yourself about your own path?

5. **What elements do you want that are deal breakers if they _don't_ happen?** As you think about this, you might sense the experience you want _not happening_ and what you might do to correct the situation. You can have what you want! There are certain things you definitely want to experience and accomplish in your lifetime. What you want is what you need.

6. **What parts of your personality are you willing to let go of without feeling any loss? What parts do you want to keep so you can use them consciously?** Take a look at how attached and unconscious you are about various aspects of your identity. What could you give away, and what aspects do you want to keep active for now?

7. **What would you call in if you knew you could have it?** Remember that the ability to do what you invoke comes along with the result.

8. **What three things do you want and need next?** This includes tools, opportunities, resources, and helpful people. Place your attention on them and ask for them. Feel their frequency and let your reality match those vibrations. Allow the three things to want and need you as much as you want and need them.

9. **What three things do you need to discover that will lead to new kinds of self-expression?** These might include having a successful relationship, being able to perform in public, taking a writing work-

shop, or jumping over fences on horseback. What will help catalyze your next level of self?

10. **What is your next courageous act?** How might you stretch beyond your comfort zone? What activities have you said you would never do? How might you-the-soul move fluidly into your body-personality and express freely and with great joy? Remember that courage isn't hard for the soul!

Becoming transparent doesn't mean you give up wanting or having ideas for creating your ideal life. It doesn't mean you walk around without a mind or self—at least not yet! It means you have and freely make choices, but you don't focus your attention in a way that blocks or stops the Flow. Go ahead and ask questions of your soul. See what you say. See what wants to occur without force. Let the harmony roll!

Wanting transparency draws it in. Imagining yourself to be transparent is the best way to feel transparent, and then everything that prevents you from being transparent rises into visibility so you can clear it. And yes, you can commit to transparency even though others are experiencing the hell realms and adding to the chaos in the world. You can engage with your own challenges and fire-walk across the coals without burning. You can quiet your mind and feel down through, and that brilliant, lit-up stuff that's beyond will come right to and through you. It sees you before you see it.

> Nature loves courage. You make the commitment, and nature will
> respond to that commitment by removing impossible obstacles.
> Dream the impossible dream and the world will not grind you
> under; it will lift you up. This is the trick. This is what all these
> teachers and philosophers who really counted, who really touched
> the alchemical gold, this is what they understood. This is the
> shamanic dance in the waterfall. This is how magic is done. By
> hurling yourself into the abyss and discovering it's a feather bed.
>
> **Terence McKenna**

Just to Recap...

As you get a taste of transparency, choose it as a way of life, and begin to acclimate to living this way, you encounter some "yes, buts." Stay centered in your home frequency to find the answers. You also find that when you've cleared your own clutter, you become aware of societal clutter, which you can clear the same way you released the blocks you thought were yours alone. After clearing your clutter, it's important to stabilize your transparency and explore the world from this perspective. As you discover the new reality stage by stage, you teach yourself through your insights by working with mindfulness and personal inquiry.

Living in a transparent world brings a quality of permeability; you may experience a blending of your senses, a lessening of boundaries, and a porousness of your body and matter itself. You become extremely sensitive to energy, develop telepathic and empathic abilities, and feel information "impressing" you. You are fluid, and your body becomes your thoughts and feelings.

Exploring the new, transparent world, you can't help but wonder where transparency is taking us. The innovations coming from horizontal transparency, where the focus is the physical world, deal with making physical changes based on the Information Age and linear perception, often leaving out the heart and soul—and the development of our own expanded human capacities. When we look at how the addition of vertical transparency will shift things we take for granted, we can see how reality itself is likely to transform for the better in the Intuition Age.

With transparency, you want to be aligned with the soul and allow your knowing and creativity to fall straight through your personality. Working with the concept of invocation is important; remember to ask for the ideas and help that is always there for you.

Living in a transparent world, the possibility of enlightenment becomes quite real. Enlightenment is a result of becoming transparent but is beyond the transparency of the mind. It is in many ways the release of the concept of self, and yet you still live in the world and partake of its physical creativity.

Chapter 9: The New Normal

Transparency Message
NO MORE STORY

no more story
no more chronology
where I lived, what I did, how I learned:
just a recitation now
perhaps when I die, I'll still have a "life review"
but maybe I won't need it
I'm feeling my mistakes and their value
and how my stiffness and softness affected others
and how my unvoiced judgments
carried across like clubs
and how my sweetness and clarity healed in unseen ways
and how the love I could not face
because it felt so excruciating
was how big I really am
every time I cried because my heart stirred and opened
every sudden catch in my flow
because an unexpected cruelty occurred
no matter how subtle
these earthly responses
all come from who I am
no story needed

Transparency

now I am as always
a pure simplicity of existence
an open eye
seeing it all
an emotional body
including every possible feeling nuance
a lit-up field of consciousness that forgives
and creates and provides and joins and leaves
I am this point of view
and so many other perspectives
that I find so mesmerizing and lovable

without a description that I try to possess
I am so relaxed!
and right in this moment, when I know this,
I also know how I am cared for, provided for,
how I fit

in the long story of humankind
weaving like one colored thread throughout
in a crazy wisdom way
zigzagging and spiraling
reversing and unfolding
what fun, this Flow
that is finished and not yet finished
in this timeless moment

Final Thoughts

I clearly hear the healthy conversations
flowing below the surface—the descriptions of deep experience,
interesting ideas batted back and forth lightly like shuttlecocks,
sacred feelings offered simply, cushioned by large quiet spaces,
nonexhausting insights understood immediately,
no ripples of discontent.
I am relieved to not have to speak it all in this one now-moment.
I can Be and feel the beauty of unfiltered soul-shine;
I love to fall in and bask in it.

Freedom! Nothing now needs be as it ever was.
Quietly, we dig out our jewels, carefully recrafting ourselves.
No one knows what transformation's patient love may yield.
Important things are improving.
We've set it all "a-spinnin."
A resonance has begun, light knowing light, the yes-yes-yes,
the weaving of you-are-me and we-are-others.
I want to say: Are you connected in the most important ways?
I mean: Am I?

Spirit says, "Even the tiny tinkling brook
knows what the rains and oceans know."

Penney Peirce

Oh, yes! I just remembered, right here at the end! My romance with transparency actually began quite some time ago, with a dream—but perhaps that dream was reminding me of something I have been focusing on for lifetimes. I have written of this visionary dream before, but truly, I only just now thought of it again! My Inner Perceiver seems to be weaving a tale for me like a mystery writer, causing me to remember and forget and remember like some turtle surfacing, then diving, then surfacing in the pond.

The dream I had is somewhat esoteric and prophetic, or perhaps it's fodder for a sci-fi novel. Anyway, it described a huge shift in our internal energy-and-consciousness reality yet didn't give me many details about the physical shift that would parallel it. I guess it's taken these ensuing years for those pieces of insight to drop into place.

My Visionary Dream of Transparency

It was sometime in the early 1990s. The dream woke me at exactly 3:00 AM, as is the case with most visionary dreams I've had, and it was as if a curtain had been parted on a very real scene:

I am camping in the desert, "holding a spot" for what seems like several weeks, just waiting and maintaining a steady vibration, following some sort of higher, intuitive orders. *[Looking at this now, I sense it was symbolic of the work I'm doing in my life—holding a space of clarity in the field, at certain locations, for a certain periods of time, stabilizing something for some purpose I am only gradually remembering.]*

My mother is with me, and as we lounge in our plastic folding chairs, she tells me she is worried about the future. I am reading a book, written in a series of different-sized dots and circles, all touching each other. The pages are literally covered edge-to-edge with a field of these spheres—some yellow, some blue, some purple—looking very much like a close-up of stained round cells under a microscope.

As I pay attention, all the spheres begin rotating. It makes perfect sense to me, and I read the book by tracking through the field, following various sequences of rotations of the spheres, like tracing the flow of oil through a complex series of gears. *[I sense that the moving spheres are a language, a diagram, a reality, and a message from higher beings. And, as I read, I realize the message is written in past tense, even though it's describing something yet to come in "earth time." My mother, in real life, was attuned to spirit but afraid of losing control. She may have represented the consciousness of partially transparent people.]*

I say to my mother, "Oh, don't worry. It's not going to be that bad. See? It says right here . . ." And I proceed to describe what the book depicts: A "cosmic event" had occurred way out in the far reaches of the universe and had set in motion this particular sequence of rotations, where the collision or spin of one celestial body—and even the tiny particles involved—affected another, and then another, and another, until the wave of spiraling energy reached our solar system and planet. When that happened—and it wouldn't be too much longer—the book says people would attribute the result to erroneous causes like photons from the sun or a magnetic pole shift. But the wave of very high frequency energy would cause a significant increase in the vibration of the earth and everything on it.

The dream scene suddenly shifts, and I am standing in a room talking to a male colleague—a healer who is dressed in a gray business suit and has just been working in the big cities of the East Coast.

"Those suits are really solid!" he exclaims. And in the dream, I think, "The business mentality is hard to get through, or maybe the bodies themselves are like suits."

He looks at me and says, "Well, you look fine; you're right on schedule."

I look down and my left arm is transparent up to the shoulder! As I see this, memory floods into me about what is really going on. We are approaching an important time in the history of the planet. There will be an "event," related to the cosmic event from the far-distant universe, that is called "The Void." I suddenly remember I've been living all my lifetimes, preparing diligently, to be able to live through this event. *[Later,*

I consciously realize I have known about this "future" event perhaps since I began incarnating on the planet, knowing it as if it has already happened.]

I'm so excited! The impact of this memory flood is stupendous and shakes me to my core. "How could I possibly have forgotten this?" I marvel. I know the event is something joyful, yet I also know many people will lose their lives. Oddly, though, this doesn't concern me too much.

Then an authoritative voice says, "To survive The Void, you must become like the void." And I know then that we are all in a process of becoming "empty" and transparent, like deep outer space—every inch of us. I know in an all-at-once-way, that to be transparent means to hold nothing to yourself, to dissolve ego, to be soft, adaptable, porous, and permeable. It means we learn to live without the need for fixed identity or a set history, and without limitation, beliefs, fear, and reactionary behavior. Those things make us too dense.

In the dream I know: During The Void, which I sense to be in the first third of the twenty-first century, there would be a powerful phenomenon akin to the stopping of time. It would primarily occur in the higher dimensions of energy-and-consciousness, yet it would affect our physical bodies. I know that as we were experiencing this "pause," we'd have no idea how long it was lasting, because time would not exist. It's like we would blink out, then blink back in again, but in the time between, the world would make a huge leap in frequency. During The Void, there would be a tremendous flood of energy running through the planes of existence, through the "energy bodies."

Those who had become transparent—in other words, those who were fluid and fully in the moment, without expectations or projections into future or past, and who held no fixed ideas—would simply flow with the situation, and wouldn't experience disruption to their normal life. They already knew the sort of timelessness or timefulness inherent in the present moment. With no holding patterns, transparent people would instantaneously adapt to the new frequency, giving them an experience of heightened divinity and Light.

But people who were still living with the concept of linear time, projecting into the future, rushing to meet deadlines, dipping nostalgically into the past, or resisting the "lightening up" process, would have their worldview shattered. Anywhere there was too much holding on or holding back or holding out, that energetic and mental fixation would act as an impurity in the system, causing an implosion. Those who were still opaque with fear and controlling behaviors would blink out but not be able to adjust to the high vibration, so they wouldn't be able to blink back in to the new reality. And they would likely die from the overload.

And yet, there was no tragedy. Those who died would not realize what had happened consciously, and they would reincarnate right away onto a planet that was of the same vibration as the one they'd just left. Their Earth would function in much the same way as it always had.

Those who blinked back in, having absorbed the huge new dose of Light, would come back to a high-frequency Earth that was more etheric yet seemed just as familiar to them, because they now matched its vibration. Neither group would suffer alienation. The souls would all still exist and be interconnected in the unified field, just as they had always been. In effect, there would be a bifurcation of the world, and two twin-like planet Earths, at two different frequencies, would exist side by side in parallel realities.

I have shared this dream with others over the years, and have found that the idea of a cosmic event and bifurcating planet has arisen in many people's minds and dreams. In fact, I recently read an article describing how, in 2016, scientists captured a 20-millisecond-long signal from the Large Magellanic Cloud (the third closest satellite galaxy to the Milky Way) that recorded the moment when two black holes slammed together. The cataclysm *sent ripples through space-time and onwards to Earth*, which instruments detected as gravitational waves.[1] Who knows if this is related to The Void event in my dream, but when I read it, I got chills.

Ken Carey, author of *The Starseed Transmissions*, speaks of something similar to "The Void" event. His vision, too, connects this event to the stopping of time; he calls it "the nanosecond of non-time." A friend of mine said she had a dream where she was inside a cocoon, very tight and alone. Suddenly, it exploded, and she was a swan swimming peacefully on a glassy lake with many other swans. She said she realized that what was coming would be an experience of greater connectedness with like-minded others—that she would no longer have to do everything alone. Another friend, sitting on the beach and staring at the sea, saw a vision of the Earth splitting into two parallel planets, separated only by a "dimension." She knew that "this was expected by many people who had prepared themselves."

Since the dream, I've had the thought that though I saw The Void event happening all at once, with immediate repercussions, it was in the nonphysical realms. In this physical world, still largely programmed to run on linear perception, it's likely that the bifurcation will occur in super-slow motion, in waves and pulses, over a period of linear time. I wonder if we are in the early stages of The Void event now, using dramatic collective experiences to challenge us to be transparent so we can integrate the intensity of the new energy. Was September 11th one of those pulses? Will more dramatic waves and pulses occur in upcoming now moments? Perhaps we are still awaiting a more dramatic global experience. Who knows?

Naïve Optimism?

As I read back through what I have written in *Transparency*, I wonder: "Am I being naïve?" There is so much chaos in this bridge time, and so many are sure it's leading to the destruction of much of humanity and a terrible shock for our planet—yet I see it as a positive thing, a vast clearing phase. I don't know exactly where my optimism comes from, but it seems to originate way, way back in time, and deep down below the surface of events and thoughts.

Perhaps it comes from the "me" who lives in that higher frequency reality we used to call the future. In this source place, sight goes away, hearing fades to a soft hum, and the tactile turns to something nearly unfeelable, like the neutral between hot and cold. What's left after the senses are gone is a shiny nugget. It's a bright little sun, the memory of the big suns in the universe and perhaps of the kind of sun the universe itself might be if we could go beyond it and look back. That's where I go when I look for the source of my naïveté. It's something about what the soul knows for sure.

I can't say enough about the difference in the two realities—the opaque, linear one and the transparent, spherical-holographic one. Everything we know in linear terms is about to change into a new kind of functioning, and we'll know it all with such added dimension that we'll have to redefine life. Yes, the ego needs to go! Yes, our human consciousness needs to be shocked into waking up and breaking out from the familiarity of its hypnotized, glazed-over, prison-cell mentality. You don't have to be shocked into it, though, because you are finding the knowledge you need, just as you need it, to wake up on your own.

When we think in linear terms, achieving the transparent world seems logistically impossible. The left brain starts cranking hard to imagine every single person touching every other person, creating a linked network of clarity that will certainly take a very long time to occur. And overcoming millennia of vengeance, violence, apathy, and suffering definitely has the odds stacked firmly against it. Steam is coming out of our ears!

But shift to spherical-holographic perception and transparency, where spirit and matter merge and intermingle, and it's easier to sense the powerful effect a high-frequency, wisdom-rich, compassion-loaded, collective inner blueprint can have on humanity. Just as enlightenment can happen in any ordinary second, just as the reality you've dreamed of can become your daily life, so transparency can come upon you and become normal— with no apparent, logical cause. It simply emerges from your own field and from the field of humanity that has reached a critical mass of clarity.

Not everyone on earth has to do all the work of becoming transparent alone. When the critical mass occurs—and perhaps this relates to my dream about The Void event—the transparent reality will seem like the next most natural thing. When the automobile, telephone, television, personal computer, and internet materialized, it didn't take long before people couldn't imagine the world without these things. So it will be with transparency.

Final Thoughts

You may not understand everything I've put in this book, but you will. You will. The acceleration will open you to it. Perhaps the already-occurred Void event is pulling you into it, bit by bit, because it's so true and inescapable. The new post-Void reality already exists at a higher frequency too, and it is teaching you, showing you easier ways to live here on earth. It all hinges on collapsing the duality between the energy-and-consciousness world and the world of form. You'll feel it—how the new transparent reality makes sense in a more comprehensive way than what you've known to date. It's the new common sense.

It doesn't really matter whether everyone else becomes transparent—just do your part. You don't need agreement from others. You can set the tone and show the way. Remember that everyone else exists inside your sphere, and when you're living in your home frequency it's like living in a world of contagious diamond light. Just including others inside your reality and letting them feel your energy and inner blueprint—at the telepathic and clairsentient level—assists in an unknowable, far-reaching way. It's up to you and it's not up to you; you are everything and can influence everything, and the collective consciousness knows what it's doing. The inevitable return to absolute Awareness has already occurred in the timeless dimensions and is guiding you to that revelation.

So don't worry, it's a waste of attention. Rest assured: We will each remember our belonging in the huge and profoundly intimate soul family via our collective home frequency. We never lost what's real and true—we just pretended to be separate. Can't you see us all now, laughing and giggling at the Cosmic Joke—that we "forgot" the truth of the gigantic universe and unified field that surrounds us, penetrates us, guides us, and makes us?! Can't you just feel us sending resounding joy-ripples throughout the universe to nurture new life?

Life as it is should be enough of a reason to laugh.
It is so absurd, it is so ridiculous. It is so beautiful, it is so wonderful.
It is all sorts of things together. It is a great cosmic joke.
Osho

Acknowledgments

This book has really had its way with me! As many authors know, you must become the thing you are writing about; you must inhale and digest the content until it takes shape in you as your juices and cells. For me, this came in stages.

In large part, I want to thank my mother, Skip Peirce Eby, whose death at the end of 2015 put me into a crisis mode that catalyzed greater transparency in so many ways. The writing process, which took most of 2016, was steeped in the spaciousness she left. I hope she is looking in on me and seeing how I have made positive use of her transition to the higher realms; hopefully, I am passing on her presence, absence, and now her refined presence to many others.

I also want to thank Guy Eby, my stepfather, for his unflagging good humor and moral support. He is a literal real-life hero, several times over, and he has inspired me. Thanks, too, to my sister Paula, who is always there for me with her wit and warm diplomacy.

Ann Lambert and Leisa Donnelly have been a wonderful support for me locally in Florida, and so have my other friends Carol Adrienne, Karen Harvey, Ann Lewis, Nina Patrick, Pam Sabatiuk and Steve Steinberg, Audra and Benjamin Russell, Christine and Peter Esdaile, Engebret Fekene and Camilla Heiberg, and Marianne deWolff and Jos

Acknowledgments

van de Veerdonk. I am grateful to Larry Wilson in Sewanee, Tennessee, for reading the manuscript and sharing his brilliant insights.

Other great conversations helped me as well: with Jon Driscoll in Santa Fe, Megan Poe and Vivian Rosenthal in New York, Jon Pellicci in Palm Beach Gardens, Mike Cowan in Houston, Roger Marsh in San Francisco, and Anca Suditu in Bucharest. In addition, I value the many great insights that came innocently from the mouths of my clients; I tried to jot them all down and integrate them throughout the book.

I want to give special thanks to Jenny Blake, who enthusiastically agreed to write the foreword for this book. Her bright and shining consciousness and personal transparency are just what we needed; a perfect pairing with the content! Beyond Words Publishing and Simon & Schuster have been behind me since the beginning, and they feel like family at this point. Thanks to Emily Han, Lindsay Easterbrooks-Brown, Emmalisa Sparrow Wood, Jen Weaver-Neist, Devon Smith, Bill Brunson, Corinne Kalasky, Jackie Hooper, Ruth Hook, and especially to Richard and Michele Cohn.

Notes

To the Reader

1. Frederic and Mary Ann Brussat, *Spiritual Literacy: Reading the Sacred in Everyday Life* (New York: Scribner, 1996), 381.

2. Penney Peirce, *The Intuitive Way: The Definitive Guide to Increasing Your Awareness* (New York: Beyond Words Publishing, 2009), 211–212.

Chapter 1

1. Jill Bolte Taylor, *My Stroke of Insight: A Brain Scientist's Personal Journey* (New York: Plume, 2009), 41, 144.

Chapter 2

1. Manilal Nabhubhai Dvivedi, trans., *The Yoga-Sutra of Patanjali* (Bombay: Tookárám Tátyá, 1890), 65.

2. Acts 1:9 (New American Standard Version).

3. *Stars Wars, Episode IV: A New Hope*, "Quotes," IMDb.com, accessed February 27, 2017, http://www.imdb.com/title/tt0076759/quotes.

4. H. G. Wells, *The Invisible Man: A Grotesque Romance* (New York: Harper & Brothers, 1897), 223.

5. "Summary of Fiscal Year 2013 Annual FOIA Reports," The United States Department of Justice website, July 18, 2014, https://www.justice.gov/oip/blog/summary-fiscal-year-2013-annual-foia-reports; "Summary of Fiscal Year 2015 Annual FOIA Reports Published," The United States Department of Justice website, March 17, 2016, https://www.justice.gov/oip/blog/summary-fiscal-year-2015-annual-foia-reports-published.

6. U. S. House of Representatives Committee on Oversight and Government Reform, "FOIA Is Broken: A Report," Oversight & Government Reform website, January 2016, https://oversight.house.gov/wp-content/uploads/2016/01/FINAL-FOIA-Report-January-2016.pdf, 1.

7. Jim Flannery, "Transparency Is Vital to Meeting Growing Consumer Demands for Product Information," Grocery Manufacturers Association website, January 25, 2016, http://www.gmaonline.org/blog/transparency-is-vital-to-meeting-growing-consumer-demands-for-product-information/.

8. "75 Customer Service Facts, Quotes & Statistics: How Your Business Can Deliver with the Best of the Best," HelpScout website, accessed April 17, 2017, https://www.helpscout.net/75-customer-service-facts-quotes-statistics/.

9. Ibid.

10. Amy Gesenhues, "Survey: 90% of Customers Say Buying Decisions Are Influenced by Online Reviews," Marketing Land website, April 9, 2013, http://marketingland.com/survey-customers-more-frustrated-by-how-long-it-takes-to-resolve-a-customer-service-issue-than-the-resolution-38756.

Chapter 4

1. Matthew 7:6 (New King James Version).

Chapter 5

1. Jon Ronson, *So You've Been Publicly Shamed* (New York: Riverhead Books, 2015), 10.

Chapter 7

1. "Sustainable Development Goals," United Nations Sustainable Development website, accessed February 4, 2017, http://www.un.org/sustainabledevelopment/sustainable-development-goals/.

2. Barbara Spraker, "Capacity-Building Resources," Women Leading the Way website, accessed February 4, 2017, http://www.womenleadingtheway.com/womens-leadership-resources-teams.html.

3. Barbara Spraker, "Conversation Circles," Women Leading the Way website, accessed February 27, 2017, http://www.womenleadingtheway.com/conversation-circles.html.

4. Dave Eggers, *The Circle* (New York: Vintage Books, 2014), 490.

5. Ilya Pozin, "How Transparent Is Too Transparent in Business," Forbes website, April 2, 2014, https://www.forbes.com/sites/ilyapozin/2014/04/02/how-transparent-is-too-transparent/#4c49f3667bac.

6. Steve Crabtree, "Worldwide, 13% of Employees Are Engaged at Work," Gallup website, October 8, 2013, http://www.gallup.com/poll/165269/worldwide-employees-engaged-work.aspx.

7. Susan Sorenson and Keri Garman, "How to Tackle U. S. Employees' Stagnating Engagement," June 11, 2013, http://www.gallup.com/businessjournal/162953/tackle-employees-stagnating-engagement.aspx.

8. Steve Denning, "Is Holacracy Succeeding at Zappos?" *Forbes* website, May 23, 2015, https://www.forbes.com/sites/stevedenning/2015/05/23/is-holacracy-succeeding-at-zappos/#5ec5ac7256dc.

Chapter 8

1. Carol Adrienne, *When Life Changes or You Wish It Would: How to Survive and Thrive in Uncertain Times* (New York: HarperCollins, 2003), 54, 55.

Chapter 9

1. Terence McKenna, *The Archaic Revival: Speculations on Psychedelic Mushrooms, the Amazon, Virtual Reality, UFOs, Evolution, Shamanism, the Rebirth of the Goddess, and the End of History* (New York: HarperCollins, 1992), 231.

2. Jason Dorrier, "Peter Diamandis: We'll Radically Extend Our Lives with New Technologies," SingularityHub.com, August 30, 2016, http://singularityhub.com/2016/08/30/peter-diamandis-well-radically-extend-our-lives-with-new-technologies/.

3. Kevin Kelly, *The Inevitable: Understanding the 12 Technological Forces That Will Shape Our Future* (New York: Viking, 2016), 99, 257.

4. Seng Ts'an, "On Trust in the Mind," from *Entering the Stream: An Introduction to the Buddha and His Teachings*, edited by Samuel Bercholz and Sherab Chödzin Kohn (Boston: Shambhala, 1993), 149.

Final Thoughts

1. Ian Sample, "2016's Best Bits: Breakthroughs In Science," *The Guardian*, December 24, 2016, https://www.theguardian.com/lifeandstyle/2016/dec/24/breakthroughs-science-2016-gravitational-waves.

Glossary

acceleration, the: A way to describe the increasing frequency of the planet and of our bodies, which has been intensifying for many years.

ascension: The ability to raise the frequency of one's body, emotions, and mind beyond the vibration of the physical world, so the body disappears into a higher dimension without physical death; the opposite of *descension*.

apportation: The motion or production of an object without apparent physical agency.

attunement: Adjusting the vibration of your body, emotions, and mind to match a particular frequency, usually of a higher vibration.

astral plane: A dimension of consciousness just beyond the physical realm, marked by lower emotion and populated by souls in transition, nature spirits or elementals, and earth-bound souls.

aura: The subtle energy around and through the physical body comprised of an individual's pattern of emotional, mental, and spiritual energy-and-consciousness; sometimes seen clairvoyantly as light or color; also known as the *personal field*.

Awareness: As used capitalized in this book, the state of enlightenment beyond dualistic awareness, and differentiated from lower-dimensional "consciousness;" the original state of unity. See *enlightenment*.

centerpoint: An emergence point for any of the billions of possible realities or identities in the universe; the place of knowing the self as an individual experience. By being in any centerpoint, one can know both the individual experience and universal experience of the whole simultaneously, via holographic perception.

clairaudience: The inner sense of hearing; to hear voices, music, and sounds without the aid of the physical ears.

clairsentience: The inner sense of touch, smell, and taste; to feel or sense nonphysical energy fields, discarnate entities, or patterns of knowledge without using the physical body; obtaining information by touching objects.

clairvoyance: The inner sense of sight; the ability to see visions, past or future events, or information that can't be discerned naturally through the five material senses. Medical clairvoyance is the ability to view the human body and diagnose disease, while X-ray clairvoyance is the ability to see into distant or closed areas.

clutter: The fear-based blockages previously stored in the subconscious mind but now emerging into the conscious mind to be cleared; contractions of energy-and-consciousness that stall, distort, or stop the Flow.

compassion: A pervasive understanding that knows love as the core of every being and situation. The virtue that gives rise to one's desire to alleviate another's suffering.

dematerialization: The process of dissolving a physical form back into the unified field; the opposite of *materialization*.

descension: The process of the body appearing in form without physical birth; the opposite of *ascension*.

destiny: Life after the soul has integrated fully and consciously into the body, emotions, and mind; one's highest frequency life, accompanied by unlimited talents, harmonious energy flow, perfect timing, and doing what one is "built for" and most enjoys.

diamond light: A way to imagine the substance of the soul; diamond light conveys the experience of purity, supreme clarity and transparency, incorruptibility, and enlightenment.

dimensions: Levels or frequencies of awareness and energy progressing from physical, to etheric (or subtle), to emotional, to mental, to spiritual, and on into levels of the Divine. As energy-and-consciousness progresses through the dimensions, greater unity is experienced.

direct experience: A live connection with the world through which one experiences situations immediately, without analysis, description, or comparison; an experience of full engagement with each experience in each moment.

direct knowing: A live connection to higher sources of information and wisdom that comes via the right brain and intuition, often all at once, as a pattern or a string of words that aren't monitored or edited by the left brain.

dissonance: The discord created when vibrations of different wavelengths meet, create instability and chaos, and demand resolution; the opposite of *resonance*.

Divine, the: A nonreligious way to refer to the Godhead, Creator, or Supreme Presence; an experience of perfect, transcendent force, truth, and love, or oneness with the universe.

ego: The sense of individuality based on separation from the whole; when the consciousness identifies as ego, fear and self-preservation are the motivators. Often associated with extreme left-brain dominance.

ego death: The process in which the dominant left-brain consciousness surrenders to the right-brain consciousness, and the personality begins to identify as the soul; the left brain becomes the servant, or implementer, rather than the "boss."

empathy: The ability to use one's sensitivity to feel "with" or "as" another person, group, or object, resulting in greater compassionate understanding.

energy body: See *light body*.

energy-and-consciousness: A term that conveys the idea that energy and consciousness are flip sides of the same coin; change one and the other changes to match.

enlightenment: The achievement of total clarity about the true nature of things; a permanent state of higher wisdom, illumination, or self-realization;

319

the awakening of the mind to its divine identity; the final attainment on the spiritual path when the limited sense of "I" merges into supreme consciousness.

etheric energy: The vibratory frequency that is one level higher than matter; a malleable form of energy that acts as a kind of "modeling clay," or energetic blueprint, for the physical dimension; also known as *subtle energy* or *ethers*.

evolution: A gradual process of development leading to a more advanced form; the progression of individual identity through relationship identity, to group identity, to identity as collective consciousness, to unity with infinite, divine awareness.

feel into: The ability to penetrate into a person, object, or energy field with one's attention, merge with it, and become it briefly; to allow subtle information to register on one's body via conscious sensitivity, as if one is the object of observation.

felt sense: The impressions or direct experience of a person, object, or energy field registered on the body and mind through conscious sensitivity.

Flow, the: The natural, continuous, fluid, wavelike movement of life and any process; a state in which one is fully immersed in what they are doing, characterized by a feeling of energized focus, full involvement, and enjoyment of the process; the oscillating evolutionary movement of consciousness from the unified field into form or vice versa.

frequency: The number of waves that pass through a specific point in a certain period of time; the rate of occurrence of anything.

frequency-match: The process of attuning one's personal vibration, whether consciously or unconsciously, to the vibration of another person for the purpose of communication.

group entity: See *relationship entity*.

harmony: A pleasing combination of the elements in a pattern that emphasizes the similarities and unity of all the parts.

hologram: A three-dimensional image (originally generated by a laser); a quantum-mechanical explanation of reality that suggests the physical universe is a giant space-time hologram in which the entirety is within each facet, leading to the concept that every moment—past, present, and possible—exists simultaneously. Likewise, every place exists everywhere simultaneously.

holographic perception: Seeing from the centerpoint of one's own self, or sphere, which allows knowledge of the centerpoint, or core truth, of any other entity as though it is oneself.

home frequency: The vibration of one's soul as it expresses through the body, emotions, and mind; a frequency of energy-and-consciousness that conveys the most accurate experience of heaven on earth as possible.

horizontal transparency: The free flow of information and innovation in the physical world, especially pertaining to corporations and government; not taking into account the spiritual, nonphysical dimensions; associated with *left-brain perception*. (See also *linear perception*.)

imaginal realm: The collective conscious and unconscious, or unified field, where all ideas exist and can be combined into any creative endeavor.

inner blueprint: The most current pattern of one's life purpose or vision; it includes a mix of love and fear, and wisdom and ignorance, depending on how much personal growth and transformation a person has experienced. This energetic pattern gives rise to the events and forms in one's physical life.

Inner Perceiver: The wisdom of the soul inside a person, sometimes known as the Revealer or Holy Spirit, that directs one's attention to notice things that aid in learning life lessons and expressing oneself authentically.

integrated self: The experience of the soul totally merged with the personality, and therefore able to see how the spiritual realm is merged with matter.

intuition: Direct knowing of what is real and appropriate in any situation without need for proof; perception that occurs when body, emotions, mind, and spirit are simultaneously active and integrated while being focused entirely in the present moment; a state of perceptual aliveness in which one feels intimately connected to all living things and experiences the cooperative, cocreative nature of life.

Glossary

Intuition Age, the: The period following the Information Age, where perception accelerates, and intuition, direct knowing, and ultrasensitivity take precedence over logic and willpower; the time on earth when soul consciousness saturates the mind, transforming the nature of reality, resulting in transparency.

involution: The process of energy-and-consciousness dropping in frequency from higher dimensions into physical form.

invocation: Calling upon nonphysical beings, as in the gods and goddesses, for assistance; calling in the wisdom one needs to proceed in life.

karma: The idea that whatever negative or positive energies one sends out come back to the sender in like kind, either in this life or a later one.

left-brain perception: Perception focused on definition, description, language, logic, analysis, compartmentalization, and security; too much reliance on this intellectual kind of knowing feels cold, heartless, or egotistical. (See also *horizontal transparency*.)

light body: A higher dimensional body that underlies or closely parallels the physical form, composed of etheric or subtle energy; often seen clairvoyantly as light. In it, the energies and functions of the chakras are coordinated, and health and illness can be discerned as transparency, color, or shadows; also known as the energy body.

liminal space: The seemingly empty space before and after the experience of crossing a threshold from one reality to another, likened to the time when the caterpillar transforms into the butterfly.

linear perception: A kind of consciousness characterized by cause-and-effect logic, the analysis of steps required to achieve a goal, and the idea that one must repeat what worked in the past to achieve the same results in the future. (See also *horizontal transparency*.)

many-worlds theory: The idea in physics that the world is split at the quantum level into an unlimited number of real worlds, unknown to each other, where a wave evolves instead of collapsing or condensing into a specific form, embracing all possibilities within it; therefore, all realities and outcomes exist simultaneously but do not interfere with each other.

materialization: The process of bringing an idea from the imaginal realm into physical manifestation; the opposite of *dematerialization*.

midbrain: The middle of the three primary divisions of the human brain, which helps process the five senses, perceptions of similarity and connectedness, and affection.

mindfulness: The practice of engaging with the reality of the moment and noticing what is being noticed with an open mind.

neocortex: The last and most evolved level of the human triune brain, divided into a left and right hemisphere; involved in higher functions such as spatial reasoning, conscious thought, pattern recognition, and language.

opaque reality: The reality caused by linear perception in which separation is one of the key elements, resulting in fear; life seems dense, slow, and full of suffering; associated with the old perception of the Industrial and Information Ages.

overlays: Unconscious, limiting beliefs one inherits in infancy and early childhood, from parents and other influential people, that emphasize particular behaviors as necessary for survival.

oversoul: A collective of a number of souls forming one merged body of knowledge, guiding incarnated beings on earth.

past and parallel lives: The idea that souls are composed of thousands of parts, many incarnating on the earth to experience individual lives. The lifetimes of one soul can be separated from each other through time, giving the impression of sequential occurrence, or several lives may exist at one time but are separated by location.

personal field: See *aura*.

personal vibration: The overall vibration that radiates from a person in any given moment; a fluctuating frequency that is a combination of the various contracted or expanded states of one's body, emotions, and thoughts.

projection: Casting one's mind into thoughts of the past, the future, fictitious realities, other locations, or other people's realities to avoid experiencing something in the present moment; blaming other people for what one doesn't want to acknowledge about oneself, or seeing traits in others that one cannot see in oneself.

psychokinesis: The process of using only the mind, with no physical intervention, to manipulate physical objects. Often called PK.

radical trust: A state of unconditional trust—that perfect experience of peaceful surrender—in everything.

relationship entity: A pooling of two—or more—people's total histories, knowledge, and talents that acts as a guide for both—or all—the participants in attaining optimal growth; it might be thought of as a small oversoul.

reptile brain: Also known as the reptilian complex, this is the first and oldest part of the human triune brain; concerned with instinct, emotion, motivation, and fight-or-flight survival behavior.

resonance: The vibration produced in an object due to the vibration of a nearby object; the regular vibration of an object as it responds to an external force of the same frequency; the opposite of *dissonance*. Waves that vibrate the same length create resonance.

right-brain perception: Perception focused on large patterns of direct knowing and direct experience, where everything is interconnected and capable of being known at once, and there is no language; it sources intuition and creativity. (See also *vertical transparency*.)

round trip: The renewing, creative flow of energy-and-consciousness from form to the unified field, or imaginal realm, and back to form again.

shape-shift: The ability to make physical changes in oneself such as alterations of age, gender, race, or general appearance, or changes between human form and that of an animal, plant, or inanimate object.

soul: The experience of the Divine expressing as individuality; the self-aware spiritual life force or essence, unique to a particular living being, carrying consciousness of all actions; the inner awareness in a person that exists before birth and lives on after the physical body dies.

spherical perception: Perception based on an inner geometry of being present at all times at the centerpoint of a large sphere of energy-and-consciousness, which is one's present moment, mind, identity, and reality.

The sphere expands and contracts depending on the frequency of one's focus, and there is nothing outside the sphere, since it embodies the entire unified field.

spherical-holographic perception: The combination of spherical and holographic perception, resulting in the transformation of individual identity and life as we have known it via linear perception. The two kinds of perception fold into each other seamlessly.

subconscious mind: Mental activity that functions just below the threshold of awareness, where all experience is stored as sensory data; the part of one's awareness where memories based on fear are stored or repressed.

subtle energy: See *etheric energy*.

synchronicity: A coincidence of events that seem to be related and can be interpreted to find deeper meaning in life.

synesthesia: A neurological phenomenon in which stimulation of one sensory or cognitive pathway leads to automatic, involuntary experiences in a second sensory or cognitive pathway.

telepathy: The transfer of thoughts, feelings, or images directly from one mind to another without using the physical senses.

teleportation: The movement of objects or elementary particles from one place to another, nearly instantaneously, without their traveling through physical space.

transformation: A complete change of physical form or substance into something entirely different; a total shift in identity and the way reality functions.

transparency: A state of clarity and authenticity caused by the soul merging fully with the personality and clearing the fear-based clutter; characterized by trust, spontaneity, and full engagement with the Flow.

transparent reality: A reality cocreated by a number of transparent people in which secrets, lies, hiding, self-protection, and other artifacts of fear are no longer present; associated with the new Intuition Age.

truth and anxiety signals: The subtle, instinctive expansion or contraction responses of the emotions and body, sometimes experienced through the five senses, that indicate either safety and truth, or danger and inappropriate action.

ultrasensitivity: The heightened bodily awareness of vibration and energy information that results from the acceleration of the planet, leading to enhanced empathic ability and other capacities like telepathy and clairvoyance.

unified field: A universal sea of energy-and-consciousness, or presence, that underlies and pre-exists physical matter; a state, force, or "ground of being" that is the absolute constant of the universe and connects everything in a single, unified experience. Gravitational and electromagnetic fields, the strong and weak atomic forces, and all other forces of nature, including time and space, are conditions of this state.

vertical transparency: The state of spiritual authenticity that results from the soul merging with the personality and guiding the life; associated with *right-brain perception*.

Index:
Exercises, Figures & Transparency Messages

Chapter 1: The Awakening

Chapter 2: Transparency

Chapter 3: The Opaque Reality

Chapter 7:
When Relationships & Groups Are Transparent

Chapter 8: No Walls, No Secrets

Chapter 9: The New Normal

Index:
Chapter Lists

Chapter 5: The Bridge Time

Chapter 6: Becoming Personally Transparent

Chapter 7: When Relationships & Groups Are Transparent

Chapter 8: No Walls, No Secrets

Chapter 9: The New Normal

About the Author

Penney Peirce is a gifted clairvoyant-empath and visionary (who spells her name in a weird way). She has been interested in the mysteries from the moment she learned to say "Why?" Today she is one of the pioneers in the transformation movement, having written trend-setting books on intuition, frequency and personal vibration, and the paradigm shift.

She is a popular author, lecturer, counselor, and trainer specializing in intuition development, inner-energy dynamics, expanded perception, transformation, and dream work. She has worked throughout the United States, Japan, Europe, South America, and South Africa since 1977, coaching business and government leaders, psychologists, scientists, celebrities, and those on a spiritual path about the hidden dynamics of what makes for true success.

She has been involved with the Center for Applied Intuition, the Intuition Network, the Institute for the Study of Conscious Evolution, The Arlington Institute (futurists), Knowledge Harvesting and Interconnecting.com, the Global Alliance for Transformation in Entertainment, and the Kaiser Institute, which trains hospital CEOs in the development of intuitive skills. Peirce is the author of:

Books

- *Transparency: Seeing Through to Our Expanded Human Capacity*
- *Leap of Perception: The Transforming Power of Your Attention*, winner of the 2014 COVR Visionary Awards for Book of the Year and Best Alternative Science & Spirituality Book, and winner of the 2014 Silver Nautilus Book Award for Science/Cosmology
- *Frequency: The Power of Personal Vibration*, 1st Runner Up for the 2010 COVR Visionary Award for Best Alternative Science & Spirituality Book
- *The Intuitive Way: The Definitive Guide to Increasing Your Awareness*
- *Dream Dictionary for Dummies*

eBooks

- *Be the Dreamer Not the Dream: A Guide to 24-Hour Consciousness* (previously in print as *Dreams for Dummies*)
- *The Present Moment: A Daybook of Clarity and Intuition* (previously in print)
- *Bits & Pieces 1: Thoughts on Emotion, Ending Struggle, and Living with the "Big Dark Hidden"*
- *Bits & Pieces 2: Thoughts on the Feminine, the Flow, Presence, and Becoming the World*
- *Bits & Pieces 3: Thoughts on Coming Trends in Education, Politics, Business, and World Events*

She is featured in various other books, including: *Return of the Revolutionaries* by Walter Semkiw, MD; *The Purpose of Your Life* and *When Life Changes or You Wish It Would* by Carol Adrienne; *The Celestine Prophecy* and *Tenth Insight Experiential Guides*, by James Redfield and Carol Adrienne; *Intuiting the Future* and *Opening the Inner Eye* by Dr. William H. Kautz; and *Breaking Through: Getting Past the Stuck Points in Your Life*, by Barbara Stanny. She appears in the film *Discover the Gift*.

About the Author

Peirce's work is open minded, practical, and sophisticated, synthesizing diverse cultural and spiritual worldviews with many years of experience in business as a corporate art director with such companies as Atlantic Richfield and American Hospital Supply Corporation. She is extraordinarily attuned to the intricacies of the mind and the dimensions of human consciousness, blending a deep understanding of natural laws with a designer's skill in structural patterning. She is known for her ability to present complex ideas in a common-sense, easy-to-understand way.

Penney emphasizes the practical aspects of intuitive development and transformation, helping people apply "direct knowing" to increase natural efficiency and their enjoyment and participation in life. Her work assists people and organizations in uncovering life purpose and action plans, understanding and easing transitions, alleviating burnout, and finding accurate answers to pressing questions. She believes that life functions according to innate natural principles, and when we live in alignment with these truths, things work smoothly and effectively.

Penney was educated at the University of Cincinnati, The New School and Columbia University in New York City, and California Institute of the Arts near Los Angeles. She lives in Florida.

Stay Involved

penneypeirce.com
Penney's website has lots of free stuff and information about her books, private sessions, and upcoming events.

- Receive Penney's newsletter: **penneypeirce.com/newsletter .htm**
- Find upcoming events: **penneypeirce.com/calendar.htm**
- Read about Penney's books: **penneypeirce.com/books.htm**

intuitnow.blogspot.com
Check out Penney's *Intuition & Transformation* blog.